# TRANSLATING DATA INTO INFORMATION TO IMPROVE TEACHING AND LEARNING

**VICTORIA L. BERNHARDT, Ph.D.**
Executive Director
Education for the Future Initiative

Professor
Department of Professional Studies in Education
College of Communication and Education
California State University, Chico, CA

EYE ON EDUCATION
6 Depot Way West
Larchmont, NY  10538
(914) 833-0551
(914) 833-0761 Fax
www.eyeoneducation.com

For information about permission to reproduce selections from this book, write:
EYE ON EDUCATION
Permission Dept.
6 Depot Way West
Larchmont, NY  10538

Library of Congress Cataloging–in–Publication Data

Bernhardt, Victoria L., 1952-
    Translating Data into Information to improve teaching and learning / Victoria L. Bernhardt.
        p.   cm.
    Includes bibliographical references.
    ISBN 978-1-59667-061-7
    1. Educational datawarehousing—United States.  2. School improvement—United
States—Data analysis. 3. Educational planning—United States—Continuous school
improvement. 4. School improvement—United States—Data tools.  I. Title: Data
Warehousing.  II. Bernhardt, Victoria L., 1952—Data warehousing to improve teaching and
learning.  III. Title

**10** 9 8 7 6 5 4 3 2 1

# Also Available from Eye On Education

# ACKNOWLEDGEMENTS

In so many ways, I have no right to be writing a book on data tools. I am not an engineer (although, I would love to be), a data architect, or someone who knows the details of the technology behind the data tools. As someone who is extremely passionate about the use of data to improve teaching and learning in education organizations, and someone who is confronted every day of my working life with questions about data analyses, data tools, and how they work together, I have written this book to answer the many questions I am confronted with every day and to put these answers into a coherent format that can help any size school district get its data in better order to improve teaching and learning.

I could not have written this book without the support and expertise of many individuals who understand the behind the scenes workings of data tools, and who have worked with school districts on these very same issues. I am privileged to know so many wonderful supportive people, including reviewers of the first draft of the book: Becky Blink, Wisconsin; Martin Brutosky, South Carolina; Lynn Caulkins, Washington; Sue Clayton, Vermont; Joe Costanza, South Carolina; Cheryl Cozette, Missouri; Donnie Coggins, South Carolina; Theron Davis, South Carolina; Michael Derman, Pennsylvania; Rob Dzoba, South Carolina; John Ferrara, Vermont; Andrea Hartman, Connecticut; Kathleen Hocker, Pennsylvania; Kris Jensen, Washington; Nancy Katims, Edmonds School District, Washington; Joe Kitchens, Oklahoma; Marcy Lauck, California; Diane Lemieux, Vermont; Sally Lyon, Missouri; Doris McWhorter, Ontario, Canada; Kathy Miller, Michigan; Karen Raney, Texas; Joy Rose, Ohio; Jessica Rummins, Michigan; Denise Sanders, Vermont; Lynn Silver, Georgia; Kathy Tokarek, Michigan; and Amy White, South Carolina. I thank numerous school districts for the use of their data or reports. These districts include: Chilton Public Schools, Wisconsin; Columbia Public Schools, Missouri; Edmonds School District, Lynnwood, Washington; Northview Public Schools, Grand Rapids, Michigan; San Jose Unified School District, California; Tyler Independent School District, Texas; Western Heights Public School District, Oklahoma City, Oklahoma; and Westerville School District, Ohio. I thank TetraData for allowing me to learn the insides of data warehousing and for letting me contribute to their products from the very beginning. I am honored to be associated with them.

In addition to reading the first draft of this book (which in and of itself was a real fete), Michael Derman, Amy White, Kris Jensen, and Joy Rose continue to support the creation of a product that will help school districts everywhere. Mike lent his expertise with his knowledge of cleaning and loading data, and supporting school districts in managing their data warehouses; Amy assisted with technical details and screen shots; Kris helped with graphics and technological understandings. As with just about everything I write, Joy lovingly edited multiple drafts and made herself available to help with any task, any time. Joy is my editor "extraordinaire."

As always, the *Education for the Future* staff, Patsy Schutz, Brad Geise, Lynn Varicelli, Sally Withuhn, Tony Capretto, and Thiago Jorge did everything imaginable to support the writing of this book. Patsy is tireless in handling my travel, contacts, contracts, and workflow, which frees me up to focus on the book while in transit and on weekends. Brad is always there to take his share of the travel and work. Lynn, one more time, did a wonderful job keeping the drafts and many edits of this book ordered and converted into a lovely layout. She really has this process nailed. Sally, Tony, and Thiago supported the work in their usual "whatever it takes" fashion.

I appreciate the work of Dave Strauss, Communications Designer, for his cover design. Thank you, Dave.

A huge thanks to my publisher, affectionately known as *Cousin Bob,* Mr. Robert Sickles, and his staff. I am grateful for all you do to support the creation and marketing of all my books. Eye on Education has to be the easiest publishing company in the world with which to work!

Thank you goes to my husband, Jim Richmond, for putting up with the ongoing writing process by letting me off the hook from indoor work and outdoor chores in the forest.

I owe so much to all of these special friends and colleagues. They are the reason this book exists and is useful. Thank you all for helping me learn. The person who writes, learns the most.

This acknowledgement section would not be complete without thanking you, the reader, and you, the school district personnel working on continuous improvement, who believe in and use Education for the Future products and processes. I am so honored to work with you and so privileged to have the opportunity to continue my learning while working with you.

I hope this book exceeds your expectations; if it does, it is because of the continuous improvement that has resulted from your insights, direction, assistance, and support all along the way.

Sincerely,
*Vickie Bernhardt*
*June 2007*

# ABOUT THE AUTHOR

Victoria L. Bernhardt, Ph.D., is Executive Director of the Education for the Future Initiative, a not-for-profit organization whose mission is to build the capacity of all learning organizations at all levels to gather, analyze, and use data to continuously improve learning for all students. She is also a Professor (currently on leave) in the Department of Professional Studies in Education, College of Communication and Education, at California State University, Chico. Dr. Bernhardt is the author of the following books, all published by Eye on Education, Larchmont, New York:

▼ *Translating Data into Information to Improve Teaching and Learning* (2007) helps school districts improve teaching and learning at all levels by analyzing and converting their data into meaningful information and reports that can inform schools, school districts, states, and the community of student progress.

▼ A four-book collection of using data to improve student *learning—Using Data to Improve Student Learning in Elementary Schools* (2003); *Using Data to Improve Student Learning in Middle Schools* (2004); *Using Data to Improve Student Learning in High Schools* (2005); and *Using Data to Improve Student Learning in School Districts* (2006). Each book shows real analyses focused on one education organizational level and provides templates on an accompanying CD-Rom for leaders to use for gathering, graphing, and analyzing data in their own learning organizations.

▼ *Data Analysis for Continuous School Improvement* (First Edition, 1998; Second Edition, 2004) helps learning organizations use data to determine where they are, where they want to be, and how to get there—sensibly, painlessly, and effectively.

▼ *The School Portfolio Toolkit: A Planning, Implementation, and Evaluation Guide for Continuous School Improvement*, and CD-Rom (2002), is a compilation of over 500 examples, suggestions, activities, tools, strategies, and templates for producing school portfolios that will lead to continuous school improvement.

▼ *The Example School Portfolio* (2000) shows what a completed school portfolio looks like and further supports schools in developing their own school portfolios.

▼ *The School Portfolio: A Comprehensive Framework for School Improvement* (First Edition, 1994; Second Edition, 1999). This first book by the author assists schools with clarifying the purpose and vision of their learning organizations as they develop their school portfolios.

▼ Currently in press: *Questionnaires Demystified: Using Perceptions Data for School Improvement* describes how to create, administer, analyze, and use questionnaires as a tool to improve teaching strategies, programs, and learning organizations.

Dr. Bernhardt is passionate about her mission of helping all educators continuously improve student learning in their classrooms, their schools, their districts, and states by gathering, analyzing, and using actual data—as opposed to using hunches and "gut-level" feelings. She has made numerous presentations at professional meetings and conducts workshops on the school portfolio, data analysis, data warehousing, and school improvement at local, state, regional, national, and international levels.

Dr. Bernhardt can be reached at:

Victoria L. Bernhardt, Ph.D.
Executive Director, Education for the Future Initiative
400 West First Street, Chico, CA 95929-0230
Tel: 530-898-4482 — Fax: 530-898-4484
e-mail: vbernhardt@csuchico.edu
website: *http://eff.csuchico.edu*

# TABLE OF CONTENTS

# FOREWORD

TetraData Corporation, a software and services company focused on using data to identify the processes that require improvement in education, is very proud to be associated with Dr. Victoria L. Bernhardt, one of the most well-researched and tireless leaders that we have met in the world of K-12 education. Our firm provides the type of technology—i.e., data warehouse, data analysis and reporting software, which facilitates the process of analyzing myriads of data relevant to the enhancement decisions that need to be made in a timely manner—that makes Dr. Bernhardt's work come alive. Though TetraData has changed over the years and Dr. Bernhardt has written a plethora of meaningful publications, we continue to share a common passion—that one day all children, parents, and education professionals will have access to the data they need to provide the best opportunities for teaching and learning at all levels of education.

In this new work, *Translating Data into Information to Improve Teaching and Learning,* Dr. Bernhardt tackles the challenging issue of helping educators acquire and align data tools that will help them do a systematic and comprehensive analysis of their data and report results in meaningful ways. Throughout her years of researching the necessity of using data to truly improve teaching and learning, Dr. Bernhardt has validated the value of gathering, analyzing, and using data that are aligned to the purposes of teaching and learning. Alignment is central to the success of an education system. And just the fact that we use the word "system" indicates that we have to be strategic and foundational in our thinking about how we structure, organize, and operate our system. Similarly, we must be strategic in thinking about the development of an "information foundation" that under girds our education system. Dr. Bernhardt masterfully explains the need for such an information foundation, vis-à-vis, data tools, and a data warehouse; and she presents examples of school districts that are doing this work.

Once the need for data tools is clearly explained, Dr. Bernhardt does a masterful job of describing the practical side of the process. She has made this book very useful for understanding the process of planning, selecting, implementing and managing data tools and a data warehouse. Equally important, she provides us with something that we have seen a number of educational systems struggle to make happen, i.e., establishing a culture and process for making the use of data a vibrant part of the education system. Otherwise, data tools, the data warehouse, and the software used to make the warehouse visible to your teachers and administrators may become ornamental rather the foundational to your education system.

This is a fine work that will be very useful to schools, school districts, educational service agencies, and state departments of education. Within those organizations, this work is designed to be read and implemented by the education leaders responsible for education outcomes, instruction and learning, financial decisions, and information technology. It is the most authoritative work that we have seen on this important education topic. Its authoritative nature comes from Dr. Bernhardt's years of dealing with data to improve teaching and learning and her thoughtful, well-researched approach to the topic.

Martin S. Brutosky
Chief Operating Officer, TetraData Corporation
a Subsidiary of Follett Software Company
300 Executive Center Drive, Suite 300, Greenville, SC 29615
Tel: 864-458-8243
*http://www.tetradata.com*

# PREFACE

For approximately 125 days each year for the past seventeen years, I have worked with educational organizations that are attempting to use data to improve teaching and learning. Each of these workdays (a total of more than 2,100 days), I have heard the following questions being asked: *What data are important for helping us improve student achievement results for all students? How do we analyze these data when the task seems so overwhelming? Are there some data we can eliminate to make our data analysis easier? Whose job is it to analyze the data, anyway? How do we get the data into the hands of teachers so they can better meet the learning needs of all students? What professional learning is needed for teachers, principals, and district leaders so they can use the data to improve curriculum and instruction?*

In the last six or so years, especially since the passage of the United States' Elementary and Secondary Education Act of 2001, known as No Child Left Behind, I have also been hearing from educational organizations that have taken the plunge and purchased data tools, particularly data warehouses, to make data accessible to all levels of staff, and to make the data analysis work easier. While some of these organizations are still asking the same questions as above, I am now hearing these additional questions: *How can we improve the quality of our data? What are the top five queries we should be making to find out what we need to do to improve teaching and learning? How will our jobs be different if we are using data and data tools effectively? How do we get everyone using data and data tools? Everyone is working very hard; can data really help us work smarter—not harder? How can data tools help us improve teaching and learning?*

My goal with *Translating Data into Information to Improve Teaching and Learning* is to answer all of these questions, in terms that anyone can understand, and to make recommendations for educational organizations planning to buy data tools to make data more accessible, easier to analyze, and more informative and useful.

My personal mission is to support educational professionals in their quest for data and to help them use data effectively to improve teaching and learning throughout their learning organizations. This book will help any school district, whether novice or advanced, get started on making data more accessible, of higher quality, easier to analyze, more informative, and more useful. It will also show school districts how to get started with purchasing analytical data tools.

## Intended Audiences

In these times of high-stakes accountability, all professional educators must learn how to gather, analyze, and use data to improve teaching and learning. This does not mean they must become statisticians. Rather, it means they must become efficient generators and consumers of data. The intended audiences for this book are school and district administrators and teacher leaders who recognize the need to use data to continuously improve teaching and learning, especially those who are considering purchasing analytical data tools. This book is also intended for college and university professors who teach educational personnel at the undergraduate and graduate levels. All professional educators must understand the impact data can make on educational quality, as well as the impact analytical data tools can have on using data.

*Translating Data into Information to Improve Teaching and Learning* complements the *Using Data to Improve Student Learning* series previously published by *Eye on Education*. Each of the books in the series shows, from the first demographic data through the implementation of a continuous improvement plan, what data analysis looks like, as well as, the benefits of using the results. The templates and examples provided on the CDs can be used with any analytical data tools.

These books are:

▼ *Using Data to Improve Student Learning in School Districts (2006)*

▼ *Using Data to Improve Student Learning in High Schools (2005)*

▼ *Using Data to Improve Student Learning in Middle Schools (2004)*

▼ *Using Data to Improve Student Learning in Elementary Schools (2003)*

I hope you find *Translating Data into Information to Improve Teaching and Learning* to be helpful as you work through the processes of using data and data tools to improve teaching at all levels and learning for *all* students.

Sincerely,

Victoria L. Bernhardt, Ph.D.

Executive Director, *Education for the Future Initiative*

400 West First Street, Chico, CA  95929-0230

Tel: 530-898-4482 — Fax: 530-898-4484

e-mail: vbernhardt@csuchico.edu

website: *http://eff.csuchico.edu*

CHAPTER **1**

# INTRODUCTION: A VISION FOR USING DATA TO IMPROVE TEACHING AND LEARNING

*A superintendent I know spoke for 99 percent of the*

*school districts in America today when he told me that*

*his district had systems to manage money down to the dime,*

*but no systems to manage the learning mission. This is the*

*most critical challenge for school districts to meet.*

**Larry Lezotte,** *Learning for All*

## A Vision for Data Tools

In every classroom, imagine starting the school year with historical data about every student—even a student just enrolled in school that morning. The data would include student achievement test results since the student's initial enrollment in school and would track information about what standards she or he has mastered, the names of the student's teachers in previous grades, the absences, discipline referrals, and more—all easily accessible electronically.

*Imagine teachers setting end-of-year goals, assessing students at the beginning of the year to understand what the students know and don't know, and measuring their students' progress toward these goals several times during the year using assessment tools that school and district personnel have selected. By revisiting and measuring their goals throughout the year, teachers are better able to decide whether they need to alter what they are doing to ensure that each student reaches those year-end goals. In addition, teachers can print report cards to send home at the same time the class grades are sent electronically to the district office. Imagine a teacher's computer dashboard alerting her/him immediately after an electronically scored assessment is given that a student is at risk of failing a standard if certain skills are not mastered.*

*At the school level, imagine students accessing a special password-driven section of the classroom database to add self-assessment data, their goals for improvement, and completed projects, and to view assessments and grades with their parents. Imagine students receiving suggestions on electronic lessons to help them learn the concepts they missed on the last assessment. Just imagine parents' delight with their ability to view or receive, on demand, progress reports about their daughter or son!*

*At the district level, imagine administrators knowing exactly which data reports are crucial for helping schools understand the impact of their processes on student learning. These enlightened districts "batch" (i.e., predefine, automatically assemble, and produce) standard reports to all schools to give them powerful information about their systems. These districts also use these data to show administrators where and when the district needs to provide new programs, professional development, technical assistance, leadership, and other resources to achieve the purpose and mission of the district. The data could ensure that a continuum of learning is maintained within and across schools.*

*Imagine school and district administrators being alerted by their computer dashboards when students are absent. Phone calls can be made to determine the reason for a student's absence and to get truant students back to school. Ongoing evaluations can be made to ensure instructional offerings are compelling enough to keep the students interested in school. Alerts can also be triggered when student information has been "misentered" into the district's comprehensive integrated information system. This system would allow administrators to check and recode records such as free/reduced lunch status. For example, if younger siblings of a high school student have been identified as qualifying for free or reduced lunch status and the high schooler has not, the alert system would identify the high school student as someone whose records do not accurately reflect her/his status. These alerts could be set to keep the district from losing dollars and to ensure the accuracy of data, the safety of children, and the effectiveness of instructional offerings.*

*Now imagine that all of this information, which helps teachers, schools, and districts perform most effectively for all students, also satisfies all the state and federal departments of education data requirements. Imagine the ability to send reports electronically to state and federal agencies with the touch of a key.*

***Imagine having the data tools that would do all these things and more....***

## Data and Data Tools are Important for Improving Teaching and Learning

Data can help teachers, principals, and school district administrators ensure a continuum of learning from preschool to elementary to middle to high school, and even to college. Data can also provide valuable information with respect to the effectiveness of instruction, professional development, financial expenditures, and specific programs and processes, districtwide and at each school.

With data, schools can monitor a continuum of learning across grade levels, in alignment with the school and district visions, and identify specific school needs. Data can give school personnel the ability to predict potential successes, as well as to intercede to prevent failure from occurring and to ensure success.

In classrooms, teachers can know exactly how a student has performed on different student achievement measures and standards when the student first arrives in class. Teachers can monitor each student's progress on an on-going basis and know exactly the knowledge and skills attained by each student as she or he moves on to the next grade. Based on data, instructional strategies can be adjusted at any time to ensure attainment of the standards by all students.

Without the use of data at each grade level and across grade levels, instructional decisions, which ultimately impact students, are based on best guesses, hunches, gut feelings, and experiences; what some refer to as gut-based decision making. Without the use of data that reflect actual learning measures and not just test scores, personnel at each grade level are probably doing the same things over and over and experiencing disappointment because they are expecting different results.

If personnel in districts, schools, and classrooms want to improve student learning and teaching effectiveness, as well as spend money more efficiently, they have to use data. If these personnel had access to quality data when they needed them and knew how to use them, the world of education would look very different from the way it looks today. If dollars could be spent only on effective programs, perhaps students would not fall through the cracks. Programs that are not working could be identified, and the resources used for these programs could be redirected to better address student learning. Lost dollars due to miscoding, missing forms, or absent students could be regained and reinvested into instructional programming.

Teachers, school administrators, and regulatory office and school district personnel need data to understand the impact of their work with schools and students. With comprehensive data analysis, educational personnel are able to understand the results of their efforts, pinpoint what is working and what is not,

*Data can give school personnel the ability to predict potential successes as well as to intercede to prevent failure from occurring and to ensure success.*

*If personnel in districts, schools, and classrooms want to improve student learning and teaching effectiveness, as well as spend money more efficiently, they have to use data.*

and tailor better learning experiences for individual students. In order to use data effectively to improve teaching and learning, educators need to acquire and use data tools.

## Purpose and Contents of this Book

The purposes of this book are threefold: 1) to describe what data can improve teaching and learning, 2) to assist educators in thinking through the issues surrounding the selection of data tools that will help them get the data they need to improve teaching and learning, and 3) to facilitate educators' understandings of quality data and reports at each educational level to improve teaching and learning. To these ends:

*Chapter 1* provides a vision for using data to improve teaching and learning and establishes the need for data tools to use data effectively.

*Chapter 2* describes the functions of today's most used data tools—student information systems, curriculum/instruction/assessment management software, and analytical data tools such as data warehouses—and how they must integrate with each other.

*Chapter 3* discusses what data will provide the information needed to improve teaching and learning.

*Chapter 4* delves into the issue of cleaning data and how to improve data quality.

*Chapter 5* explains analytical data tools such as data warehouses and highlights issues learning organizations must think through as they plan to transform data into information to improve teaching and learning.

*Chapter 6* covers the topics of data discovery and data mapping; both of which are necessary to prepare data to connect into a warehouse or any other analytical data tool.

*Chapter 7* provides tips on selecting analytical data tools.

*Chapter 8* looks at whether you should create your own inhouse analytical data tools or go with an outside vendor; it also provides an example of a district that created tools itself.

*Chapter 9* offers advice on how to create a culture that values the use of data and data tools.

*Chapter 10* addresses reporting and using data results to improve teaching and learning.

*Chapter 11* gives an account of who must get trained on the data tools and who should have access.

*Chapter 12* answers questions about managing the data tools or warehouse—how much time it will take, how many people it takes, and what is included.

*Chapter 13* reports on school districts using data warehouses to improve teaching and learning.

*Chapter 14* offers recommendations on how to get started with a data warehouse to improve teaching and learning.

*Appendix* contains the *Education for the Future Continuous Improvement Continuums* for districts and schools.

*Glossary of Terms* lists the terms used throughout the book and other terms that educators will encounter as they learn more about data tools, data warehouses, and data analyses.

*References and Resources* lists the references used to write this book, along with additional resources.

## Summary

We can imagine educational learning organizations using data, thoroughly and effectively, to improve teaching and learning. If we can imagine it, then we should be able to make it happen. In fact, some districts are realizing this vision today, as you will see in some examples later in this book. To make this vision a reality, learning organizations need data tools. *Translating Data into Information to Improve Teaching and Learning* describes how school districts can improve teaching and learning at all levels by analyzing and converting their raw data into meaningful information and reports that can also inform schools, school districts, states, and the community about student progress.

# CHAPTER 2

# DATA TOOLS FOR IMPROVING TEACHING AND LEARNING

There is no doubt that the Elementary and Secondary Education Act of 2001, commonly known as No Child Left Behind (NCLB), has impacted educators' uses of data in the United States. In fact, every American school district now knows that improving student learning requires the collection, analysis, and use of data. With the use of data comes the need for tools, particularly student information systems, curriculum/ instruction/assessment management tools, and data analysis tools. Tools are necessary to get needed data into the hands of teachers, without having to wait for the district data "expert" to provide the data and the answers. Many districts do not have data "experts"; therefore, teachers just do not get the data.

Excellent tools to keep track of data and to ensure that all students meet learning standards are available now to do all those things imagined in Chapter 1; the hard part is figuring out which data tools you need, what functions you want them to provide, and which tool(s) you need first. These choices can get confusing. Technology companies claiming they are devoted to education spring up every day. Some companies focus on student information and data warehouse products; others specialize in curriculum, instruction, or short-cycle assessment management. Although some companies claim to do it all, none do—at this point. There may never be a system that does all these things because the technology, engineering, and focus behind each of these systems are very different. School districts need to make sure that any data tools they purchase will "integrate" with any other system. (A discussion of systems integration via the School Interoperability Framework, or SIF, appears later in this chapter.)

*With the use of data comes the need for tools, particularly student information systems, curriculum/instruction/assessment management tools, and data analysis tools.*

*Excellent tools to keep track of data and to ensure that all students meet learning standards are available now.*

*School districts need to make sure that any data tools they purchase will "integrate" with any other system.*

It is inevitable that school districts will eventually want all three types of data tools—student information systems, curriculum/instruction/assessment management, and data analytical tools or data warehouse. The question is, which tools do districts need to buy first to do the job and to make efficient use of increasingly limited resources?

As school districts take steps to acquire and effectively use data tools to improve teaching and learning, they must put the necessary infrastructure in place first. Infrastructure consists of the network and the hardware to run data tools, as well as the tools that will gather the majority of the data that will be used to improve teaching and learning. The tool that is the most essential part of the infrastructure is a district-integrated *student information system*. This is an excellent place to start if a school district does not already have a stable, effective, or efficient way to gather data from schools daily.

> *The tool that is considered the most essential part of the infrastructure is a district-integrated student information system.*

Once a district has a student information system in place, the product the district buys next often depends on who is on the committee to investigate data tools. Teachers and many administrators will always want curriculum/instruction/ assessment management tools next; data "experts" and some administrators often want a data warehouse management system next. Ultimately, districts buy whichever of these systems they did not buy in the first or second round of purchases of data tools.

Knowing that school districts will want all three types of data tools eventually, it is important to consider the big picture of how the tools will fit together. That big picture, the one that will do everything imagined in Chapter 1, combines a district's transactional and analytical systems through a systems integrator to allow for the intersection, analysis, and reporting of all data, as illustrated in Figure 2.1. The transactional systems are those that handle the day-to-day operations of collecting, processing, and storing operational data, such as a web-based student information system to gather daily information in an easy-to-manage way. Districts need a system that brings together all data in one district-integrated database—as opposed to separate or site-based databases. Transactional systems are also human resources, financial, plant, equipment, and department-specific databases. Analytical systems are software and databases that assist with the learning mission through tools that help ensure curriculum alignment, instruction and practice coherence, and the assessment of learning standards.

## Figure 2.1
# INTEGRATED DATA WAREHOUSE

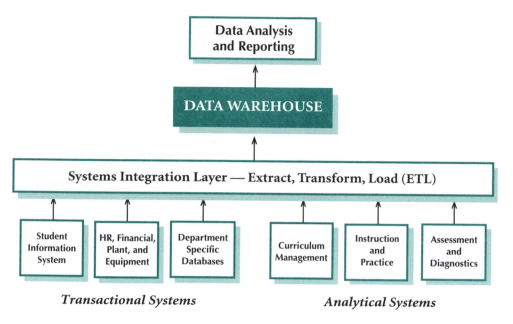

Let's look at the three general types of data tools to understand what the products do and what to look for when purchasing each of them.

## Student Information Systems

Student information systems are transactional or operational databases that house mainly demographic and student achievement data collected on a daily or regular basis. Transactional databases automate repetitive collection of data. In schools, these transactions include data such as class attendance, tardies, discipline referrals, enrollments, scheduling, and grades. Some student information systems have portals for parents to access their children's data. Some allow teachers to enter student grades easily and to set up, administer, and score ongoing assessments. Student information systems help with scheduling students and groups of students into classes. Some will also house human resources data, such as teacher employment demographics, and other items shown as transactional systems in Figure 2.1.

Before the advent of electronically-linked student information systems, teachers used paper and pencil to tally student absences. They sent the paper to the office secretary who, at some point during the day, entered the information into a database or spreadsheet. The data were used to figure out the school's average daily attendance but were seldom used for anything else. Now, student information systems can electronically link classrooms to the overall school database for instant updating, practically taking class roll on their own. Some systems show the class lists in alphabetical order (or a graphic layout of students' desks) on the computer screen. The teacher clicks on each student name or desk to take attendance, and the system enters into the database the names of the students and the class period for which attendance is being recorded. Teachers and administrators can see trends in absences: by student; by school or district; and by time of day, day of the week, or day of the month. A well-designed student information system enables school personnel to study important measures of student engagement, such as attendance, discipline, and suspensions, and to fully analyze problems before attempting a solution. However, without good district procedures for regulating how, what, when, and by whom data are entered into the system, the information might not be useable. Individual schools should not determine how data are entered (more on this in Chapter 4).

*Individual schools should not determine how data are entered into student information systems.*

A student information system that organizes routine and repetitive demographic data is ultimately very important for data analysis to improve teaching and learning. A school district will want to purchase one student information system for the entire district and ensure that the data gathered at each school site will roll-up to the school district database.

When purchasing a student information system, a district must be very clear on what the system does with the data at the end of the year and how many years of data the system will hold. Generally, student information systems are designed only to store and look at annual slices of data; this is one way they differ from data warehouses. Most systems will allow the district to archive all the data at the end of the year and start fresh in the fall. However, some systems will erase the previous year's data as the new year's data are entered. Many districts that assumed their information systems were storing years of student demographic information have been very disappointed to find only the current year's data available when they tried to access information from past years. Check with the student information system vendors on the scalability of the system—its ability to add fields and archive data—and how easy it is to generate reports and to retrieve information once the data have been entered.

Student information systems organize the data all schools need to gather regularly for a particular year, such as attendance of students, teachers, and administrators; discipline referrals; number of students by gender or ethnicity/race; number of students qualifying for free/reduced lunch; language fluency; home language; homelessness; mobility; retention; courses offered; courses assigned to different students and teachers; master schedules; report cards; transcripts; course grades; safety/crime/drug use statistics; health/immunizations; programs (after school, summer school, preschool attendance, service learning, special education, advanced placement, honors, etc.); family living situation; high schoolers taking college courses; middle schoolers taking high school courses; honor roll; and education of parents. Student information system modules also exist for gathering teacher data, such as number of years of teaching, assignments, certifications, training, and attendance. Many districts need to use these modules to analyze teacher data. *These are some of the data every school needs to be gathering to get a clear idea of who its students and teachers are and to get a glimpse into its school processes. A student information system is different from a data warehouse in the way it handles time and its ability to link all appropriate data from multiple sources to a specific student.* Figure 2.2 is a table showing what a student information system (SIS) is, what it is not, what to look for in a SIS, and SIS options.

*A school district will want to purchase one student information system for the entire district and ensure that the data gathered at each school site will roll-up to the school district database.*

*A student information system is different from a data warehouse in the way it handles time and its ability to link all appropriate data from multiple sources to a specific student.*

**Figure 2.2**
# STUDENT INFORMATION SYSTEM

| *What a Student Information System Is* | *What a Student Information System Is Not* |
|---|---|
| ◆ A transactional, or operational, database that gathers and houses basic school data, typically student demographics, enrollments, attendance, disciplinary incidents, grades, and class schedules, and, sometimes, assessment results, financial, and human resources data<br>◆ A system that handles time in annual slices and typically does not combine multiple years in the same database | ◆ A data warehouse<br>◆ A curriculum/instruction/assessment management tool, although it could have some of these pieces<br>◆ A system that allows for longitudinal data analysis (multiple years), although some are coming onto the market |

### *What to Look For in a Student Information System*

- ◆ Web-based, with roll-up functions to a single database (i.e., the ability to aggregate each school's data into an overall school district database)
- ◆ Ease of use (consistency, control, security)
- ◆ Excellent security assurances
- ◆ How many years of data it can retain in the system (what happens to last year's data when a new year begins? Archiving?)
- ◆ Class scheduling abilities
- ◆ Scalability—make sure the system has enough fields to gather all the data you want now and will want in the future, and that it can handle the number of students in the school district, over time
- ◆ The complete package—training, ongoing support, project management
- ◆ Reporting—ease of access, use, and querying
- ◆ Options you want, such as a parent portal, scheduling, grade books (see other options below)
- ◆ Non-proprietary
- ◆ SIF compliance: can integrate with other SIF-compliant curriculum/instruction/assessment management tools and data warehouses; general integration and modularity to other systems

### *Student Information System Options*

Besides being transactional databases for daily demographic data, student information systems now come with several options. Please be clear on what you want your system to do before talking with vendors. Do not let the options get in the way of your main purpose for purchase. Some options include:

- ◆ A parent portal that allows parents access to their child's progress
- ◆ Grade book (basic or standards-based)
- ◆ Report cards
- ◆ Scheduling program—critical for high schools
- ◆ Ability to customize fields
- ◆ Ability to generate different types of schedules (i.e., block, standard, etc.)
- ◆ Ability to gather ongoing assessment results
- ◆ Ability to gather human resource and financial data
- ◆ Ability to generate customized reports
- ◆ Digital portfolios
- ◆ Ability to integrate digital photos and generate photo ID cards

# Curriculum/Instruction/Assessment Management Tools

Curriculum/instruction/assessment management tools typically allow users to align K-12 curriculum to standards, provide instruction and curriculum resources and assessments, and measure student performance against standards. Some curriculum/instruction/assessment tools store shared lesson plans and connect teachers in school districts globally. Curriculum/ instruction/assessment management tools are neither student information systems nor data warehouses.

Curriculum/instruction/assessment management tools help teachers analyze student performance on ongoing assessments and reveal how closely student learning matches the content presented in class. Such systems might—

*Curriculum/instruction/ assessment management tools are neither student information systems nor data warehouses.*

- ▼ provide standards-based lesson plans and resources to help teachers deliver standards-based instruction and to help students learn specific topics;

- ▼ provide ongoing assessments that are standards-based and aligned to the high-stakes assessments;

- ▼ help teachers align classroom instruction to lesson plans and curriculum frameworks;

- ▼ help teachers and schools align lessons and assessments to standards; and

- ▼ help teachers align curriculum across grades.

*Teachers in Northern School District use a curriculum/instruction/assessment management tool to create their own pre-assessments from a huge selection of test items that are similar to those found on their state standardized assessment. All students take pre-assessments online, and teachers get the results soon after so they can quickly see which standards students know and which standards need further clarification. The curriculum/instruction/assessment management tool suggests lessons for covering material that most students answered incorrectly on various assessments. It also links to education web sites for material that a smaller group of students failed to master. Teachers can assess students as many times as they wish throughout the year, and students can monitor their own learning.*

When purchasing a curriculum/instruction/assessment management tool, make sure you are clear on what you want such a tool to do (Figure 2.3). There are so many options, you want to make sure what you purchase is modular so you may add to it as other tools that will assist with curriculum, instruction, and assessment are released.

Figure 2.3

# CURRICULUM/INSTRUCTION/ASSESSMENT MANAGEMENT SYSTEM

| *What a Curriculum/Instruction/Assessment Management System Is* | *What a Curriculum/Instruction/Assessment Management System Is Not* |
|---|---|
| ◆ Tools to manage K-12 standards-aligned curriculum, provide instruction and curriculum resources and assessments, and measure student performance against standards | ◆ A student information system <br> ◆ A data warehouse <br> ◆ A longitudinal data analysis tool |

### *What to Look For in a Curriculum/Instruction/Assessment Management System*

- ◆ Quality tools that allow easy use
- ◆ SIF compliance: can integrate with other SIF-compliant student information systems and data warehouses; general integration and modularity to other systems
- ◆ Total package—training, ongoing support, project management
- ◆ Web-based
- ◆ Excellent security system
- ◆ Scalability—make sure the tool can handle all that you want it to be able to do. Can it handle the number of concurrent users and students in your district?
- ◆ Reporting—ease of access, use, and ad-hoc querying
- ◆ Immediate reporting of results
- ◆ Non-proprietary
- ◆ Alignment of content to state standards

### *Curriculum/Instruction/Assessment Management System Options*

New curriculum/instruction/assessment management tools are springing up every day, and new features are added on a regular basis. Some current options include:
- ◆ Tools to align the district's curriculum to state or other standards
- ◆ Storage and retrieval area for lesson plans
- ◆ Recommendations for remedial lessons
- ◆ Suggestions for standards-based lesson plans
- ◆ Item bank of questions for creating assessments (How many items are in the item bank? How many are actually aligned or correlated to your state's standards?)
- ◆ Ability to integrate pre-packaged test content from textbook publishers or other sources
- ◆ Suggestions for curriculum, instruction, and assessment resources
- ◆ Virtual schools/online education
- ◆ Digital media
- ◆ Professional learning for teachers
- ◆ Interoperability with student information and other systems

## Data Warehouses

Data warehouses are analytical databases that store many years of data and enable school districts to analyze data across different data systems, such as student information systems, databases of student achievement test results/school program/process data, and information about student, parent, and staff perceptions. Business Intelligence (BI) or analytical tools are needed with a warehouse to provide school districts with statistical capabilities such as analyzing longitudinal data, disaggregating data, and following cohorts of students over time, as well as other more sophisticated statistical analyses. Combining BI/analytical tools with a robust data warehouse is powerful for following students' education histories backward, regardless of what schools they attended (as long as that information is in the warehouse). For example, educators can identify all the students who dropped out of a particular high school in a given year and then compare factors in these youths' education histories for all previous years, noting any common characteristics. Such information could be invaluable in lowering a school's dropout rate by identifying programs and strategies to keep students in school.

With a data warehouse, schools can analyze the impact of instructional programs and processes on teaching and learning. For example: *Evergreen School District used its data warehouse to analyze student achievement results by demographics, by instructional methods, and by preferred student learning styles. Using this tool, Evergreen teachers quickly saw that their students from low-income backgrounds learned more effectively when teachers presented content in an active, hands-on format. Teachers also saw that high school girls in the district were enrolled in more Advanced Placement classes and were getting significantly higher GPAs than were high school boys. Deeper analyses of past successful approaches could indicate teaching strategies that would be more successful with boys.*

Data warehouses can connect directly to student information systems and curriculum/instruction/assessment management systems so a school district is able to receive regularly updated data in the data warehouse. Some data warehouses have dashboards for users to get instant and ongoing information that they determine to be most important. Look for easy to use BI/analytical tools that truly integrate any database system in your district when selecting your data warehouse. (Chapter 7 covers how to select a data warehouse.)

*With a data warehouse, schools can analyze the impact of instructional programs and processes on teaching and learning.*

> *Data warehouses allow longitudinal and comprehensive data analyses with multiple variables from multiple sources.*

Educational data warehouses allow the manipulation and integration of multiple databases connected to one another through individual student and teacher identification numbers and through class schedules that link students to teachers. An excellent educational data warehouse will link student demographic and grading data from a student information system to standardized student test scores that might come from a testing company, to program/process and human resource data from separate databases, and to curriculum/instruction/assessment management systems. One can access these different types of data for an individual student without re-entering the basic student information each time. Educational data warehouses often have a dashboard (Figure 2.4) or a scorecard that will show administrators or teachers, on their computer screens, any data they want to monitor on an ongoing basis via a password-protected portal. Data warehouses allow longitudinal and comprehensive data analyses with multiple variables from multiple sources. Figure 2.5 reviews what an educational data warehouse is, what it is not, what to look for in an educational data warehouse, and options available.

## Figure 2.4
## DATA WAREHOUSE DASHBOARD

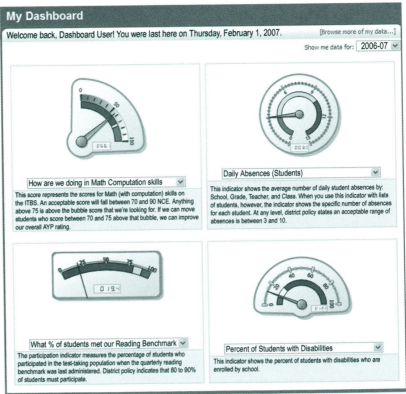

Adapted from TetraData, a subsidiary of Follett Software Company. Reproduced by permission.

**Figure 2.5**
# EDUCATIONAL DATA WAREHOUSE

| *What an Educational Data Warehouse Is* | *What an Educational Data Warehouse Is Not* |
|---|---|
| • A tool that allows longitudinal and comprehensive data analysis with multiple variables from multiple sources<br>• A reporting tool | • A student information system—you need to use a system other than the data warehouse to gather your ongoing school data<br>• A curriculum/instruction/assessment management tool; however, it should be able to integrate with such a component<br>• An operational or transactional system (such as human resources or student information system), but a data warehouse can integrate and use those data analytically |

### What to Look For in an Educational Data Warehouse

• Quality BI/analytical tools that allow easy querying and use
• SIF compliance: general integration and modularity to other SIF or non-SIF-compliant systems; can integrate with curriculum/instruction/assessment management and student information systems
• Total package—data import tools, data storage, data analytic tools, training, ongoing support, project management
• Web-based
• Excellent security system
• Architecture Data Capacity/Scalability—make sure the system has enough fields to gather all the data you want now and will want in the future and that it can handle the number of students in the school district, over time
• Reporting—ease of access, use, and querying
• The use of a generally accepted industry software platform
• Multiple role-based tools to meet the needs of every user
• Ability to manage your own data
• Ability to export data to other applications for statistical analyses
• Unlimited capacity for adding, relating, and analyzing data sets
• A technology that is specifically built for education and that has a multi-year history of successfully servicing the needs of education customers (versus a technology that was built for business and is being forced-fit to meet education requirements)

### Educational Data Warehouse Options

Data warehouse tools are appearing on the market with new and improved capabilities. Some of the options that anyone in the market for a data warehouse will have to sort through include:
• Dashboard or score card that is user-defined
• Ability to automatically update data from student information systems and curriculum/instruction/assessment management tools every day
• Ability to do sophisticated statistical analyses
• Ability to perform special analyses, such as root cause and value-added
• Ability to generate pre-determined reports for every educational level

## Tips on Enlightened Purchasing

*Selecting the right data tools requires planning and research.*

Selecting the right data tools requires planning and research. Many school districts hope to discover one company that will provide a student information system, a curriculum/instruction/assessment management tool, and a data warehouse all in one. Few companies, if any, offer all three, although some student information systems offer a partial curriculum/instruction/assessment management tool; and some data warehouse companies partner with curriculum/instruction/assessment management and student information system providers to include these capabilities with their products. School personnel can become frustrated as they seek tools in which all three components work together.

Here are some suggestions to help relieve some of the frustration for effectively selecting data tools:

*Be clear about what you are looking for.* Inevitably, as you begin to shop for one kind of data tool, vendors will talk about the other two as well. Be clear about what tools you are interested in purchasing when you start looking. Do you want a student information system, curriculum/instruction/assessment management tools, a data warehouse—or all three? Do you want to buy them all at once or one at a time? If you need a recommendation, I suggest getting the student information system first. Do not feel as though you have to buy all pieces from the same company. A cooperative vendor should help you secure partnerships with other vendors. If your school district cannot afford all three systems, do not be afraid to talk with the vendors about your dilemma. They may be able to adjust prices or propose cost-saving strategies, such as collaborating with other districts in your area to share a server, which would decrease the per-pupil cost of a data system. One data tool company might also join forces with another company to offer your district incentives to buy both products. Be honest with vendors about the amount of money you can afford to spend on tools; they may be able to help you stretch your resources.

*Involve a team with broad membership in the selection process.* Include teachers, administrators, and information management personnel in selecting data tools. Be sure the people who will use the particular product most are represented. One district made the mistake of buying a data warehouse preferred by the teachers, who were the majority on the buying committee. The district's data analysis person was left with a product that did not do what she needed it to do. Many extra hours were spent customizing the data warehouse, and it was still so cumbersome that the district eventually replaced this tool. Another district had administrators purchase an electronic "lesson planning tool" without consulting teachers. That tool was never used. Make sure the vision and expectations for the tool, including what it will not do, are documented for everyone who will use it .

*If the student information system is the first tool you should purchase, what is the second one?* Which tool you buy next depends upon what the district and its staff see as the next step in the transformation from impression-based to data-informed decision making. If your district does not have a means of assessing student learning on an ongoing basis, you might want to invest in a curriculum/ instruction/assessment management tool. If you are conducting ongoing assessments by hand and think you want to use a curriculum/instruction/ assessment management tool to automate this process and you want a data warehouse eventually, you might discover that you can go directly to the data warehouse tool if the vendor has an easy process for loading assessment data.

*Do not attempt to set up several new tools at once.* Setting up any new tool is labor intensive. Setting up more than one is beyond most district's capacities. Converting to a new Student Information System often uncovers data problems that can be fixed before a warehouse is purchased or built.

*Research possible vendors—and have them come to you.* Look into potential vendors' stability, financial status, dedication to education, and longevity serving education customers. Invite them to meet with you in your district or at your school. Do not be timid about asking to see data tools at work. Such tools are a big investment, and you want to know that they will do what you need them to do in your environment.

*Do not automatically go to the lowest bidder.* Stay aware of what you need a data tool to do and the total package. If a company with a less desirable product offers to lower its price, go back to the company you really want to work with and discuss possible pricing options. Often a reduced price also reflects a reduced product that will entail other costs later on. Make sure you are comparing the total cost of the product, including maintenance fees.

*Be sure the tools can talk with one another.* Look for the tools to be SIF compliant. The Schools Interoperability Framework (SIF) is a collaboration of school data stakeholders that sets data exchange standards to enable software packages to communicate with one another. SIF-compliant data tools, which should have this term on the label, interact as one system; data that are entered into one of the data tools can be entered into the other tools automatically, with specified business rules. For example, with a SIF-compliant student information system, curriculum/instruction/assessment management tool, and data warehouse, a student's name and identification number would have to be entered only once. The name and identification number would automatically be entered into all the other systems. Do note, however, *SIF moves data. SIF does not clean data.* If you have dirty data in one system, you could be moving dirty (or inaccurate) data around in every other system. See Chapter 4 on cleaning your data. (Visit *http://www.sifinfo.org* for more detailed information on SIF and a current list of companies that offer SIF-compliant products.)

*Make sure the tools are modular and expandable.* As you purchase elements of your total package, make sure that the tools can expand to handle multiple years, increasing enrollments, and additional data fields you might want to add at a later date. Also, make sure other tools can be integrated into the total package.

*Buy only tools that manage and share data using non-proprietary architecture.* Avoid proprietary software which is engineered so you cannot integrate tools from other vendors. Any of the tools you purchase should be scalable and based on generally accepted industry architecture (e.g., MS SQL Server, Oracle, XML, etc.).

*If you have some old tools that are not SIF compliant, do not throw them out just yet.* Most quality data warehousing companies are able to connect just about any system to their warehouses using what the industry calls extract, transform, and load (ETL) tools. Check with the data warehouse vendor about how you can use non-SIF compliant or ETL tools.

*Purchase tools from vendors that have a solid total package.* Look for a great company with a tool that does what you want it to do, provides quality training, and has excellent ongoing support, including online support and user conferences. Project management is an often overlooked service that is critical to the success of your implementation; ask for a detailed project management and implementation plan. Consider these elements, as well as your staffing cost-savings, as you calculate the Total Cost of Ownership (TCO). You may pay more for the initial total package; but, in the long run, you will get more effective use out of your investment and more for your dollar.

*Talk with current users.* Ask lots of questions, not only about the products, but also about the people with whom you will be working. Will these vendors follow through with their promises and be there to support you through all parts of the process? How does the company deal with problems? Do they play the "blame game" or pragmatically go about solving the problem? Ask for three to five references of school districts that have used the product for more than one year. Do not think you have to speak only with districts that are the same size as yours. The work is the same whether you are working with 5,000 students or 50,000. Contact these users to learn of their experiences with the tools and the vendor.

*Ask the vendor what the district will be required to do or to provide in order to be successful.* A good, reputable company will not be afraid to tell you what you need to provide from the district side of the project.

## Do We Really Need a Data Warehouse?

There are data tools on the market that can connect disparate databases and data sources. The amount of work and knowledge it takes to do this often requires a dedicated engineer. These solutions are effective only if they can connect all sources of data, longitudinally, *and* help manage the quality of the data. A data warehouse generally does a more complete job for the typical school district. (See Chapter 8 for more on this topic.)

## Summary

Data can make the difference in improving teaching and learning. We want teachers and administrators to use data to improve teaching and learning in every classroom in every school. In order to get educators to use data, we need to get the data into their hands with the least amount of effort on their parts. Data tools are necessary. The three most often needed and used types of tools are student information systems, curriculum/instruction/assessment management tools, and data warehouses. Many hope that one product will do all three things; however, right now, they are three distinct tools with three distinct roles. Nevertheless, SIF-compliant data tools are able to interact as one tool.

With data tools, teachers and administrators are able to know which students are meeting which learning standards and which strategies will assist teachers in helping each student learn and succeed. Data tools are necessary for analyzing data to improve teaching and learning at all levels and in all schools. Acquiring these tools calls for a big investment in dollars and in time. Involving the right people in selecting the necessary tools will ensure that you will find a good fit with a vendor and will ensure that the tools will be used. Realize that you are making a ten-year commitment (hopefully), not just a two or three-year decision. Choosing the right vendor-partner could be one of the most important decisions you will make with regard to improving teaching and learning.

CHAPTER 3

# DATA THAT WILL IMPROVE TEACHING AND LEARNING

What data should school districts include in their data analyses that will help improve teaching and learning? Since teaching and learning are at the heart of the business of education for any school district, deciding what data to include in its comprehensive data analyses to help improve teaching and learning is of utmost importance as a data warehouse is being planned. Data are numbers that represent measurements, observations, or a variable. Data analysis is the act of transforming data into useful information to facilitate decision making.

When asked what data are important for data-driven decision making, most schools and school districts say student achievement results. School districts believe they are being data-driven when they have analyzed the dickens out of their state assessment results. In some states, school districts feel they are being data-driven when they analyze the dickens out of their state assessment results *and* use some benchmark assessments to help students prepare for the state test. Test scores, however, are only the beginning of data-driven decision making. Other elements, such as demographics, perceptions, and school processes, impact student achievement in various ways. Test scores are a good start, but they fall short of providing all the information needed for sound decision making.

## Student Achievement Results

Just because test results are the measures that some stakeholders choose to hold schools accountable for teaching and learning does not mean that these data are the most useful measures to schools for *improving* teaching and learning. Data that seem to be the most important to our stakeholders as measures of teaching and learning are some of the least useful when trying to *improve* teaching and learning.

Certainly test score analyses are important. In fact, in a perfect world, schools would use both formative and summative assessments to ensure that all students are learning. If only summative assessment data are studied, however, solutions for improving the scores might be incomplete.

Test scores tell us some things about the quality of educational programs, but test scores alone just do not provide enough information to make decisions about improving the quality of these programs. Test scores are outcome measures. To understand how to change these outcomes, schools need to know the inputs of the programs, what is being implemented, and how things need to change to get different results. Programs and individual strategies that are being used to deliver the curriculum must be carefully monitored and evaluated. Districts and schools need to know details about who the students are and what they and other stakeholders think about what the district and the schools are doing to help them succeed. Schools need to know the impacts of the programs, what is being implemented, and understand how things need to change to get different results. Different results will never be achieved if schools keep doing the things they have always been doing. Only by having change driven by a wide variety of data that are readily available will different results be achieved.

Demographic, school process, and perceptions data, along with student learning measures, can help schools know if what they are doing is meeting the needs of the students, and what they need to do differently to get different results. These four data categories are discussed on the pages that follow. Figure 3.1 shows these four measures as overlapping circles. The overlapping circles show how the data categories can intersect in numerous ways. (For more on the four circles, see *Data Analysis for Continuous School Improvement* [Bernhardt, 2004].)

> *Just because test results are the measures that some stakeholders choose to hold schools accountable does not mean that these data are the most useful measures to schools for improving teaching and learning.*

## Figure 3.1
# MULTIPLE MEASURES OF DATA

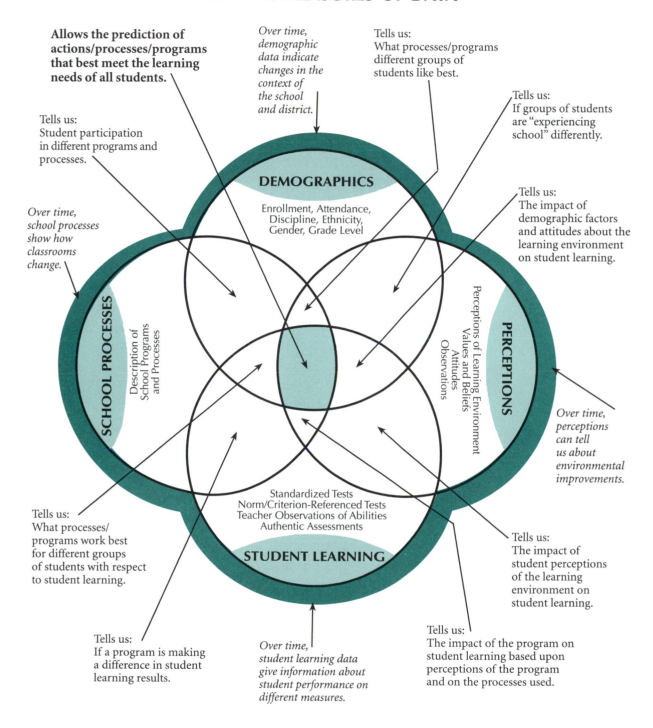

**Allows the prediction of actions/processes/programs that best meet the learning needs of all students.**

*Over time, demographic data indicate changes in the context of the school and district.*

Tells us:
What processes/programs different groups of students like best.

Tells us:
If groups of students are "experiencing school" differently.

Tells us:
Student participation in different programs and processes.

Tells us:
The impact of demographic factors and attitudes about the learning environment on student learning.

*Over time, school processes show how classrooms change.*

**DEMOGRAPHICS**

Enrollment, Attendance, Discipline, Ethnicity, Gender, Grade Level

**SCHOOL PROCESSES**

Description of School Programs and Processes

Perceptions of Learning Environment
Values and Beliefs
Attitudes
Observations

**PERCEPTIONS**

*Over time, perceptions can tell us about environmental improvements.*

Tells us:
What processes/programs work best for different groups of students with respect to student learning.

Standardized Tests
Norm/Criterion-Referenced Tests
Teacher Observations of Abilities
Authentic Assessments

**STUDENT LEARNING**

Tells us:
The impact of student perceptions of the learning environment on student learning.

Tells us:
If a program is making a difference in student learning results.

*Over time, student learning data give information about student performance on different measures.*

Tells us:
The impact of the program on student learning based upon perceptions of the program and on the processes used.

*Example Demographic
Data to Gather*

- *Number of schools,
  administrators, students,
  and teachers*
- *Safety/crime data*
- *Class sizes: student-teacher
  ratios*
- *Student living situation,
  family structure, and size*
- *Preschool attendance*
- *Student gender, ethnicity,
  free/reduced lunch status,
  language fluency*
- *Student/teacher attendance*
- *Student mobility, retention,
  dropout rate*
- *Teacher years of experience,
  degrees, ethnicity, gender,
  languages spoken, turnover,
  retirement projections*

*Enrollment in:*

- *Title I/schoolwide*
- *Extracurricular activities*
- *After-school programs/
  summer school*
- *Gifted, AP classes*
- *Tutoring/peer-mentoring*
- *Community-support services*
- *Counseling opportunities*
- *Special education*
- *Interventions*

## Demographic Data

Demographic data provide descriptive information about the district, the schools, students, parents, administrators, and staff. Demographic data include enrollment, attendance, discipline, grade level, ethnicity, gender, native language, number of years of teaching, qualifications, etc. By looking at demographic data over time, we can observe trends and glean information for purposes of predicting and planning.

Demographic data give us a glimpse of the system and how the district organizes itself for success. Demographic data, which also include enrollment by program offering, can begin to tell us about program implementation and the culture of school, including how students are treated and moved around the system. For example, the percentage of students by gender and ethnicity in special education ought to be the same as the percentage of students by gender and ethnicity for the entire school. Think about enrollment in special education or advanced placement; does enrollment in these programs reflect the demographics of the school and the district? By monitoring these demographic results and keeping the intentions of the programs clear, schools can make sure they are using interventions appropriately.

Longitudinal demographic data often stay basically the same, unless something happens in the community, such as an influx of immigrant families, or new policies go into effect, or if the leadership becomes either inadequate or highly effective.

I believe it is important to create a data profile or a comprehensive picture of all demographic data from the most general to the most specific for the district and for each of the schools within the district. These profiles will begin to tell the story of the system. *Using Data to Improve Student Learning in School Districts* (Bernhardt, 2006) shows a complete data analysis for a real school district and reveals what the data indicate about how to improve the system to impact teaching and learning. Most demographic data are readily available for import into a data warehouse via student information systems.

## School Processes

School processes define what learning organizations, and those who work in them, are doing to help students learn: what they teach and how they group, teach, and assess students. School processes include curriculum, programs, instruction and assessment strategies, interventions, responses to interventions, and all other classroom practices. To change the results the district and schools are getting, administrators and teachers must document what processes are being *implemented*. That information must be aligned to the results they are getting in order to understand what to improve to get different results and to share how they are getting their successes. To truly know if a reading program is successful or not, we have to know how reading is taught in each classroom in every school.

School processes are the hardest measures to quantify. This is a task we all have to work on to really comprehend the impact of our processes and to understand how to improve teaching and learning. If the implementation of specific processes is not being measured or monitored, those processes are probably not being implemented. Districts and schools must devote time to the management and assessment of school processes so successful processes can be shared and unsuccessful practices can be redesigned or eliminated. Measuring processes is one of the most important actions we can take to improve K-12 education. Processes are all those curriculum elements, instructional strategies, and programs that we have extensive control over in education. However, they are some of the hardest parts to measure.

Quantifiable school process information could include: walk-through assessments, program enrollments (as mentioned in the demographic section above), course programs and interventions, flow charts, amount of time allotted for a subject, and specific classroom observations. School process data can be entered into a data warehouse through flat files, spreadsheets, databases, or by coding program information (e.g., noting specific program participation) along with student and teacher information in the student information system.

*Example School Process Data to Gather*

- ◆ *Curriculum*
- ◆ *Programs*
- ◆ *Instructional strategies*
- ◆ *Assessment strategies*
- ◆ *Interventions*
- ◆ *Responses to interventions*
- ◆ *All other classroom practices*

*Measuring processes is one of the most important actions we can take to improve K–12 education. Processes are all those curriculum elements, instructional strategies, and programs that we have extensive control over in education. However, they are some of the hardest parts to measure.*

## Perceptions

*Example Perceptions Data to Gather*

- *Students' perceptions of the learning organization*

- *Staff perceptions of the learning organization*

- *Parents' perceptions of the learning organization*

- *Community perceptions of the learning organization*

- *Perceptions of program implementation*

- *Alumni perceptions of learning experiences*

Perceptions data help us understand what students, parents, staff, and others think about the learning environment, a program, or a process—or how students learn, and what different constituents believe it would take to improve teaching and learning. Perceptions can be gathered through questionnaires, interviews, focus groups, and/or observations. Perceptions are important because actions reflect what people believe, perceive, or think. Perceptions data can also tell us what is possible with respect to change.

Perceptions about learning styles, teaching styles, or program implementation might include an identification number or name so that this information can be analyzed with additional data from the three other measures of data. (Sometimes preferred learning and teaching styles are considered a demographic.)

Perceptions data can also be gathered anonymously so respondents do not feel someone can track non-positive, albeit honest, responses to survey questions. If names or any sort of identification are not required, those perceptions data might not be included in the data warehouse or only go in as group aggregations. Some school districts put their aggregated questionnaire results in the warehouse to allow access to the results and to create the opportunity to cross these data with other data, even if the data cannot be linked to individuals. They can be linked to schools and grade levels if these demographic data are requested.

Perceptions data can be entered into a data warehouse through a questionnaire database, flat files, a student information system, or the same data tool that allows a school to gather ongoing assessment data. (Visit the Education for the Future website at *http://eff.csuchico.edu* for questionnaire resources and services.)

## Student Learning

Student learning describes the outcomes of our educational system in terms of standardized test results, grade-point averages, standards assessments, diagnostic assessments, assessments "of" and "for" learning, and ongoing or short-cycle assessments. Schools often use a variety of student-learning measures, sometimes separately, without thinking about how these measures interrelate.

Student-learning results must be disaggregated by demographics and school processes, systematically and comprehensively, and then analyzed to ensure that all students are learning and to ensure that school processes are meeting the needs of all students. These analyses can be further understood by taking perceptual data into consideration.

Student learning results can be entered into a data warehouse through flat files provided by the testing companies, through the student information system, or through any other data tool that assists with assessments of and for student learning.

> *Example Student Learning Data to Gather*
>
> ♦ *Standardized test results*
>
> ♦ *Grade-point averages*
>
> ♦ *Standards assessment*
>
> ♦ *Diagnostic assessments*
>
> ♦ *Assessments "of" and "for" learning*
>
> ♦ *Ongoing or short-cycle assessments*

## Input/Process/Outcome

Let's think about the most common data elements organized in terms of *input, process,* and *outcome.* In other words, of the most common data elements, which ones represent *inputs* or *givens;* which ones reflect our *processes* or *systems;* and which ones are *outcomes* or *results.* Figure 3.2 shows about 30 common data elements (not exhaustive) grouped by *Input/Process/Outcome.* A brief discussion follows the graphic.

## Figure 3.2
# INPUT, PROCESS, OUTCOME (IPO) DATA ELEMENTS

| Input / Givens → | Process / System → | Outcome / Results |
|---|---|---|
| Student Background | Purpose, Mission, and Vision | Student Achievement Results |
| Staff Background and Qualifications | Leadership/ Policies | Student and Teacher Attendance |
| Parent–Community Characteristics | Curriculum | Student Behaviors |
| Perceptions: Preconceived Notions, Expectations | Program Offerings and Access | Student Attitudes |
| Learning Styles Preferences | Staffing Assignments | Teacher Attitudes |
| Teaching Styles Preferences | Instructional Strategies and Materials | Graduation Rates Dropout Rates |
| Core Values and Beliefs | Assessment Strategies and Materials | Student Careers |
| Student Learning Standards | Professional Learning, Planning, and Collaboration | Student Success in College |
| | Parent– Community Relationships | Parent–Community Attitudes |
| | Physical Environment | District/School Climate |
| | Financial Allocations | |

*Note.* From *Translating Data into Information to Improve Teaching and Learning,* by Victoria L. Bernhardt, 2007, Larchmont, NY: Eye on Education.
Copyright © 2007 Eye on Education, Inc.

## Input—The Givens

It behooves us to understand very clearly whom we are serving and to employ the most highly qualified teachers and staff to best serve our students and their needs. The *inputs* are what districts and schools need to take into consideration as they create processes and systems for teaching and learning. Input data elements set the context of the organization, are at the core of who we are, and are often difficult to change. Input data elements include, but are not limited to, the following (Note: the *italicized* words in parentheses indicate where these data elements appear in the four circles, shown as Figure 3.1):

▼ Student backgrounds (e.g., gender, ethnicity, language fluency, free/reduced lunch status, disability, number of years in the system) *(Demographics)*

▼ Characteristics of parents/community *(Demographics)*

▼ Who the teachers and administrators are (e.g., gender, ethnicity, number of years teaching experience, qualifications, understanding of student needs) *(Demographics)*

▼ Preconceived notions/expectations *(Perceptions)*

▼ Learning preferences (student learning styles) *(Demographics)*

▼ Teaching styles preferences *(Demographics)*

▼ Values and beliefs of everyone in the organization *(Perceptions)*

▼ Student learning standards *(School Processes)*

## Process—The System

*Process* data elements are the actions that learning organizations plan and implement to get the outcomes they are striving to achieve. Given whom we have as administrators, teachers, students, parents, and community, what processes will get us to our desired outcomes? Clearly, a district purpose, mission, and vision, along with what we expect students to know and be able to do (standards), should lead all efforts.

These guiding principles, along with the following, make up the system:

▼ Leadership

▼ Policies

▼ Financial allocations

▼ Curriculum

▼ Instructional strategies

▼ Instructional materials

▼ Assessment strategies

▼ Program offerings and access

▼ Staffing assignments

▼ Professional learning

▼ Parent/community relations

▼ District and school environments

Effective and high-quality processes are based on an understanding of input data elements and the relationships of the three—*input, process,* and *outcome.*

## Outcome—The Results

*Outcome* data elements describe the results of the processes a learning organization puts in place, given the inputs. In other words, the outcomes we get are dependent upon the processes we employ for our students, teachers, and administrators. District and school outcomes include:

▼ Student achievement results *(Student Learning)*

▼ Student and teacher attendance *(Demographics)*

▼ Student behaviors *(Demographics)*

▼ Student attitudes *(Perceptions)*

▼ Teacher attitudes *(Perceptions)*

▼ Graduation rates, dropout rates *(Demographics)*

▼ Student careers after high school *(Demographics)*

▼ Student success in college *(Demographics)*

▼ Parent-community attitudes *(Perceptions)*

▼ District/school climate *(Perceptions)*

Any time one wants to know if a data element is an outcome or not, just ask if a school can get different results from the same student (e.g., behavior) via different teachers, and if so, you know it is an outcome of the processes or strategies used. For example, many teachers would argue that student behaviors and attitudes are givens. However, just about every teacher would agree that different teachers get different behavior and attitudes from the same student(s), just as different administrators can get different attitudes from teachers. It follows then that teachers' and administrators' strategies are processes and that attitudes and behaviors are outcomes.

## Looking at Input/Process/Outcome Data

Looking at data elements as *Input, Process,* or *Outcome,* we can see several things:

1. How few *givens* truly exist in a learning organization. Sometimes educators think there are many data elements that are beyond their control, when there are actually very few that are not changeable. Some inputs, such as teaching preferences, are hard to change. However, through careful planning, professional learning, and collaboration, we can change these inputs.

2. Given how few *input* data elements exist in most learning organizations, educators should know what these inputs are. Knowing the input data elements is critical for creating appropriate processes to achieve outstanding results or outcomes.

3. *Processes* are how learning organizations get their results, given the *inputs.* Teachers have beliefs about which processes impact student learning, and they turn those beliefs into actions in their classrooms. How these actions get implemented is often dependent upon who is implementing them. To assess the impact of processes, learning organizations have to know the degree to which processes are being implemented. It is very important to gather data on these data elements. Processes are hard to measure, but it is necessary to measure and analyze processes if we want to change outcomes or results.

4. *Outcomes* are the results of our *processes,* given the *inputs.* Many times staffs consider outcomes, such as student behavior and attendance, as inputs or givens. As the example on the previous page indicates, if we can get different results from the same student with different teachers—or even students—behavior and attitudes are outcomes of our processes. If staffs consider these outcomes only as givens, they are probably thinking there is nothing they can do to impact student behavior and attitudes when, in reality, they can do a great deal, depending on the strategies or processes, they use.

5. At some point in time, outcomes will be used as inputs to improve processes and systems. The more the data elements are known and analyzed, the more these elements will fall into multiple categories.

In short, to understand how to determine the impact of processes on the inputs, and to know what to change to get better results, data elements from all three groups (inputs/givens, processes/systems, outcomes/results) must be gathered and analyzed in relationship to each other.

## What Data Analyses Are the Most Important for Educational Organizations?

If 100% student proficiency of all student groups is desired (as stated by NCLB), every organization, starting with federal and state departments of education, should be helping school districts, schools, and teachers gather and use data that will help all educators know how to improve what they are doing to get to 100% student proficiency. This requires more than test scores. While learning organizations have to look at all data to understand their systems and to make sure processes are in place to benefit student learning, there are some specific analyses within those profiles that will particularly help each organizational level improve teaching and learning. By analyses, we mean transforming the data into more useful information for decision making. Below is a discussion and outline of different analyses by organizational level, posed as questions, starting with the classroom and working up to the United States Department of Education. The data required to perform the analyses and to answer these questions are shown in the second columns of Figures 3.3 through 3.6.

## Classroom Analyses

*At the classroom level, teachers need to answer two major questions: "Are all students learning what is being taught?" and "Will what is being taught help all students learn what they are expected to know and be able to do?"*

At the classroom level, teachers need to answer two major questions: *Are all students learning what is being taught?* and *Will what is being taught help all students learn what they are expected to know and be able to do?*

Teachers need to understand how each student prefers to learn and what teachers must do to create a continuum of learning that makes sense for students. Student learning measures can help teachers see if all students are learning; process and perceptions data, combined with student learning measures, can help teachers understand what needs to be altered in their teaching strategies to meet the needs and learning styles of all students. Student demographic data can help teachers know if there is a student group that requires special attention, different instructional materials, or has different ways of learning. Staff standards assessments can help everyone see if all teachers are teaching to the standards and creating a continuum of learning that makes sense to students, as well as what teachers think it would take to improve their teaching and the learning of all students. Figure 3.3 is a table of Classroom Analyses.

**Figure 3.3**

# CLASSROOM ANALYSES

| Data Questions | Data Needed |
|---|---|
| • *Are ALL students learning what is being taught?* | • Student learning: Ongoing assessments, grades, standards assessments by demographics, and by individual student and class<br>• Student perceptions of teaching and learning, by gender, ethnicity, and grade levels<br>• Student demographics (as a disaggregation)<br>• School processes: What is being taught; how is it being taught? |
| • *Will what is being taught help ALL students learn what they are expected to know and be able to do?* | • School processes: What is being taught; how is it being taught?<br>• Student learning: Results across time, disaggregated by demographics<br>• Student perceptions<br>• Student demographics (as a disaggregation)<br>• Student learning standards |
| • *How do students prefer to learn?* | • Student perceptions: Student learning styles<br>• Student learning: Ongoing assessments, grades, standards assessments, by individual student and class<br>• Student demographics (as a disaggregation)<br>• School process assessment (could be questionnaires or classroom observations) |
| • *Is there a continuum of learning in place for ALL students?* | • Staff perceptions: Standards implementation questionnaire<br>• School process assessment (measured through observations, questionnaires, flowcharting)<br>• Student learning results by and across grade levels and over time<br>• Student demographics (as a disaggregation) |

## School Analyses

At the school level, teachers and administrators need to know on an ongoing basis how they are doing, if the system is setup for success, and that they are creating instructional congruence—a continuum of learning that makes sense for all students. If there is no instructional congruence, the data analyses need to illustrate why not. School process data, staff perceptions, and student learning results by teacher and student can help a school see where there might be effectiveness issues, and if all staff are collectively meeting the purpose and mission of the school. To this end, administrators need to know if staff members are on the same page with the mission and vision and how to get them on the same page.

Staffs must look at the data at a school level to enable teachers to be successful in every classroom at every level (Figure 3.4).

*At the school level, teachers and administrators need to know on an ongoing basis how they are doing, if the system is setup for success, and that they are creating instructional congruence— a continuum of learning that makes sense for all students.*

## Figure 3.4
## SCHOOL ANALYSES

| Data Questions | Data Needed |
|---|---|
| • *How are we doing as an educational organization?* | Data profile of:<br>• Demographics    • Perceptions<br>• School Processes    • Student Learning |
| • *Is the system set up for success?* | • Student learning: Ongoing assessments, grades, standards assessments, by student demographics<br>• Staff demographics: Number of years of teaching, by grade level<br>• Student, staff, and parent perceptions<br>• School processes, by student demographics (e.g., program enrollments, by gender and ethnicity) |
| • *How are we doing with respect to NCLB?* | • Student learning: Percentage of students proficient, by demographics<br>• Adequate yearly progress (AYP)<br>• Demographics: dropout rates, attendance, etc. |
| • *How are we doing with respect to the school vision, mission, goals, and plan for continuous improvement?* | • School processes: What is being taught, how is it being taught, which teachers need to change their processes? (measured by classroom observations, standards implementation, questionnaires)<br>• Student learning: Ongoing assessments, grades, standards assessments<br>• Student, staff, parent perceptions: What needs to change to improve?<br>• Demographics: To ensure we are serving those whom we have as students |
| • *Does a continuum of learning exist that makes sense to ALL students? If a continuum of learning does not exist, why not? (Instructional coherence, vertical articulation)* | • Student learning results across grade levels and over time, by teacher and by student demographics<br>• Staff perceptions: Standards implementation questionnaire, climate questionnaire<br>• School process assessment: To determine how individual teachers are teaching and what instructional strategies teachers are using; classroom walk-through data<br>• Demographics by student learning: To determine if a continuum of learning exists for all students |
| • *Is everyone on staff on the same page with respect to school improvement; if not, why not?* | • Staff perceptions: Standards implementation questionnaire; climate questionnaire<br>• School process assessment: To ensure that there is a shared vision with implementation and evaluation structures in place<br>• Student learning results across grade levels<br>• Staff demographics: Number of years of teaching or qualifications |
| • *To what degree are programs and strategies being implemented?* | • School processes, by teacher<br>• Program enrollment, by student demographics |
| • *How effective are programs/ processes with respect to improved student learning?* | • School processes, by degree of implementation, by student learning results, by teachers |
| • *What is the cost-effectiveness of approaches that lead to student learning (e.g., value-added)?* | • School processes, by financial allocations, by student learning results |
| • *How effective are our teachers with respect to student learning results?* | • Student learning, by teacher, by content area, by student demographics |
| • *Does the school meet the needs of ALL students?* | • Student learning, by student demographics, by grade level and student<br>• Student perceptions |

## School District Analyses

First and foremost, districts want to know that all their schools are helping all students become proficient and that all students are improving each year. Student learning results by demographics, over time, by school, can yield that information. In addition, districts usually want to know how the school district is doing with respect to similar districts. If these are all the data districts look at, however, they are looking at their systems with hindsight.

To become proactive in providing assistance to schools to meet the desired outcomes, districts must look comprehensively at all four categories of data and provide leadership with respect to what the data ought to look like. For example, demographic profiles of each school can tell district leaders about program equity and effective building and district leadership. Demographic profiles show which students schools place in special education and which students are allowed in gifted programs. The discipline data give indications of how students are treated and how a school is led. To provide leadership, the district must review these numbers and discuss, support, shape, and monitor what these numbers need to look like. Looking systematically across the district and schools, district leadership can provide appropriate professional learning for staffs as well. Staff members may need training in analyzing data and in using the data to change their own instructional practices to ensure that all students are learning and meeting the standards. Figure 3.5 is a table of School District Analyses.

*To become proactive in providing assistance to schools to meet the desired outcomes, districts must look comprehensively at all four categories of data and provide leadership with respect to what the data ought to look like.*

**Figure 3.5**
# SCHOOL DISTRICT ANALYSES

| Data Questions | Data Needed |
|---|---|
| ◆ *How are we doing?* | Data profiles of the district and all schools:<br>◆ Demographics ◆ Perceptions<br>◆ School Processes ◆ Student Learning |
| ◆ *Is the system set up for success?* | ◆ Student learning: Ongoing assessments (summative and formative), grades, standards assessments, by student demographics, by grade level and school<br>◆ Staff demographics: Number of years of teaching, by grade level, by school<br>◆ Student, staff, and parent perceptions, by school and demographics<br>◆ Student demographics by school processes, by grade level and school |
| ◆ *How are we doing with respect to NCLB, and are all schools and programs getting students to proficiency and improving each year?* | ◆ Student learning: Percentage of students proficient by demographics, by school, over time |
| ◆ *How are we doing as a district system compared to similar districts?* | ◆ Student achievement, by student demographics, compared to similar districts (usually available on state websites) |
| ◆ *How are we doing with respect to the school district vision, mission, goals, and plan for continuous improvement?* | ◆ School processes: What is being taught, how is it being taught, which teachers need to change their processes? Does the mapping of our curriculum and instruction processes make sense?<br>◆ Student learning: Ongoing assessments, grades, standards assessments, summative assessments<br>◆ Student, staff, parent, and administrator perceptions: What needs to change to improve?<br>◆ Demographics: To ensure we are serving those whom we have as students |
| ◆ *Has a continuum of learning been created that makes sense to ALL students? If not, why not?* | ◆ School learning results across grade levels and over time, by teacher, and by student demographics<br>◆ Staff perceptions: Standards implementation questionnaire, climate questionnaire, organizational learning questionnaire<br>◆ School process assessment: Classroom observations, or assessments to determine how individual teachers are teaching<br>◆ Demographics, by student learning: To determine if the continuum of learning makes sense for *all* students |
| ◆ *Is everyone on staff on the same page with respect to school and district improvement; if not, why not?* | ◆ Staff perceptions: Standards implementation questionnaire; climate questionnaire by school; organizational learning questionnaire<br>◆ School process assessment: Is there a shared vision with implementation structures in place; what professional learning will help?<br>◆ Student learning results across grade levels, by school<br>◆ Staff demographics: Is there a difference by number of years of teaching or qualifications, by school? |
| ◆ *To what degree are programs and strategies being implemented?* | ◆ School processes, by teacher<br>◆ Program enrollment, by student demographics |
| ◆ *What is the cost-effectiveness and program effectiveness of approaches that lead to student learning, for ALL students?* | ◆ School processes, by financial allocations, by program, by student learning results, by demographics |

**Figure 3.5** *(Continued)*
# SCHOOL DISTRICT ANALYSES

| Data Questions | Data Needed |
|---|---|
| • *How are we going to predict and prevent failures and to predict and ensure successes?* | • Demographics<br>• Student learning<br>• Student, teacher, and parent perceptions, by school<br>• School process assessment |
| • *How effective are our teachers with respect to student learning results?* | • Student learning, by teacher |
| • *How effective are our leaders?* | • Demographics, by school<br>• Student learning, by demographics, by perceptions and processes, by school<br>• Student, teacher, administrator, and parent perceptions, by school |
| • *Do established policies make sense? Does district administration provide leadership so all staffs know what we want results to look like?* | • Comprehensive data profile, by district, and by school, that lays out all data elements for scrutiny |
| • *Does the school district meet the needs of ALL students?* | • Student learning, by student demographics, by grade level and school<br>• Student, staff, administrator, and parent perceptions |

*Note:* Many disaggregations will be multiple. For example: by gender, ethnicity, and gender and ethnicity together.

## State and Federal Analyses

We want State and Federal Departments of Education to move from compartments and departments monitoring compliance, asking for the same data over and over, to educational organizations that understand and support school districts and schools in addressing the needs of the whole child. The data that need to be gathered from school districts and schools should help them achieve 100% proficiency for all students, foremost; secondly, the data should support the evaluation of programs and strategies.

States must look at demographic data to understand how to plan for increases and decreases in enrollment across the state, student needs, and teacher quality/shortages. State Departments of Education usually want to compare school district student achievement results to know which districts are getting good results and which districts need to improve. With quality data gathered and analyzed, we should be able to determine how effective districts get their results—what works and what does not work, and the costs of different strategies. At the same time, the data will reveal why some districts are not getting good results and what needs to be altered to get better results. The United States Department of Education can look at these same analyses by state or by school district within states.

It would be ideal if requests by Federal and State Departments of Education for helpful data were timely and non-redundant. It would also be ideal if districts were given support and resources to submit their data so they do not have to spend time and effort correcting inaccurate data. The Data Quality Campaign has done a great job leading this cause (See *http://www.dataqualitycampaign.org*). Figure 3.6 is a State and Federal Analyses table.

> *The data that need to be gathered from school districts and schools should help them achieve 100% proficiency for all students, foremost; secondly, the data should support the evaluation of programs and strategies.*

**Figure 3.6**
## STATE AND FEDERAL ANALYSES

| Data Questions | Data Needed |
|---|---|
| • *How are states doing with respect to NCLB, and are ALL school districts (within a state) getting students to proficiency and improving each year?* | • Student learning: Percentage of students proficient by demographics, by state and school district, over time<br>• Adequate yearly progress (AYP), by demographics |
| • *How are we doing as a state, compared to other states?* | • Student achievement by student demographics compared to other states<br>• Adequate yearly progress (AYP) |
| • *How do school districts compare with respect to effectiveness and efficiencies? How do effective districts get their results? Which districts are struggling and why?* | • Student learning results, by school district<br>• Demographics to understand context<br>• School processes by school district<br>• Student, staff, and parent perceptions |
| • *What works and what does not work with respect to programs and strategies?* | • Student learning results, by school district<br>• Demographics to understand context<br>• School processes, by school district<br>• Student, staff, and parent perceptions |
| • *To what degree are programs and strategies implemented?* | • School process measurement, by school district and grade level<br>• Program enrollment, by student demographics |
| • *How cost-effective are approaches that lead to student learning?* | • School processes (programs, strategies), by financial allocations, by student learning results |
| • *How are students performing in college, or in their careers, by district?* | • Demographics to describe which student went to which college<br>• Perceptions of students' experiences, by high school, by college<br>• Student learning (GPA), by college, by high school and GPA, by subject area |
| • *How are we going to predict and prevent failures and to predict and ensure successes?* | • Demographics<br>• School processes<br>• Perceptions<br>• Student learning |

## Summary

Because student learning takes place neither in isolation nor only at school, we cannot use test scores as the only measure to determine the effectiveness of our programs and strategies. Multiple measures must be used to understand the multifaceted world of learning from the perspective of everyone involved. Demographic, perceptual, school process, and student learning data can help us understand the system that is producing the results we are getting and, at the same time, help us know what has to change to get different results. Different analyses of these data can give us the powerful information we need to make the appropriate decisions for students.

CHAPTER **4**

# IMPROVING THE QUALITY OF DATA

B ill Gates, Chairman of the Board and Chief Software Architect for Microsoft Corporation, is credited with saying—*The first rule of any technology used in a business is that automation applied to an efficient operation will magnify the efficiency. The second is that automation applied to an inefficient operation will magnify the inefficiency.*

We know the use of data can provide information to make any school district more efficient and effective. We also know that it takes data tools to help get the necessary analyses in an efficient manner. While data tools can support the quest for efficiency, the only way organizations can become more efficient and effective with their analysis of data in the long run is to have data that are accurate, valid, and timely—in other words, organizational efficiency and effectiveness relies upon data quality.

> *We know the use of data can provide information to make any school district more efficient and effective.*

## Data Quality

> *Data are of high quality "if they are fit for their intended uses in operations, decision making and planning."*
>
> **J.M. Juran**
> (Industrial Quality "Guru" who focuses on quality management.)

*Data quality* is a broad term for the accuracy and usefulness of data and the way in which data enter and flow through a data system. Most of us think of error-free data entry when we think of data quality. It is true that inconsistent data entry is often the cause of poor data quality; however, how we define, gather, store, manage, and move the data also affect data quality.

The characteristics of high-quality data and some of the questions we need to answer to get to these characteristics include:

**Accuracy:** *Do the data correctly describe what they are meant to describe?* Look for errors in entry, field-length errors, wrong characters, and values that are out of range.

**Completeness:** *Do we have all the data? Are all the records complete?* For example, many times data clerks do not input ethnicity for students, unless they have been trained to do so.

**Uniqueness:** *Are there two elements that are the same?* First and foremost: Check to see that all students and teachers have unique identification numbers. Unique means one number is assigned to one individual and is never used again.

**Consistency:** *Are the data free from contradiction? Do the data have the same values in different data sources?* For example, the data to describe gender should be consistent in every data source. If your district is using "M" and "F" for gender, any records that use "m" and "f" to indicate gender should be corrected.

**Timeliness:** *Are the data entered and available at the most useful times?* For example, if formative assessment data are not available to teachers shortly after the assessments are given, those data will never be used.

**Relevance:** *Do the data reflect what we are trying to measure?* This might be the hardest issue to come to grips with if the data have not been assessed for a long time. Are the data logically connected and important to collect? This issue is related to decisions that have to be made, to reports that have to be submitted, and to the process rules, discussed on the following pages.

**Flexibility:** *Can the data be easily used to satisfy a wide variety of purposes and specific questions (summary as well as detailed information)?* For example, make sure the way attendance is collected is appropriate for showing a daily rate for individual students and the school, and that averages for the day, week, month, quarter, semester, and year can also be provided.

*The characteristics of high-quality data include:*

- *Accuracy*
- *Completeness*
- *Uniqueness*
- *Consistency*
- *Timeliness*
- *Relevance*
- *Flexibility*

# How Data Quality is Most Often Compromised

Organizations that work with school district data say that data quality is most often compromised in these ways:

### Inconsistent or incorrect use of identification numbers (IDs)

▼ Same ID number is given to two different students

▼ Student ID number is changed when student changes buildings

▼ When a teacher takes over a class, same teacher ID number is used in the schedule as in the previous year

▼ Same ID numbers are used for teachers in different buildings

▼ ID numbers for withdrawn teachers are used for incoming teachers

▼ ID numbers for teachers change with the change of the school year

▼ Teacher ID number used in schedule (from SIS) not the same ID number used in personnel system to track teacher information

### Missing, incorrect, or duplicate values

▼ Student information is incomplete for many students (for example, ethnicity or gender not filled in)

▼ Schools do not track teacher information (certificate level, professional development) consistently

▼ No electronic version of elementary enrollment data (homeroom assignments)

### Incorrect assessment information

▼ When IDs are bubbled into the score sheet by students, many have digits transposed, are incomplete, or not entered at all

▼ When IDs are entered by teacher, ID for a student with the same or similar name is entered instead of the correct one

### In general

▼ No one in a district has clear knowledge of the condition of the district's data

▼ Inconsistent data-entry practices occur from building to building

▼ Schools do not keep (or code) information on interventions or programs

> *Data quality is most often compromised in these ways:*
>
> ♦ *Inconsistent or incorrect use of identification numbers (IDs)*
>
> ♦ *Missing, incorrect, or duplicate values*
>
> ♦ *Inconsistent data-entry practices occur from building to building*

## Improving Data Quality

Data quality must be systematically assessed and measured and errors must be remedied before the data are used or moved into a data warehouse. Every district has dirty data that need to be cleaned and the cost of hiring outside people to do so is prohibitive for most districts. So, typically, district staff must clean up existing data, starting with the most recent year and working backward in time. Furthermore, procedures and practices for entering new data must be implemented to ensure that the data going forward is of high quality from the beginning, reducing the effort needed to ensure high-quality data in the future.

Improving the quality of data throughout a school district can be a daunting task. Enormous quantities of data are often spread over many departments with different technologies. A data quality program is essential for ensuring data quality within an organization. A good data quality program should have these elements:

▼ A data manager: Someone in charge of the data and data quality

▼ An assessment of the data quality

▼ Clear data definitions and process rules

▼ Protocols and procedures for gathering and entering quality data

A discussion of these four elements follows.

## A Data Manager: Someone in Charge of the Data and Data Quality

Someone has to have the overall responsibility for understanding all the data, maintaining the quality of the data, and ensuring that data-quality guidelines are being adhered to. To understand all district data, where the data are, what the data are supposed to do, and then make sure they are clean is a major responsibility. The data manager must work closely with the technology staff that moves the data and with the program staff that will report the data or use data to make decisions. The data manager must be able to discuss the importance of accurate data entry with data entry staff and clearly communicate how the data will be used in the end. Data entry staff must know their accurate entries can make a significant impact on decisions.

*Data quality must be systematically assessed and measured and errors must be remedied before the data are used or moved into a data warehouse.*

*A good data quality program should have these elements:*

♦ *A data manager: Someone in charge of the data and data quality*

♦ *An assessment of the data quality*

♦ *Clear data definitions and process rules*

♦ *Protocols and procedures for gathering and entering quality data*

Additionally, individuals within the organization must be assigned to "own" and take responsibility for the data associated with their departments. For example, the District Special Needs Program Director must own the special-needs data and ensure that everyone throughout the district understands the intent of the Program and the data associated with it. The owner of the data must monitor the data to make sure they reflect what the district wants the program to accomplish, and if they do not, then make adjustments.

## An Assessment of the Data Quality

The first steps in assessing data quality are to take a very careful look at all data in your data systems—student information system, test files, databases, etc.—to profile them and to clean them with respect to the characteristics of high-quality data described on the previous pages. Figure 4.1 shows an example of part of a data profile for a district.

Figure 4.1 lists several demographic data sources and describes the layout and the organization of five files within one data source—a student information system. A district should create this type of profile and analysis for all data sources. (More on this in later chapters.)

*Individuals within the organization must be assigned to "own" and take responsibility for the data associated with their departments.*

Figure 4.1

## EXAMPLE SCHOOL DISTRICT PROFILE OF DATA SOURCES AND DATA

| Source System Name | Type of Data Housed in System | Hosted by Vendor or District |
|---|---|---|
| | Student Information | |
| | Human Resources | |
| | Financial | |
| | Discipline | |
| | Special Education | |
| | Transportation | |
| | Language Development | |
| | Special Programs | |
| | Cafeteria/Child Nutrition | |

| General Student Information System (SIS) — *Partial Example* | | |
|---|---|---|
| **Record Structure** | **File Organization** | **File Layout** |
| One record per student for each school attended within a single year. | Time periods: 2005-06 2006-07 2007-08 | The student file contains the following data – time period, school number, student ID, student test ID, last name, first name, middle initial, mailing address, birth date, social security number, active status, grade level, gender, ethnicity, English proficiency, lunch status, gifted qualified, gifted served, gifted services received, special education services received, home language, bilingual status, summer school status, alternative school status, previous school attended, assigned school, homebound status, migrant status, homeless status, education level of mother, education level of father, inter-district transfer, intra-district transfer, zip code, geographical code, Title I reading status, Title I math status, homeroom teacher ID (for elementary students with no schedule). |
| **Record Structure** | **File Organization** | **School Data** |
| One record per school within a single year. | Time periods: 2005-06 2006-07 2007-08 | The school file contains the following data—district number, school number, state school number, school name, Title I status, school type. |
| **Record Structure** | **File Organization** | **Course Data** |
| One record per course for each school within a single year. | Academic time periods: 2005-06 2006-07 2007-08 | The course file contains the following data—time period, school number, course ID, state course ID, course name, state course name, subject area, department, level. |
| **Record Structure** | **File Organization** | **Course Data** |
| One record per course grade within a marking period for each school within a single year. | Academic time periods: 2005-06 2006-07 2007-08 | The schedule file contains the following data—time period, school number, student ID, course ID, state course ID, section, term, period, class size, grading period. |

## Clear Data Definitions and Process Rules

To be understood, useful, and used, data must reflect school district processes; and everyone must know how to use the data correctly. Establishing clear data definitions and identifying data owners will help ensure that data are used and transformed consistently within the prescribed intentions of any process. Data dictionaries typically provide information on the structure and definition, as well as the content, of data elements. Figure 4.2 shows an example outline for data-element definitions which, when completed for all data elements and compiled, will become a data dictionary. Data dictionaries should document the data owners, along with the descriptions, guidelines, length, format, data types, data calculations, content rules, and modes of access for the district's data.

> *To be understood, useful, and used, data must reflect school district processes; and everyone must know how to use the data correctly.*

### Figure 4.2
### EXAMPLE DATA ELEMENT DEFINITIONS OUTLINE

| Data Element Name | Data Element Definition |
|---|---|
| Description | This is a short description of the data element being sought. |
| Guidelines | These are any unique conditional uses, procedures, or implementation and reporting rules about this data element. Not all data elements will have guidelines. |
| Length | This is the maximum length of the data field in the database. |
| Format | This is the required reporting format. Data elements that do not have a specified format will not display "Format." |
| Data Type | This is the data type required. Only *Date* or *Alphanumeric* are acceptable. |
| Content Rules (Codes) | This is additional information about how this data element is to be constructed. Not all data elements will have content rules. |
| Data Owner | Who "owns" or is responsible for this data element. |

Figure 4.3 shows the Figure 4.2 outline completed for a data element containing a district of responsibility code. The definition tells the data handlers what the code is used for as well as the parameters of the code.

**Figure 4.3**

## EXAMPLE DISTRICT OF RESPONSIBILITY CODE DEFINITION

| Data Element Name | District of Responsibility Code |
|---|---|
| Description | The 12-digit code assigned to a Local Education Agency (LEA) by the State Education Agency (SEA) for uniquely identifying the LEA. |
| Guidelines | This is the LEA that has responsibility for reporting on the status of the student for accountability purposes under No Child Left Behind (NCLB). This is not necessarily the school district in which the student resides. |
| Length | 12 characters |
| Data Type | Alphanumeric |
| Content Rules (Codes) | The Basic Education Data System (BEDS) Code is assigned by SEA and can be found on the SEA website. |
| Data Owner | Administrator X |

Figure 4.4 displays an example definition for grade-level code. This example defines the codes and provides information for selecting the correct code.

## Figure 4.4
# EXAMPLE GRADE LEVEL CODE DEFINITION

| Data Element Name | Grade Level Code |
|---|---|
| Description | The instructional level for the student as determined by the school district. |
| Guidelines | Grade-level reporting has specific rules for various collection sets:<br><br>*SIS:* Use the current grade level for the student at the time that the student identification data set is compiled.<br><br>*Student Enrollment:* For students without disabilities, use the grade level assigned at the date of enrollment.<br><br>For students with disabilities, use the grade level assigned by the Committee on Special Education (CSE) or the Committee on Pre-School Special Education (CPSE) on the date of enrollment. Students with disabilities who are identified by the CSE or the CPSE as State Alternative Assessment (SAA) eligible must be reported as ungraded.<br><br>For students in an Alternative High School Equivalency Preparation Program (AHSEPP) or a High School Equivalency Preparation Program (HSEPP), use a grade level of "GED." No other students should be reported with a grade level of GED. |
| Length | 4 characters |
| Data Type | Alphanumeric |
| Content Rules (Codes) | For this element, the grade ordinal will be used in the data warehouse. The codes shown are suggested. |

| Description | Ordinal | Code | Description | Ordinal | Code |
|---|---|---|---|---|---|
| Kindergarten | KDG | K | Grade 9 | 9th | 9 |
| Grade 1 | 1st | 1 | Grade 10 | 10th | 10 |
| Grade 2 | 2nd | 2 | Grade 11 | 11th | 11 |
| Grade 3 | 3rd | 3 | Grade 12 | 12th | 12 |
| Grade 4 | 4th | 4 | Ungraded K-6 | K-6 | K-6 |
| Grade 5 | 5th | 5 | Ungraded 7-12 | 7-12 | 7-12 |
| Grade 6 | 6th | 6 | Preschool | PRES | PS |
| Grade 7 | 7th | 7 | Pre-Kindergarten | PREK | PK |
| Grade 8 | 8th | 8 | GED | GED | GED |

## Protocols and Procedures for Gathering Quality Data

School districts must establish protocols and procedures for gathering and entering data in a high-quality fashion. These protocols need to include descriptions of what events trigger an entry (or modification) of a record in the student information system and how and when to enter the data correctly. Figure 4.5 shows an example protocol for entering a new record into a student information system. This would be used for entering a new record when a new student enters the district or school. (Protocol designed by Rebecca Blink, Chilton, Wisconsin, discussed in Chapter 13.)

### Figure 4.5
### SIS DATA ENTRY PROTOCOL

| *The following is a list of fields that must be entered when setting up a new student record:* | |
|---|---|
| **Field Names** | **Field Protocols** |
| Last Name | If name has a space, e.g., *Van Oss*, put the space in |
| First Name | |
| Middle Initial | Capital letter *with* a period |
| Grade | |
| Gender | |
| Student ID | Allow SIS to assign this ID number randomly—do not change |
| Mailing Address | |
| City | |
| State | Abbreviation as used by U.S. Postal Service |
| Zip Code | 9 digit |
| Parent/Guardian Name | |
| Telephone | Include area code: xxx-xxx-xxxx |
| Birthday | yyyy-mm-dd |
| Social Security Number | No spaces |
| Ethnicity | (See protocol) |
| Entry Date | yyyy-mm-dd |
| Entering Grade | PreK-12 |
| Graduation Year | yyyy |
| Enter Teacher Number | Homeroom teacher, all buildings |
| ESL Level | |
| Locker | |
| District of Residence | |
| School of Residence | |
| Last School | (If a district school) |
| Primary Language | Will default to English. Only change if applicable; otherwise leave as English. |
| Home Language | Will default to English. Only change if applicable; otherwise leave as English. |

Figure 4.6 displays an abbreviated example of student information system procedures for filing attendance reports. The procedures are very specific, so all data entry clerks know exactly what they need to do and when.

## Figure 4.6
## EXAMPLE SIS PROCEDURES

| Filing System | |
|---|---|
| *15th Day of Attendance* | You must have a file labeled as Membership and Attendance Report 15th Day. File all reports for the 15th day in this folder. |
| *45th Day of Attendance* | You must have a file labeled as Membership and Attendance Report 45th Day. File all reports for the 45th day in this folder. |
| *90th Day of Attendance* | You must have a file labeled as Membership and Attendance Report 90th Day. File all reports for the 90th day in this folder. |
| *135th Day of Attendance* | You must have a file labeled as Membership and Attendance Report 135th Day. File all reports for the 135th day in this folder. |
| *180th Day of Attendance* | You must have a file labeled as Membership and Attendance Report 180th Day. File all reports for the 180th day in this folder. |
| *Pre-code* | You must have a file labeled as Pre-code. File all reports for Pre-code in this folder. |

| Procedures: Log into SIS as REGISTRAR1 USER | |
|---|---|
| *Attendance Reports* | These reports must be generated beginning after attendance has been completed on the 15th day and periodically thereafter.<br><br>**Master Classification List:**<br>1. Retrieve the **State Reports** toolbar.<br>2. Click on the **Launch** button.<br>3. Choose **Master Classification List – Student** from the pull-down list.<br>   a. Change sort to **By Grade.**<br>   b. District name is **Green County.**<br>   c. Day number is **15, 45, 90, 135, or 180.**<br>   d. Select the appropriate grade range for your school.<br>   e. Click the **Setup** button.<br>      Click in the circle to the left of **Landscape,** click the **OK** button.<br>4. Click the **Print** button. At the print window, click the **OK** button.<br>5. When the report is completed, click the **Close** button.<br>6. Compare this report against the attendance blue cards, verifying each student's enrollment data and/or withdrawal date.<br><br>If proper procedures have been followed, the withdrawal date on the **Master Classification List** should be the same date as the withdrawal date on the **Attendance Blue Card.**<br><br>**This report should be given to each special education teacher to verify that each special education student is listed on the teacher's Pupil Classification Roster. Teachers should make changes/additions on the report and on the appropriate Pupil Classification Roster, if necessary, and return items to the Attendance Clerk so the information can be corrected in the SIS.** |

**Figure 4.6** *(Continued)*

## EXAMPLE SIS PROCEDURES

| Procedures: Log into SIS as REGISTRAR1 USER | |
|---|---|
| *Membership and Attendance Worksheet* | This report will print by grade level.<br>1. Retrieve the **State Reports** toolbar.<br>2. Click on the **Launch** button.<br>3. Choose **Membership and Attendance Worksheet** from the pull-down list.<br>   a. Day number is **15, 45, 90, 135, or 180.**<br>   b. Leave **Grade** blank to include all grade levels.<br>   b. District name is **Green County.**<br>   c. Click the **Setup** button.<br>     Click in the circle to the left of **Landscape,** click the *OK* button.<br>4. Click the **Print** button. At the print window, click the *OK* button.<br><br>If your school has homerooms that contain "mixed grade levels," it is recommended that you compare the total number of absences per grade level on the **Attendance Blue Cards** to the **Membership and Attendance Worksheet.**<br><br>If your school has homerooms that do not contain "mixed grade levels," follow the procedures below for verifying information:<br><br>   First, the **Add/Drops New** column should be checked against the **Attendance Blue Cards.** Each date that shows an add on the **Membership and Attendance Worksheet** should correspond with an entry of **E, E1, or E2** on an **Attendance Blue Card.**<br><br>   Second, the **Add/Drops Drop** column should be checked against the **Attendance Blue Cards.** Each date that shows a drop on the **Membership and Attendance Worksheet** should correspond with an entry of *W* on an **Attendance Blue Card.**<br><br>   Third, the **Attendance** absence column should be checked against the **Attendance Blue Cards.** These numbers should match. If they do not, you must find the mistake, either on the **Attendance Blue Card,** or in the *SIS,* and correct.<br><br>   Fourth, the **Membership** (by classification) columns should be checked against the **Pupil Classification Rosters.** Any change in the number of students classified in any of these columns should be documented by an entry on a **EFA Pupil Classification Roster.** If a student has more than one classification, the **Membership and Attendance Worksheet** will list only the highest weighted classification. |
| *Membership and Attendance Data Verification Report* | This report will print by grade level.<br>1. Retrieve the **State Reports** toolbar.<br>2. Click on the **Launch** button.<br>3. Choose **Data Verification Report** from the pull-down list.<br>4. Click the **Print** button. At the print window, click the **OK** button.<br>5. When the report is completed, click the **Close** button.<br><br>**If you have errors on this report, you must correct those errors and run this report again. Continue this until the report has no errors.** |

Once the policies and procedures are put into place, documentation of policies, processes, and procedures must be made available, data clerks must be trained, and the implementation of the procedures must be monitored. District processes for data entry may need to change to ensure consistency and accuracy.

## Summary

Data can help learning organizations become more efficient and effective, as long as the data are accurate, complete, unique, consistent, timely, and relevant—in other words, of high quality. To improve data quality, at least one person in a school district must know all the data sources and what they contain. Once the contents of the sources are clearly identified, they can be profiled, assessed, and improved.

Definitions, process rules, protocols, and procedures for entering data will support the gathering of quality data. Data entry staff members must be trained on all of these processes and procedures, which will need to be monitored to ensure that quality data are maintained in all data sources.

The data tools you use and data analyses you generate can only be as good as the data in them. Please be sure your data are of high quality. Start with your most important data and most current year and work your way back in time until all data are clean.

*District processes for data entry may need to change to ensure consistency and accuracy.*

*The data tools you use and data analyses you generate can only be as good as the data in them.*

CHAPTER 5

# PLANNING FOR A DATA WAREHOUSE TO TRANSLATE DATA INTO INFORMATION TO IMPROVE TEACHING AND LEARNING

Throughout this book, the discussion has focused on how important it is for education personnel to use data to improve teaching and learning. That work can be fairly straightforward and logical—as long as one has access to the data and the tools for the data analysis work. To perform comprehensive data analyses to improve teaching and learning, a school district needs to connect *demographic, student learning, school process,* and *perceptions* data (when administered with identifiers), usually by way of numerous databases and flat files. (These four categories of data are described in Chapter 3.) The usual way to make that connection is with a data warehouse. There are tools that will allow districts to intersect databases without the warehouse (such as a zone integration server described in Chapter 8). For the purposes of this chapter, the term *data warehouse* will be used. This does not exclude the other tools that will do the same things. Planning for a data warehouse or for the integration of data sources and tools involves the same steps.

In the very near future, every school district in the country, and in other countries, will be using some sort of data system to access and intersect many different data elements, not just to meet state and federal mandates but to help teachers improve their teaching for improved student learning. Data warehouses are designed and needed for manipulating, updating, and analyzing multiple databases that are connected via individual student and staff identification numbers. Figure 5.1 shows a graphic of how a data warehouse connects multiple data sources through an *extract, transform, and load* (ETL) process to data

*In the very near future, every school district in the country, and in other countries, will be using some sort of data system to access and intersect many different data elements, not just to meet state and federal mandates but to help teachers improve their teaching for improved student learning.*

**58** | **CHAPTER 5**
**Planning for Analytical Data Tools to Translate Data into Information
to Improve Teaching and Learning**

warehouse analysis tools. Data warehouses often have query analysis and reporting tools. If not, tools would need to be connected to the warehouse. This chapter will help educators understand how to plan for a district data warehouse or a data integrator.

### Figure 5.1
## EDUCATIONAL DATA WAREHOUSE

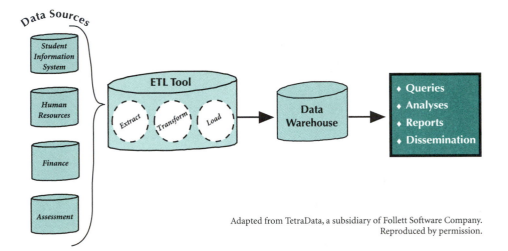

Adapted from TetraData, a subsidiary of Follett Software Company.
Reproduced by permission.

# Planning for a Data Warehouse

When most districts realize that looking at just student achievement data is not enough for understanding the impact of their processes and programs on student learning, they determine they must buy a data warehouse with analytical tools to provide the information they need to make decisions to improve teaching and learning. Once school districts recognize that they need a data warehouse to improve teaching and learning, they often enter "emergency" mode and become eager to buy a piece of software and begin inputting data. This good sense of urgency can be wasted if the proper groundwork is not performed. Some districts find themselves needing to start over with their warehouse because they didn't begin with a clear understanding of what a warehouse is or does, did not have a comprehensive plan, and because they did not realize a data warehouse is a process, not a product. The design and successful implementation of an effective data warehouse requires careful planning and the utilization of data warehouse experts. A thorough analysis of your data warehouse needs should be completed before purchasing any product or contracting with any vendor.

Designing a data warehouse, or thinking through all the issues involved in order to understand which data warehouse solution to commit to, is a time-consuming task that needs to be done with care and attention to the details.

Figure 5.2 is a Data Warehouse Needs Analysis Form that can help school districts think through the purposes, uses, and requirements of a data warehouse so they can plan for and choose an appropriate data warehouse solution. Shown in what appears to be a linear process, the thinking through of data warehouse needs is really a cyclical process. The cyclical aspect comes into play when many issues become clearer in the ensuing steps and must be revisited more than once. A discussion of the major steps follows the form.

*A thorough analysis of your data warehouse needs should be completed before purchasing any product or contracting with any vendor.*

**60** | CHAPTER 5
Planning for Analytical Data Tools to Translate Data into Information
to Improve Teaching and Learning

**Figure 5.2**

# DATA WAREHOUSE NEEDS ANALYSIS FORM

| | |
|---|---|
| **1. Establish a Data Warehouse Project Team** | |
| Identify who should be on the committee to assist with the design of the data warehouse. | |
| Clarify the role of the committee members, including timelines. | |
| **2. Define the Scope of the Data Warehouse** | |
| Determine the mission and vision for the data warehouse. | |
| Describe purposes, uses, users, and data requirements. | |
| **3. Determine Data Readiness** | |
| Identify the databases, hardware, and software that are being used in the district and schools. | |
| Describe the current networking configuration specifications. | |
| Describe the data that are currently available. | |
| Determine how much has been budgeted for a data warehouse. | |
| **4. Determine Desired Data: Data Discovery** | |
| Determine the data you want to include in the data warehouse. | |
| **5. Determine Who is Going to Do the Work** | |
| Select the data warehouse team and a project manager. | |
| Identify who will be responsible for pulling together the data to input into the warehouse. | |
| Identify who will produce the standard reports and the process for acquiring the reports. | |
| Identify who will maintain and host the data warehouse. | |
| **6. Determine the Levels of Access** | |
| Determine the levels of access, who will have access at each level, and how access will be obtained. | |
| **7. Select a Data Warehouse Vendor** | |
| Invite vendors to talk with the selection committee. Evaluate vendors' proposals. Select a data warehouse vendor. | |

## 1. Establish a Data Warehouse Project Team

The first step in planning for the data warehouse is to establish a data warehouse project team to—

▼ Define the scope of the warehouse

▼ Determine data readiness

▼ Determine desired data to include

▼ Determine who is going to do the work

▼ Determine levels of access

▼ Recommend a data warehouse vendor

*Identify who should be on the committee to assist with the design of the data warehouse.* As district or school personnel think about selecting a data warehousing system to analyze data to provide information to improve teaching and learning at the classroom, school, and district levels, a committee comprised of people with diverse backgrounds and uses for data needs to be created. Such committee might include:

▼ classroom teachers (although they should not be in the
majority because they have very limited and specific uses
for the warehouse)

▼ information technology staff

▼ school and district administrators

▼ program administrators

▼ current data specialists for the district

▼ staff from the Chief Financial Officer's Office

▼ clerical assistants for data entry

▼ district, county, and/or regional education representatives

▼ school board members

▼ other data users

It is important that people in all parts of the organization know that this planning work is going on so anyone with special interests, abilities, uses for, or knowledge of existing or desired data can join the committee or provide input into the process. If all appropriate representatives cannot meet in person, a means of handling collaborative discussions has to be made available. If the project team is not all-inclusive, the district runs the risk of seeming to impose top-

<div class="sidebar">

*Establish a Data Warehouse Project Team*

♦ *Identify who should be on the committee to assist with the design of the data warehouse*

♦ *Clarify the role of the committee, including timelines*

</div>

**62** | **CHAPTER 5**
| **Planning for Analytical Data Tools to Translate Data into Information
to Improve Teaching and Learning**

down decision making and of not considering all district needs, uses, and purposes up front. The district also runs the risk of making critical errors because the perceptions and needs of all users were not taken into consideration. The needs of all stakeholders currently and potentially involved will be important to the future acceptance and success of the data warehouse project.

*Clarify the role of the committee members, including timelines.* Committee members must clearly understand their common mission, role, and timelines for completing this work. It is essential to document the role of the committee and each member's responsibility so users of the warehouse will understand the context of the final report. The following questions should be considered:

▼ Is the committee's role to recommend a data warehouse solution to another group or to make an independent decision to purchase and implement a data warehouse system?

▼ What are the budget considerations?

▼ When will the work be done?

▼ Who will make the final decision?

▼ Who will sign the contract?

▼ Who will manage the project implementation?

These first two steps—identifying committee members and clarifying their role—the role of the committee—are vital to the success of a data warehouse, and they should not be rushed. Spending time in selecting committee members and clarifying their roles will help ensure that subsequent steps will run smoothly and efficiently.

> *Define the Scope
> of the Data Warehouse*
>
> ♦ *Determine the mission and
> vision for the data warehouse*
>
> ♦ *Describe purposes, uses, users,
> and data requirements*

## 2. Define the Scope of the Data Warehouse

*Determine the mission and vision for the data warehouse.* Determining the mission and vision for the data warehouse is basically clarifying its purpose and desired uses. Clarity of the mission is as important to the design, implementation, and maintenance of a data warehouse as it is for an entire organization. A mission provides a focus for the project and keeps everyone grounded. A mission and vision need to be identified by the committee selected to design the data warehouse and revisited on an ongoing basis as a data warehouse vendor is selected. The mission and vision will also need to be revisited when all members of the committee have met and the uses and users of the data warehouse have been determined.

*Describe purposes, uses, users, and data requirements.* After the mission and vision have been determined, the purposes for creating and using the data warehouse must be identified. This list will grow as all data warehouse possibilities are realized. Then priorities will have to be assigned. For example: *In a first round of discussions, a school district data warehouse committee indicated that the purpose of a school district data warehouse is to provide the school district with information that will help educators know how each school, grade level, and content area is performing with respect to school district benchmarks and the state test so additional support may be provided where needed. Later in the planning process, other purposes for this same data warehouse were identified for schools in the district to access information about student achievement to ensure that all students are learning regardless of race/ ethnicity, gender, language fluency, special learning needs, or economic background; to provide teachers with historical student achievement data for all their students prior to the beginning of a new school year; and to give teachers access to ongoing student achievement data throughout the school year.*

The committee must ask and answer many questions, such as:

▼ What are the desired uses of the data warehouse?

▼ Who must have access to the data warehouse in order to do their jobs?

▼ Who should have access to information to improve the way they are doing their jobs?

▼ How will security be maintained with multiple users?

▼ Will there be users with minimal technological skills and experience? How will their skills be improved?

▼ Will data warehouse managers be needed?

▼ How will potential users access the data warehouse (e.g., computer in classroom, access via the Internet from any computer at any time)?

The committee must also determine what data elements are required to support the desired uses. For example, if one use is to provide analyses to the State Department of Education for categorical programs, what data must be identified, gathered, and analyzed to meet this purpose? A review of Chapter 3 will provide a starting point for these discussions.

**64** | CHAPTER 5
| Planning for Analytical Data Tools to Translate Data into Information
to Improve Teaching and Learning

*It is critical that the district outline the mission, vision, purpose, and priorities before contacting vendors.*

*Determine Data Readiness*

♦ *Identify the databases, hardware, and software that are being used in the district and schools*

♦ *Describe the current networking configuration application*

♦ *Describe the data that are currently available*

♦ *Determine how much has been budgeted for this work*

Another important consideration is access. Should a grade-three teacher be able to examine his current students' achievement scores on various measures over the three years prior to arriving in grade three, regardless of what school they attended in the district? Should high school teachers be able to view their students' grades in all subject areas, as well as how they performed in middle school?

These important considerations will probably uncover new information essential to the project team's planning, or suggest additional people to add to the data warehouse design committee.

It is critical that the district outline the mission, vision, purpose, and priorities before contacting vendors. Otherwise, the district may easily lose focus on what it needs when vendor demonstrations show attractive features that are not essential to the purpose of the data warehouse. Clarity of data requirements can help districts find the vendors with the best fit for them. It is important that a vendor hears and understands the specific needs of the district.

## 3. Determine Data Readiness

Examining the technology, data sources, data, and budget that currently exist in the district and are readily available will help determine the readiness of the warehouse project.

*Identify the databases, hardware, and software that are being used in the district and schools.* To understand how existing data can be imported into a data warehouse, currently used database programs and their capabilities must be analyzed. Find out what is being used, where, and for what purposes. This information will identify what is available and will clarify the level of compatibility among district, school, and classroom software and hardware. We have seen districts purchase data warehouses that they expect schools to access, only to find that the schools do not have the hardware or software to connect to the main system. These analyses will also identify whether there is software being used that merely needs to be augmented or hardware that needs updating. A district must do whatever is possible to ensure that schools can access and use the district data warehouse. If the appropriate software and hardware are not available at the school level, their purchase must be included in the data warehouse budget or some other budget. Figure 5.3 provides an outline for considering source systems, the type of data housed in the system, and how and where the source system is housed.

**Figure 5.3**

## DEMOGRAPHIC SOURCE SYSTEM

| Source System Name | Type of Data Housed in System | Hosted by Vendor or District |
|---|---|---|
| | Student Information | |
| | Human Resources | |
| | Financial | |
| | Discipline | |
| | Special Education | |
| | Transportation | |
| | ESL | |
| | Special Programs | |
| | Cafeteria/Child Nutrition | |

66 | CHAPTER 5
Planning for Analytical Data Tools to Translate Data into Information
to Improve Teaching and Learning

*Describe the current networking configuration specifications.* A comprehensive data warehouse will require the use of your district and school networks and will place demands on both bandwidth and firewalls. Your district might need to upgrade its networking system. This is a major budgetary consideration and a key issue in data warehouse design, access, and implementation. Sometimes school districts blame problems on defective warehouse applications when the issue is really their network. Figure 5.4 asks questions related to current networking configurations.

## Figure 5.4
## NETWORKING CONFIGURATION APPLICATIONS

| Question | Response |
|---|---|
| Can you accommodate VPN/Remote Access? | |
| What is your network topography? | |
| What is your bandwidth connection to the Internet? T1 or better? | |
| Do you want the vendor to host the solution? | |
| What staff resources will you be able to provide from your district to help with building and implementing the warehouse? | |
| Do you have any predefined report requirements? What are your plans for the warehouse solution in providing reports? | |
| Do you have experience with a Train-the-Trainer deployment approach? | |
| What is your roll-out strategy? Who is your target audience? | |

*Describe the data that are currently available.* Consider the data that are currently available, their sources, and the compatibility of those sources with different types of hardware and software.

▼ What data does the district have and in what format?

▼ What data do the schools routinely gather electronically and otherwise?

▼ What is the *quality* and accessibility of data in the student information system? (Figure 5.5 asks questions related to student information systems.)

▼ What do the county/regional/state departments of education have that you might want in your data warehouse?

▼ What kinds of information can you get from the state data system?

▼ What can you get digitally from commercial test vendors or online data agencies?

▼ Are there important data elements that are not in electronic format? Some districts may have local assessments that have not been gathered electronically in the past. A plan to enter those data into electronic format will have to be put into place.

You may find a wealth of data available that, for some reason or another, were unknown to all potential users.

It is important to make sure that existing data are cleaned (i.e., missing data completed, student and staff identification codes aligned, etc.) and made meaningful and usable. District processes for data entry may need to change to ensure consistency and accuracy. (See Chapter 4 for more details about improving data quality.)

*Determine how much has been budgeted for this work.* How many financial resources are available for data warehouse development, training, and maintenance, and how much money will be needed to do it right? If new hardware, software, and networking are required for the schools, make sure these are included in the budget. Chapter 11 discusses who gets trained and when.

68 | CHAPTER 5
Planning for Analytical Data Tools to Translate Data into Information
to Improve Teaching and Learning

**Figure 5.5**

## GENERAL STUDENT INFORMATION SYSTEM (SIS) QUESTIONS

| Question | Answer |
|---|---|
| Is the current SIS school-based or district-integrated? | |
| Are all schools using the same SIS? | |
| If school-based, how often are the schools rolling up their data into the district-integrated system? | |
| What is the name of the current SIS(s)? | |
| Who is your SIS administrator or expert? | |
| What is the underlying database of the current SIS? | |
| Is a database schema available? | |
| Do you self-host your SIS or is it hosted elsewhere? | |
| What is the data consolidation and backup strategy for the data, both historical and current, in the current SIS(s)? | |
| What is the platform for your current SIS(s), e.g., Windows, Unix, Mac? | |
| How long has the current SIS been live? | |
| What are the historical data formats and structures from your SIS? | |
| How many years of data are reliable in the current SIS? | |
| How many years of data do you anticipate, including from your current SIS in your warehouse solution? | |
| Does your current SIS data include a district-unique Student ID? | |
| Does your current SIS data include a state-unique Student ID? | |
| Does your unique Student ID in your SIS match the Student ID in all of your other source systems? | |
| Do your current SIS data include a district-unique Teacher ID? If not, please explain how you identify unique teachers. | |
| If district-unique, does the Teacher ID match the Teacher ID in all of your other source systems? | |
| Are all students scheduled in the current year? If not, which students are and how are those students linked to a teacher? | |

## 4. Determine Desired Data: Data Discovery

The data discovery piece of the data warehouse design requires reflective work about steps already covered. Knowing what you know

now about potential data warehouse users and uses, existing data sources and their data structures, what data need to be included in the data warehouse? This work is called *Data Discovery* by many data warehouse vendors and is covered in greater depth in Chapter 6.

As you consider what data to include, think of questions you will want to answer with data, programs you will want to evaluate, theories to research, etc. Additionally, Chapter 3 describes what data are important for improving teaching and learning. You might want to review this chapter to help guide your data discovery.

*Determine Desired Data:
Data Discovery*

♦ *What data need to be included
in the warehouse?*

## 5. Determine Who is Going to Do the Work

Determine who is going to perform the work required in selecting, managing, implementing, and maintaining a data warehouse that will meet the stated mission and vision. This will be a major ongoing budget issue.

***Select the data warehouse team and a project manager.*** The design of a comprehensive data warehouse is an important task, and one that requires data warehouse expertise. Determine a local project manager and involve the individual(s) who will be responsible for the design, implementation, and maintenance of this data warehouse system as early in the process as possible. A good vendor will also have a project manager on its end. It is highly recommended to have a knowledgeable data warehouse manager as part of the district data warehouse team.

The data warehouse project manager should be knowledgeable about relational databases and data warehouses. She/he should know how to program desired reports and queries and understand a variety of school-based data. School district data warehouse project managers should have coursework and/or experience in computer science, statistics, education, data warehousing, data security, and possess good communication skills. It is important that the project manager be able to listen to and understand users' needs and the desired uses of data,

*Determine Who is
Going to do the Work*

♦ *Select the data warehouse
team and a project manager*

♦ *Identify who will be
responsible for pulling the
data together to input into
the warehouse*

♦ *Identify who will produce
the standard reports and
the process for acquiring
the reports*

♦ *Identify who will maintain
and host the data warehouse*

**70** | **CHAPTER 5**
**Planning for Analytical Data Tools to Translate Data into Information
to Improve Teaching and Learning**

and be able to suggest ways to gather the appropriate data. It might also be necessary for your project manager to have public relations/marketing talents to get the word out and to generate excitement for this major endeavor. Your situation may also require a systems programmer who will focus on the operating system and the hardware, as well as an additional networking person. Hardware and networking skills are not the same as data skills. The current school district "techie" might not have the skills to manage a data warehouse project. (Chapter 12 goes into more detail about managing the warehouse.)

Data will need some structural work to achieve a flow between new and old data and new and old software. Data analysts will need to be deployed to clean up the data, verify their accuracy and consistency, and make the data compatible and relatable. You will want a system that can spit out exception reports that identify data problems to the data entry clerks every day. Cleaning the data includes creating verification routines to help find inaccuracies, eyeballing the data for duplications and inconsistencies, understanding the data elements to know when an inappropriate number is a keyboard-entry problem or some other error, and knowing how to "fix" data problems. These data analysts will need to work closely with school clerks to get the clerks to "own" the data, so that the data are clean going into the student information system. (Chapter 4 covers how to set up processes and procedures for entering quality data from the outset.)

*Identify who will be responsible for pulling the data together to input into the warehouse.* How often you need to do reports, how mobile your student population is, how often you will want the data refreshed in the warehouse, and how you want the task to be accomplished will dictate who will be responsible for importing or inputing the data into the data warehouse. If teachers and school administrators desire classroom-specific data for use, the data warehouse project committee will need to recommend who will perform the data entry and how it will be performed. Consistency, accuracy, security, timelines, and confidentiality are important considerations. This question of responsibility requires reflecting on the purposes and uses of the data warehouse and understanding the way data will be retrieved. If it is determined that classroom data will be input routinely, the data warehouse system will have to have procedures for gathering and importing data regularly into the system.

> *Hardware and networking skills are not the same as data skills. The current school district "techie" might not have the skills to manage a data warehouse project.*

*Identify who will produce the standard reports and the process for acquiring the reports.* Who will be responsible for producing standard reports—those reports that need to be generated and updated each reporting period that can now be automated with the data warehouse? Additionally, what will be the process for teachers and administrators to acquire such reports?

In most cases, the person creating the reports will need to have programming skills (i.e., SQL, scripting, design). The curriculum and instruction director usually cannot create these types of reports.

Querying, questioning the data warehouse to produce analyses, was once the hardest part of the entire data warehouse equation. Now, data warehouse products have easy-to-use data-analysis tools. Ad hoc querying without programming is available. However, when you get to the point of knowing what types of reports you will want to generate, a standard report can be created and distributed on a regular basis. (Chapter 10 discusses reporting.)

*Identify who will maintain and host the data warehouse.* Just as with any other hardware and software, someone needs to be in charge of the maintenance, error reporting, trouble-shooting, and security of the data warehouse system. This individual needs to have data warehouse expertise and familiarity with the district's data, the schools' needs, and overall reporting needs. Ideally routine maintenance should take place during off-school periods to avoid service slow-downs or disruption to the district's work. (Chapter 12 describes what it takes to manage a warehouse.) It could also be that your district determines that it wants the chosen vendor to maintain the data warehouse server. The downside to the vendor maintaining the data warehouse server might be that no one in the district would be able to take it over without a lot of training. Additionally, a vendor might charge more than the district believes the service is worth. If the district is managing its own data, it would be better if it hosted its own warehouse.

## 6. Determine the Levels of Access

Once the data to include in the data warehouse and the standard reports have been determined, a plan of action for communicating information learned from the data will need to be established. Security is a major consideration in determining who will have access to the data warehouse. Determine who will need the data warehouse information

*Determine the Levels of Access*

- *Who will have access at each level*
- *How access will be obtained*

**72** | **CHAPTER 5**
| **Planning for Analytical Data Tools to Translate Data into Information
to Improve Teaching and Learning**

and how they can get it. This is of major importance to the final selection of the data warehouse solution. You will want to find a vendor that will help with security mapping.

### 7. Select a Data Warehouse Vendor

*Select a Data
Warehouse Vendor*

♦ *Invite vendors to talk with
the selection committee*

♦ *Evaluate vendors' proposals*

♦ *Select a data warehouse
vendor*

Only after you are clear about why you want a data warehouse and how your district plans to use it should you invite vendors in to talk with the data warehouse selection committee. Vendors' visits could confuse the committee if the background work is not done first. The visits will give you valuable information to consider, however. Chapter 7 lays out criteria for selecting a data warehouse, and all members of the selection committee should become familiar with these criteria.

## Summary

When districts realize that looking at just student achievement data is not enough for understanding the impact of their processes and programs, they also realize they must buy a system like a data warehouse with analytical and reporting tools to provide the information they need to make decisions to improve teaching and learning. A smart school district will think through the uses, users, and issues regarding implementation and maintenance before purchasing a data warehouse.

CHAPTER **6**

# DATA DISCOVERY AND DATA MAPPING

Chapter 3 describes what data and data analyses will help educational organizations improve teaching and learning. Chapter 4 explains how to profile and assess your data and improve their quality. Chapter 5 discusses how to plan for analytical data tools or a data warehouse. This chapter is devoted to ensuring that the quality data in data sources are ready for an analytical data tool, or data warehouse, to perform the analyses described in Chapter 3 and to create the reports described in Chapter 10. The key terms and data transformation processes that are described in this chapter are *data discovery* and *data mapping*.

## Data Discovery

Data discovery is the process of determining which data elements districts will want to include in their data warehouses. Data discovery includes identifying the decisions that have to be made, asking the questions that have to be answered, developing the theories that have to be tested, and creating the reports that have to be generated; then determining if the district is currently tracking these data, determining where they are being kept, and assessing the quality of the data. Data discovery could also include cleaning dirty data. The process of data discovery also helps districts understand the dynamics of their organizations. Data discovery starts with the highest aggregated information (e.g., students, staff, assessments) and then proceeds to more detailed data that further describe the aggregate, such as student last name, first name, identification number, etc.

*The process of data discovery also helps districts understand the dynamics of their organizations.*

## Data Mapping

> *Data mapping is the process of creating data element linkages between a data source and a destination.*

Data mapping is the process of creating data element linkages between a data source and a destination. Data mapping includes the process of defining the entities and attributes we want to include in our data tool/warehouse and aligning our source data with those entities and attributes. The destination in this case is a data warehouse. Data mapping supports the data discovery process of determining the data you want to analyze, the sources of those data, and the values contained in the relevant data elements.

### Data Mapping Terms

When preparing data to use in a data analysis tool, we need to determine what data we want to include and the characteristics and values of those data elements. The first step is to identify the aspects of the educational enterprise about which we want to answer questions and determine relationships. If we want to know whether student attendance correlates with achievement, we need to have data on both attendance and achievement in our data tool. Since we are dealing with relationships, we need to identify the *entities* and the *attributes* within our data. *Entity* describes the object about which we want to collect information, such as student, staff, and/or assessments. Each entity has certain characteristics that define it. These characteristics are often called *attributes*. *Attribute* refers to the kinds of information we want to track about the entities. Some attributes of the entity *student* would include last name, first name, and identification number. The numeric or alphanumeric values of the attributes may be called values, occurrences, instances, or members. There is variation in this terminology, as Figure 6.1 shows. Different data warehouse or database companies use varied terms. The terms *entity, attribute,* and *instance* are being used by the National Center for Education Statistics as it creates a National Data Model, and these terms will be used here. (See *www.NCES.org* for information about the National Data Model.)

**Figure 6.1**
## DATA DISCOVERY TERMS

| NCES Data Model (Example) | Definitions | Traditional Database | Other Data Models | | | |
|---|---|---|---|---|---|---|
| **Entity** (*Student*) | The object about which we want to collect information. | Table | File | Entity | Object |
| **Attribute** (*Last Name*) | Characteristics that define the entity. | Table | Item | Element | Attribute |
| **Instance** (*Bernhardt*) | The value of the attribute. | Value | Value | Occurrence | Member |

Figure 6.2 is a table of generally recommended entities and attributes for a school district data warehouse. These are the data attributes that generally allow staffs to answer the important questions for supporting effective data-driven decision making.

In order to translate the data collected throughout the district into useful information for decision making, the data must be transformed from how they are collected initially into the format that will allow for their effective use in the data tools. The recommended entities and attributes must be defined, their data source members must be identified as they appear in their data sources, and they must be linked to the way the users want them to appear in the data tools. This is a tedious job that must be done completely and accurately as a guide for the transformation and troubleshooting of all data. Any data company should be able to help with this work.

Figure 6.2

## RECOMMENDED ENTITIES AND ATTRIBUTES

| Recommended Entities | Recommended Attributes |
|---|---|
| **Student** | Student identification number |
| | Student name *(last name, first name, middle initial)* |
| | School identification number |
| | Birth date |
| | Gender |
| | Grade level |
| | Ethnicity |
| | English proficiency |
| | Lunch status |
| | Socioeconomic status |
| | Student test identification number |
| | Social Security Number |
| | Active status |
| | Gifted qualified |
| | Gifted served |
| | Gifted services received |
| | Home language |
| | Language Development Services |
| | Drop Out Prevention |
| | Community Service |
| | Student Assistance Program |
| | Summer school status |
| | Alternate school status |
| | Previous school attended |
| | Assigned school |
| | Homebound status |
| | Migrant status |
| | Migrant education |
| | Immigrant status |
| | Immigrant education |
| | Homeless status |
| | Homeless education |
| | Special education tag |
| | Education level of mother |
| | Education level of father |
| | Father's employer |
| | Mother's employer |
| | Sibling(s) |
| | Inter-district transfer |
| | Intra-district transfer |
| | Resident district |
| | Zip code |
| | Geographical code |
| | On track to graduation |
| | Title 1 Reading status |
| | Title 1 Math status |
| | Interventions (Retentions) |
| | Homeroom teacher code |
| | Teacher identification number *(for elementary students with no schedule)* |

**Figure 6.2** *(Continued)*

# RECOMMENDED ENTITIES AND ATTRIBUTES

| Recommended Entities | Recommended Attributes |
|---|---|
| **Student** *(Other)* | What they want to do when they graduate<br>Employment during school<br>Perceptions<br>Learning styles |
| **Staff** | Teacher identification number<br>Administrator identification number<br>School code<br>Name<br>Gender<br>Ethnicity<br>Birth date<br>Social security number<br>Active status<br>Certificates<br>Endorsements<br>Years of experience<br>Years/months in district<br>Highest degree level<br>Hours toward next degree<br>Teaching in certificate area<br>Job description |
| **Classroom Implementation** | Results of observations *(Formal and informal)* |
| **District** | District identification number<br>State district number<br>District Name |
| **School** | School identification number<br>State school number<br>School name<br>Title 1 status<br>School type<br>Feeder pattern |
| **Assessments** | Test administration dates<br>All scores<br>Grades tested<br>Points possible<br>Points received<br>Percent correct<br>Proficiency level<br>All test indicators |

**Figure 6.2** *(Continued)*

# RECOMMENDED ENTITIES AND ATTRIBUTES

| Recommended Entities | Recommended Attributes |
|---|---|
| **Course** | Course name<br>School identification number<br>Course identification number<br>State course identification number<br>Course name<br>State course name<br>Subject area<br>Department<br>Level |
| **Class** | Period<br>Section<br>Term<br>Class enrollment |
| **Schedule** | Course status *(active, non-active)*<br>Section<br>Period<br>Maximum class size<br>Actual class size<br>Grading period |
| **Course Grades** | Grade<br>Grading period<br>Course status |
| **GPA** | Cumulative GPA<br>Weighted GPA<br>Yearly GPA<br>GPA grading period |
| **Credits** | Credit category<br>Credit subject<br>Credits earned<br>Term |
| **Advanced Placement** | Score type<br>Score |
| **Student Attendance**<br>*(Daily detail, daily summary, period detail, period summary)* | Attendance code<br>Attendance date<br>Days absent<br>Days enrolled<br>Days present<br>Days excused<br>Days unexcused<br>Days tardy<br>Reason absent<br>Reason tardy |
| **Teacher Attendance** | Days absent<br>Days present<br>Membership days |

**Figure 6.2** *(Continued)*

## RECOMMENDED ENTITIES AND ATTRIBUTES

| Recommended Entities | Recommended Attributes |
|---|---|
| **Discipline** *(Detail, summary)* | Infraction date<br>Infraction type<br>Infraction location<br>Infraction code<br>Disposition type<br>Disposition code<br>Referred by *(including the teacher number so that it can be tied back to the teacher)*<br>Number of days<br>Number of times |
| **Extracurricular Activities** | Athletics<br>Music<br>Theatre<br>Academic<br>Clubs |
| **Mobility** | Entrance date<br>Exit date<br>Exit reason<br>Inter/intra status |
| **Special Education** | Primary disability<br>Secondary disability<br>Tertiary disability<br>Special education status<br>IEP status<br>Accommodations<br>Modifications<br>Instructional setting<br>Resource Specialist Placement<br>Special Day Class<br>Special education services recommended<br>Special education services provided<br>Referred by<br>Enter date<br>Exit date |
| **Professional Development** | Course category<br>Course title<br>Course instructor<br>Course date<br>Hours<br>Continuing education units earned |

Figure 6.3 shows an example of how data mapping of some of these entities and attributes might look. The first two columns are the entities and attributes identified in Figure 6.2. The third column defines what types of data we are working with, such as enumerated (lists), alphanumeric, or date. The source values define what the instances are called in the data source files. The instances in Figure 6.3 show how the source members will appear in the data tools. These definitions are necessary ahead of time to avoid time-consuming and data-corrupting errors when moving data into any type of tool. The definitions also help when troubleshooting problems.

## Figure 6.3
# EXAMPLE SCHOOL DISTRICT DATA MAPPING

| Entities | Attributes | Data Type | Source Values | Instances |
|---|---|---|---|---|
| Student | Student code | Enum | | |
| | Student name | Alpha | | |
| | School code | Enum | | |
| | Birth date | Date | | |
| | Grade level | Enum | P | Preschool |
| | | | KA | Kindergarten |
| | | | KP | Kindergarten |
| | | | K | Kindergarten |
| | | | 01 | Grade 1 |
| | | | 02 | Grade 2 |
| | | | 03 | Grade 3 |
| | | | 04 | Grade 4 |
| | | | 05 | Grade 5 |
| | | | 06 | Grade 6 |
| | | | 07 | Grade 7 |
| | | | 08 | Grade 8 |
| | | | 09 | Grade 9 |
| | | | 10 | Grade 10 |
| | | | 11 | Grade 11 |
| | | | 12 | Grade 12 |
| | | | #Any other # | Grade unknown |
| | Gender | Enum | F | Female |
| | | | M | Male |
| | | | #Any other # | Gender Unknown |
| | Ethnicity | Enum | 01 | American Indian or Alaskan |
| | | | 02 | Asian |
| | | | 04 | Black |
| | | | 03 | Filipino |
| | | | 06 | Hispanic |
| | | | 07 | Pacific Islander |
| | | | 05 | White |
| | | | 08 | Multiple or No Response |
| | LEP | Enum | LP | Limited English proficient |
| | | | EO | English only |
| | Lunch status | Enum | F | Free |
| | | | R | Reduced |
| | | | Paid | Not free/reduced |

## Summary

When districts decide they want to engage in comprehensive data analyses with the assistance of data tools, they find they need to know up front what questions they want to answer, what analyses they want to perform, and what data can answer those questions and provide the desired analyses. This process is called *data discovery*. When they are clear on what data are needed, districts must determine and document where the data are located, the data sources, and their format. This is the process of *data mapping*.

Data mapping takes the data you need to answer the questions you have generated and meticulously presents them in a comprehensive way so that anyone using the warehouse can understand both where the data came from and their format. Thereafter, the data can be connected by the data tools to get the information you desire in the format that is most useful to you. Transforming how data in the data warehouse is structured is a critical part of the process of being able to analyze data, generate reports, and improve teaching and learning.

> *Transforming how data in the data warehouse is structured is a critical part of the process of being able to analyze data, generate reports, and improve teaching and learning.*

CHAPTER **7**

# SELECTING ANALYTICAL DATA TOOLS TO IMPROVE TEACHING AND LEARNING

While all three types of data tools mentioned in Chapter 2 are important for education organizations to acquire, this book focuses on analytical data tools to access, intersect, and analyze vast amounts of data. School district personnel and teachers will need to go through needs assessments to match curriculum/instruction/ assessment management tools with their curriculum, instruction, and assessment programs. Information Technology (IT) departments, with input from administrators and teachers, will need to determine which student information system will work for the district. A data warehouse is a complete and complex tool that provides analyses never before possible within learning organizations, which is the potential this book explores.

Districts must invest in analytical tools, such as data warehouses, to allow central office and school personnel to analyze and use the data that will improve teaching and learning for all students. We recommend that school districts buy the tools from vendors and not attempt to build them themselves. Discussion on this topic appears in Chapter 8.

*Districts must invest in analytical tools, such as data warehouses, to allow central office and school personnel to analyze and use the data that will improve teaching and learning for all students.*

## Do We Really Need Comprehensive Analytical Data Tools?

If you can answer *yes* to any of the following questions, your school district needs a data tool, such as a data warehouse, and you need this book to learn more about acquiring and using a data warehouse:

▼ Do district personnel who want to use specific data have to get what they need from separate department administrators, as opposed to a central location?

▼ Do teachers and school administrators have only paper results of students' scores on high stakes tests?

▼ Is it difficult for teachers to access electronically student progress throughout the year?

▼ Is it difficult or nearly impossible to regroup, or disaggregate, your student achievement results electronically in your district or to "re-roster" results by next year's class users and teachers?

▼ Is it impossible to look at a student's historical files electronically?

▼ Does your district use data to produce compliance reports, but never digs deeper into the data to uncover reasons for the results it is getting?

A *yes* answer to any of these questions indicates that your district has not yet made the commitment to gather, analyze, and use data in an effective and efficient way that will improve teaching and learning throughout the organization.

## Purposes for the Data Warehouse

There are four major purposes for education organizations to invest in a data warehouse or to acquire analytical data tools. (For the rest of the chapter, the term *data warehouse* will be used to represent all comprehensive and data tool solutions.) These four purposes include:

1. **To make data accessible:** A data warehouse makes it possible for important data sets that can help improve teaching and learning to be available to all levels—classroom, school, district, as well as state and federal organizations. For the data in a data warehouse to be useful and usable at all levels, the data must be understandable (labeled correctly and in meaningful ways). The analytical tools that assist with the data analysis work must be intuitive, easy to use, and fast.

2. **To make data consistent:** The process of building a data warehouse can help make information from one part of the organization match information from all other parts of the organization, or help match data from organization to organization, as a result of making all the data accessible. To do this, the data must be agreed upon, gathered, and labeled consistently and completely. This should be done through the student information system.

3. **To be an adaptive and resilient source of information:** A data warehouse needs to be up-to-date, reliable, and valid. For the data warehouse to be useful, it must adapt continuously to meet users' needs.

4. **To be a secure depository of accessible information:** Another purpose for the data warehouse is to manage the security of sensitive data and grant access to only those individuals who have clearance or need for specific information. While data warehouses provide access like never before, the access should never be available to all people within the organization: access must be "managed."

> *Data Warehouse Purposes*
>
> ♦ *To make data accessible*
>
> ♦ *To make data consistent*
>
> ♦ *To be an adaptive and resilient source of information*
>
> ♦ *To be a secure depository of information*

## Selecting the Data Warehouse

Many vendors have confused education personnel about the issue of data warehouses—saying their products can do all that a district wants. As was mentioned earlier, no one tool can do everything, at this time.

If your school district does not have a comprehensive analytical data tool right now, there are some capabilities—not necessarily in this order—you might want to think about when researching a solution:

1. **Accessibility at different levels.** Most often, districts prefer all data stored at the district level, with accessibility at the school and classroom levels. You must decide how you will manage and maintain security and whom you want to access the information. Thinking through the uses of the data will help districts know how strict or how tight security has to be. For example, when first thinking about access, districts often determine that schools should be able to access only their own information. However, highly proactive data analyses requires looking at longitudinal data at individual student levels, which would require schools to have access to other schools' data. Having the data accessible at all levels does not mean that teachers and school administrators should be expected to perform all the analyses. Successful districts determine the most important analyses and provide them in report form to their schools and teachers, allowing school personnel the time to use the data and to dig deeper into the data. (Reporting the results is discussed in Chapter 10.) If teachers are trained to use the data tools and given time to use them, they will dig deeper into the data and get answers they have never before been able to receive to questions regarding student progress toward meeting standards. (More on this in Chapter 11.)

2. **Ability to build graphs automatically.** You want to be able to view the data as tables to check for accuracy; however, you want the data analysis tool to build graphs for you, as well. If you want staffs to review the data, it is wise to put the data in picture form, as much as possible, so everyone can see the resulting information in the same way. Not all analyses are most easily read in a graph, however. The more complex the analysis, or the more levels of disaggregation (e.g., special education enrollment by disability, grade level, gender, and ethnicity), the more difficult it is to create/view a graph that is understandable. Tables are the best display for those analyses.

*Successful districts determine the most important analyses and provide them in report form to their schools and teachers, allowing school personnel the time to use the data and to dig deeper into the data.*

3. **Disaggregation and digging deeper on the fly.** When you perform an analysis that is starting to show interesting information or pose significant questions, you want to be able to analyze quickly and easily at the next deeper levels to understand how the results were obtained. You will also want to see if the results hold true for all student or staff groups—in other words, you will want to disaggregate your data. When disaggregating data, we are looking at aggregate data (from the whole group) broken down into smaller component groups of the whole, such as boys compared to girls. Additionally, it is necessary to be able to "drill down" to more detailed information: for instance, we want to have the ability to click on a graph or a table cell and access the list of students, or staff, that makes up that number.

4. **Point and click or drag and drop technology that is intuitive and fast.** We want teachers and administrators to be able to use data tools without having to refer to a manual for every analysis. The technology is available now to make complex data analysis work intuitive, easy, and fast.

5. **The ability to generate standard or customized reports with a click of a button.** Some reports have to be generated every year, such as School Accountability Report Cards, Title 1 reports, and school profiles. If the same information is required each year, the data analysis product should allow you the flexibility to recreate any report you want without spending a lot of time on it. When districts determine the information that is most important for schools to use, they should be able to create reports that can be "batched" for all the schools. In other words, a district-level educator should be able to create one report format that can be automatically populated with each school's data without creating each school report individually. Of course, the more complex the need, the more difficult the reporting tool. Do not let vendors tell you that they have all the reporting possibilities thought out for you. You need the flexibility to create your own reports. It is nice that they have most reports considered; however, they do not know what will appear as an issue for you in the future—nor do you.

*Do not let vendors tell you that they have all the reporting possibilities thought out for you. You need the flexibility to create your own reports. It is nice that they have most reports considered; however, they do not know what will appear as an issue for you in the future—nor do you.*

6. **The ability to follow matched and unmatched cohorts—the same students or group of students—as they progress through their educational careers.** This is a complex analysis for data analysis tools. Most vendors will tell you they can do this. You must learn to say these words when you speak with vendors—*Show Me!* By matched cohorts, we mean following the same students over time to understand their educational experiences and individual growth. If an educational system is adding value to *all* students' education, all students should be making progress each year, and the schools should be able to document this progress.

   By *unmatched* cohorts, we mean following a group that might have some mobility, such as the Class of 2014, through their educational experiences to understand how they are doing or to predict and prevent some occurrences. As an example, if we want to know how to prevent high school dropouts, we should be able to isolate our analysis to the dropouts from the past and work our way backward through the warehouse (as long as the data are in the warehouse, regardless of the school within the district the students attended) to understand the common characteristics of those who dropped out. That way we can also look for current students with those characteristics and do something different to prevent dropouts from occurring. Accomplishing such an analysis is not an easy proposition. It takes much consideration about who gets access to what data. For example, this would mean that schools would be able to see other schools' data. These analyses require unique identifiers for students and clean data.

   School districts also want to follow students forward to understand the impact of grade levels, programs, schools, processes, etc.

7. **Longitudinal analysis capabilities.** This might sound like a "no brainer," but there are products on the market that can perform analyses on data only one year at a time. (Most student information systems hold only one year of data.) This is probably a good indication that you are dealing with flat database architecture and not a true complex data warehouse. There are also some data warehouse tools that have the ability to perform longitudinal analyses, but you might not be able to see the analyses on the screen. Again, ask the vendors to show you a longitudinal analysis. Never buy a data warehouse that cannot do longitudinal analyses and show past years' comparisons on the screen at the same time.

*Never buy a data warehouse that cannot do longitudinal analyses.*

8. **True integration of disparate systems.** The main benefit of a comprehensive data analysis tool, such as a data warehouse, is being able to cross-tabulate, intersect, or analyze together previously disconnected data. A true data warehouse can combine your student information system with your state testing data, ongoing assessments, professional development information, process information, and any other data you want to include.

You can buy a data warehouse that the vendor pre-builds in "data cubes" using common data elements such as student achievement results and demographic data. This approach is fast and efficient. However, most school districts outgrow this approach very quickly and want the flexibility of a true relational database management system, where each data element is stored once but is connected to all other data elements. This type of system gives you the ability to access and cross-analyze all data elements and not be limited to pre-determined reports.

Also, you do not want your data warehouse to take your state testing data, disaggregate it by the demographics marked on the test, and give you reports, as some vendors might lead you to believe. You want your data warehouse to use the most accurate data at all times. The most accurate demographic data should be in your clean student information system and include more demographics than the test captures; plus the student information system should continuously refresh data. You want to ask vendors about the potential integration with your existing databases, especially your student information system, and about their partnerships with vendors of these tools.

*Note:* Some districts struggle with the public relations fallout when information published by their State Departments of Education is not as accurate as information in the district warehouse. The reasons the data could vary include the following. Sometimes—

   ▼ The persons or system providing the data to the state are not using the data warehouse as their source for data;

   ▼ State reports reflect district status as of a particular date, while information in one's warehouse is current and always changing to reflect real daily changes, such as new enrollments; and

▼ The district people compiling the data were not appropriately skilled to know how to send accurate data to the state. (Submitting data to the state cannot be left to school secretaries or data clerks to figure out on their own. Those entering data must have the necessary training and time to do the job).

It is important to identify the discrepancies and acknowledge them; know why they exist, then use the correct data with an explanation about why it is correct.

9. **Extensibility.** The data warehouse product you want to purchase needs to be developed on a platform built to support future school district needs and growth. The application needs to be scalable, reliable, extensible, and developed with an open, integrated approach that supports other applications. Be careful not to buy a data warehouse to solve only this year's problems. These are expensive systems that should be able to cross disparate data analysis systems to answer just about any data question you have in your schools or district. You cannot, and should not, go through this purchasing process every year. Buy for the long haul. Remember, this effort is a journey, not a destination.

Several other factors should also be considered when selecting a data warehouse.

1. **You must like the people selling the product.** If you do not trust or like the people who sell the data warehouse, you probably will not like the engineering and customer service end of the company either. Companies hire people to carry out their mission and philosophy. Creating a data warehouse is a long-term, intensive, hands-on proposition. In fact, it is a process, not a product. If the sales people promise to send you information and they never get back to you, you will probably feel as left alone when it comes to creating your warehouse. You will want to listen very carefully to their answers to your questions regarding flexibility of the final product to meet your needs. Additionally, data warehouse vendors that really want your business will come to you—just ask. If they will not come to you, do not buy their product! There are companies that want to come to you to see your systems and to know what you need to make their product a success in your location. Certainly a company can do some product demonstrations using web sharing tools; however, at some point, the company should be willing to come to your location to meet you, to answer your specific questions, and to see your technological setup.

> *Creating a data warehouse is a long-term, intensive hands-on proposition. In fact, it is a process, not a product.*

Companies that will not come to you because of your location should not have your business. These issues reflect the company's responsiveness to your needs.

2. **Determine how long it will take to get an operational data warehouse.** Most data warehouse vendors can now get you a first iteration of your warehouse in 90 to 120 days—as long as the data extraction and transformation goes well. This depends on the size of your district, the amount of data—number of years, number of different types of data elements, number of sources—and the quality of your data. If the engineers have to keep calling you for labels or to return data because they are obviously not clean, the number of days required will increase. How the data will be updated and where it will be stored also figures into this equation.

3. **Ensure that the product can be updated as often as you want.** Comprehensive data analysis via the data warehouse seldom takes place every day. There are some data elements that you will want to track every day, such as assessments, mobility, and attendance, which can be tracked via your student information system, unless you want to cross those disparate data elements mentioned earlier. In that case, you might want a data warehouse that uploads data every night or every week. Get clarity from the vendors with regard to the updating and costs associated with it. If you decide on something other than daily or weekly updating, make sure that the schedule accommodates your wishes. For example, you will want your state testing results back as soon as you can get them; so make sure the uploading schedule is consistent with this desire. Some school districts have begun to keep two warehouses—one for research and analysis with identified dates, and one that refreshes every night. Be clear how often you want your warehouse updated.

4. **Whom do you want to host the warehouse?** This question must figure prominently into the selection of a solution. The host school district or educational service agency can manage the server that houses the data warehouse, or the vendor can host the server for you. The thinking about this has changed in the past few years from vendors helping districts host their own servers to vendors giving the districts breaks in price if the vendors host the servers. This is because many of the vendors are logging a good portion of their time in support services helping districts with server management. Many district networks are very slow, which is frustrating to the users, who may be

---

*Companies that will not come to you because of your location should not have your business.*

---

*Questions to Ask Vendors*

- *How long will it take to get our data warehouse operational?*

- *Can the product be updated as often as we want?*

- *Who can host the warehouse?*

- *How much support will be available?*

- *Can small districts form consortiums and share the use of a data warehouse in order to bring down the cost per pupil?*

- *What do other school districts that purchased from the vendor say about the vendor?*

used to faster Internet access from home connections, and can lead to non-use. It might be most efficient to allow the vendor to do the hosting. It is easier and faster for the vendor's engineers to update your data, their software, and their programming from their hosting center. Also, having the vendor host the server provides the district with lower total cost of ownership. Just make sure *you* own the data and will get them all back without hassle when your contract ends. Additionally, you will want to check out the vendor's security protocols. The biggest downside of districts not hosting their own data warehouse is that the district could get lax with the data ownership and not provide adequate time for management. (Chapter 12 discusses managing the data warehouse.)

5. **How much support will be available?** A data warehouse is a whole new way of thinking and working. You will want the possibility of face-to-face, email, telephone, website, remote web-based, and just about any other types of technical support thinkable, at hours that are convenient to you. In addition, it would be good to have web forums and/or users' conferences available to discuss the challenges and uses of the warehouse with other users. In addition to vendor support, districts should put together a team of "first responders" to understand the issues and to attempt to deal with them before contacting the vendor. "First responders" will learn more about the warehouse and be able to answer questions that reappear. Support will not just be about technical issues. Support includes help as users think through analyses and how to produce something valid and meaningful.

6. **Small districts can form consortiums and share the use of a data warehouse in order to bring down the costs per pupil.** Most data warehouses are priced on a per pupil basis. Small districts often find the data warehouse pricing to be off limits for them. Some data warehouse companies will work with small districts to combine efforts to get the costs down for them. Each district still gets access only to its own data through the data warehouse security procedures. (Two examples appear in Chapter 13.)

7. **Talk with other school districts that purchased the product you are considering.** It would be great if you could find districts that are in varying stages of using the product you are considering buying. However, listen carefully to their complaints about the product. It might not be the product; it might be the district's own data or

networking system. Many school districts state unhappiness with their data warehouses because they think they should be easier and faster to set up than they are. Districts are also often hoping for more useable data. A data warehouse requires complex engineering—it is not a plug and play software program that can be up and running in the same day. The usable data are usually more about what the school district has given the data warehouse company to work with than what the company does with the data. (Chapters 5 and 6 discuss getting data in appropriate formats for their most effective use.)

In addition to thinking about what your district might want from a vendor, you need to be prepared to dedicate staff resources to get the data available for loading into the warehouse and to troubleshoot data issues, as well as support the management of the warehouse once it is set up.

> *A data warehouse requires complex engineering—it is not a plug and play software program that can be up and running in the same day.*

## Summary

What makes the difference in schools successfully improving teaching and learning versus schools that do not succeed in improving teaching and learning is the effective use of data. Many times the reason schools and teachers do not use data to this end is that the data just are not easily accessible to them; and, when they are, the data may not be in a form that will help them achieve the analyses for which they are planning. They might have a vision about the value of gathering, analyzing, and using data, but not yet have the skills necessary for such analyses.

Comprehensive analytical tools, such as a data warehouse, can link all school and school district information together to create analyses that allow the understanding of the impact of different programs and processes on improving teaching and learning, and the identification of differences that may occur related to student groupings (e.g., gender, ethnicity, poverty, language proficiency).

A data warehouse can link all school and school district information together to allow users to analyze and use data in an effective and efficient way to improve teaching and learning throughout the organization. Selecting a data warehouse calls for a commitment to invest the financial and human resources necessary to acquire a warehouse that will make data accessible and consistent and be a secure depository of information. It is a process that requires careful thought as to what the district needs and how the needs can best be met. Careful selection of a data warehouse will ensure its use as a proactive tool to improve teaching and learning.

> *What makes the difference in schools successfully improving teaching and learning versus schools that do not succeed in improving teaching and learning is the effective use of data.*

CHAPTER **8**

# BUILD IT YOURSELF OR BUY FROM A VENDOR

Many school districts now have excellent Information Technology (IT) staffs that tell their administrators that they can build a data warehouse in-house for less than they can purchase a warehouse from a vendor. There is no doubt that wonderful IT staffs can do the work. The challenge is the amount of time it takes for them to develop the warehouse, produce meaningful reports, and then keep the warehouse working. Additionally, we have to consider what happens with the work the IT staffs were originally hired to do while they are building this major tool and the work that we need them to do to prepare the data for any warehouse, whether the district builds it or buys it. The homegrown data warehouse often takes years to develop, years that could be spent preparing and analyzing the data and making improvements to teaching and learning based on the data. Furthermore, a homegrown data warehouse may not be cheaper than a purchased one, especially when you figure in the salary and benefits of additional staff the district would have to secure to do the work the IT staff members would be doing if they were not creating a warehouse. To add to this, unless the district has security/network administrators, web developers, and database administrators, it is almost impossible to create a system as robust as what is available for purchase.

We mean no disrespect for the capabilities of the IT staffs out there. We are suggesting that there are now competent vendors available who can deliver a loaded data warehouse in approximately three months. Remember, when the IT staffs are working on creating a warehouse, their duties of focusing on data availability and preparations for the warehouse are not being done.

> *The homegrown data warehouse often takes years to develop, years that could be spent preparing and analyzing the data and making improvements to teaching and learning based on the data.*

IT staffs make or break the successful implementation of the data warehouse, even if it is bought from a vendor. Data warehouses continually evolve, and IT staffs are needed to help them evolve. District administrators need to bring the IT staffs into the conversations about buying data warehouses early and often and to enlist their support. Below are two scenarios that bring home some of these points.

### Scenario 1

*A 20,000-student district was having a "battle" with its IT department about whether to build its warehouse in the district or to go with a commercial vendor. The superintendent's gut reaction was to go with a vendor to get the warehouse up and running, then use the talents of the local IT staff to ensure that it gets built right and that it will be used well. The superintendent wanted the IT staff to create automated reports required of the district and to make data available to teachers. The IT staff members fought hard to build the warehouse themselves.*

*The IT staff members were first asked how they currently work with school staff to use the data they now provide for schools. Members of the IT staff looked up and sadly replied, "We can hardly get the required reports done, let alone get requested reports done. We never get to the school level." The answer to that first question suggested that an outside vendor was probably the way to go. If the IT staffs cannot get requested reports done now, they will have a very difficult time getting required reports done while or after building and implementing a data warehouse. In addition, the IT staff members thought they could get the data warehouse created in one year, which almost always means at least three.*

### Scenario 2

*Another district had an IT staff that advised the superintendent's council to purchase a data warehouse through an outside vendor. The IT staff members worked with the district program staff directors (e.g., special education, English language development, curriculum and instruction) to ready their data for import, worked with them to create the reports they needed, and after the warehouse was used for awhile, helped the district grow the warehouse. When asked if something else could be added to the warehouse that was feasible for improving teaching and learning, these IT staff members always said, "We can do that." What a dream it was to work with this district. The district got the data warehouse up and running within six months, by buying from an outside vendor; the IT staff ensured the security and cleanliness of the data; and the District Leadership Team made sure that someone on staff owns each piece of data that goes into the warehouse. Every year that warehouse has grown. The IT staff members create automated and standard reports to meet federal, state, and district requirements, and provide a school profile for each school in the district. The district establishes performance measures for each component of the district to judge effectiveness, efficiency, and progress. In their last iteration, the district administration and IT staff worked together to establish standard reports to link all district and school programs' effectiveness to financial data. This data warehouse will ultimately link student performance to program effectiveness/efficiency and teacher quality.*

Going with an outside vendor does not mean that there is no longer a job for the IT staffs. There is a huge need for the IT staffs to remain close to the data warehouse project to help the district automate systems and reports and to create new reports for schools to use to improve teaching and learning. (More on creating reports in Chapter 10.) Even with the commercial data warehouse comes implementation at the local level that will consume IT staffs' time. Some of the work required in getting the data warehouse up and running, and keeping it maintained, include getting the data ready to import into the warehouse, establishing and monitoring security and implementation practices, authenticating reports, training individuals to use the warehouse, and creating standard reports to automate the work that needs to be done each year. The district really needs to concentrate on these elements and leave the building of the warehouse to the vendors.

## Tough Political Issues

The first scenario, in the previous section, brings up some tough political issues. When the IT staff and district leadership do not see eye-to-eye, will they ever really be able to work together? This scenario could take two to three times longer to implement than expected because the vision for the warehouse was never shared. What do you do in this case? How are the teachers and administrators ever going to work with the IT staff to get the analyses they need to improve teaching and learning? This is a hard place for the district to find itself. Strong district leadership is needed to ensure that this type of infighting does not get in the way of acquiring a tool that will help improve teaching and learning. Conducting needs assessments and involving participants from various groups in the selection process should help to alleviate these issues. The focus must be on how the warehouse can improve what goes on in schools every day, and the IT staff must consider itself a valuable ally in the process—not just someone who is called upon when the network or a computer doesn't work.

The second scenario describes an almost ideal situation. The district establishes a clear vision, goes with an outside vendor, and the IT staff is onboard with making the vision a reality. This takes strong leadership, a very clear vision, and staff using the warehouse and pushing its limits.

Scenario 3, below, describes a district that built its own data warehouse, because it could not find a vendor with a product that was able to do what the district wanted to be able to do with its data. Superintendent Joseph Kitchens describes what occurred in the Western Heights Public School District (WHPS) in Oklahoma City, Oklahoma *(http://www.westernheights.k12.ok.us/)*.

### Scenario 3

*Why a data warehouse was needed. With the approval of NCLB and its subsequent implementation across the nation, schools have found it necessary to develop and deploy new robust accountability systems capable of providing undeniable evidence of student academic success.*

*The Western Heights Public School District Leadership Team determined that to provide for the appropriate instructional support of teachers and students in a competency-based testing environment, a very substantial change in the way student data are created, stored, and used would be required. The need to build or configure a data warehouse emerged from an instructional vision linked to the Oklahoma graduation test initiative called Achieving Classroom Excellence (ACE).*

*With the implementation of the ACE Initiative, the District would be organizing criterion or benchmark testing for over 3,500 students each quarter in over 1,250 course sections per quarter. It was, therefore, absolutely imperative that a highly-functional data warehouse be developed. It was also essential that the District establish highly effective processes and procedures, referred to as electronic pulls of data, between various assessment vendors and the district data warehouse. The data warehouse also had to be developed in a manner that supported all federal and state reporting requirements.*

*Building the warehouse. The District's development team for a data warehouse included the Superintendent, the Assistant Superintendent, the Chief Technology Officer, three Instructional Technologists, the district's Director for Student Assessment, the Manager for the Student Information System, and the .Net Application Information Management Specialist. Additionally, the District intermittently retained the services of select Oklahoma State University College of Education researchers.*

*The staff of Western Heights Public Schools carefully selected and deployed applications that would truly improve district reporting, both in regard to school improvement applications and state and federal reporting guidelines. The District wanted to make sure all of its data systems were interoperable within the district network. Because the systems were built by different vendors, we needed a new capability that would allow for the exchange of common information and data among systems. To our great relief, we found that the Schools Interoperability Framework (SIF) was all about establishing common protocols for data exchange among disparate systems. For instance, under SIF protocols, when the name of a student is entered in the student information system, that name is distributed by what's called a SIF agent to all other management systems. This greatly improves the quality of data in all systems and reduces the possibilities of data errors. When the attributes of SIF are strictly enforced and followed in association with the deployment of a SIF-compliant data warehouse, reporting flexibility and conformance with the National Center for Education Statistics (NCES) Common Core of Data (CCD) are greatly enhanced.*

*Western Heights set out to build a system that would proactively indicate instructional needs for students and support the distribution of instructional interventions (robust content), while simultaneously meeting the reporting requirements of both NCLB initiatives and state reporting. To accomplish these tasks, we deployed a SIF-compliant SIS and then deployed several SIF-compliant instructional management systems. Three Zone Integration Servers (ZIS) were also developed and deployed to manage data traffic among multiple SIF agents supporting district software applications. With the effective deployment of the district ZIS accomplished, the District could proceed with the development and deployment of a SIF-compliant data warehouse.*

*A private vendor was retained for the purposes of developing and deploying the necessary SIF agents and Zone Integration Servers necessary to support the data warehouse. Once the supporting ZIS architecture was in place, the district retained the services of the same vendor group to actually construct the data aggregator and associated data warehouse. The vendor was also retained, with assistance from both district and Oklahoma State University research staff, to develop and deploy advanced reporting processes that would create a robust and meaningful set of dynamic real-time reports for parents, students, and teachers.*

*Maintaining the data warehouse.* The CTO and the Information Management Specialist of the District share the responsibility of maintaining the data warehouse with the private vendor. The data warehouse is located on district premises. Many of the data retained in the warehouse are pre-programmed for deposit in the data warehouse, utilizing a SIF agent that has been developed by the vendor. The vendor has also developed a Zone Integration Management Tool to provide the staff with constant updates regarding the status of SIF-based data transfers and to indicate which student data are not being properly exchanged among operating systems.

When the district technology team meets to discuss the infusion of new data objects into the Total Information Management System of Western Heights Public Schools, the discussion of data management is a critical initial discussion:

▼ Do we already have access to data that will answer the question(s) being posed? If this is not the case, which management group will create the data?

▼ Who will have the right to review the data, and how will the data be stored, and under what circumstances will the data be used?

▼ Additionally, who will build the reporting, what other existing data objects will be necessary to build the desired report, and who will have access to view the associated reporting?

*Using the system.* The District has established a robust assessment package to accurately predict which students are in need of instructional intervention and what areas of instruction or/state standards specifically need to be addressed on behalf of each student. Electronic results for all district assessment packages and for the Oklahoma State Testing Program/End of Instruction (OSTP/EOI) are retrieved electronically from the appropriate vendors and then deposited in the district's data warehouse.

Norm-referenced results are used to predict which students are likely to have future problems on OSTP or EOI assessments. The actual remedial instruction effort is driven by prioritizing the results of student performance on benchmark assessments. The teachers' rank-ordered listing of student performance demonstrates which state standard each student is having difficulty mastering. Reports have also been developed to group students of similar abilities in grades 2 to 10.

*Parents are given a report card that shows each student's grade in each course, plus student performance on each quarterly benchmark assessment. The report card also indicates the level of mastery attained or not attained on each state standard. This type of reporting can only be accomplished by simultaneously using multiple data sources from diverse assessments in conjunction with disparate applications.*

*WHPS staff firmly believes that ACE requires a systemic change in the way that the instructional program of the School District is designed and operates. The District has developed efficient practices to get all relevant instructional data in the hands of teachers, parents, students, and administrators in real time through the development of a parent/teacher/ student portal to support sound and informed educational intervention.*

***Key elements of success.*** *All school stakeholders, especially teachers and administrators, want to see and use student performance data on a regular basis. The key for getting teachers involved in using the system is to have a report portal that is constantly updated with valued data in near real time. If it takes more than a day to view assessment results, the whole process is just too slow for action-oriented teachers who have students with great instructional need. In the Western Heights data warehouse, this has meant the building of valued dynamic student performance reports that can be distributed, on a near-real-time basis, using the unique scheduling of each student and teacher in combination with security protocols to preserve the confidentiality of all stakeholders. Robust staff training is inherent with this implementation model. Over three years, each teacher received 32 hours of training per year before the effort could reach full potential.*

*In the end, the initiative has been successful in every way. Student academic achievement across the district has increased by 32% over the past four years. And, to make the cake a little sweeter, the District has enjoyed a return on investment of $3 for each dollar invested. Excellent data warehousing can and should result in better fiscal management of the district dollars.*

## Summary

Many products are on the market for educational data warehousing, with many more coming online every year. The technology is getting more user-friendly and the vendors more knowledgeable about what schools need in data warehouses, analysis, and reporting. At the same time, school districts are hiring many talented IT people. These IT people often want to create a data warehouse and most certainly are capable of doing so. The time and dollar factors, as well as the district vision for the use of data, weigh heavily into the decision about the best approach to acquiring a data warehouse. Most districts need their IT staffs to focus full time on getting the data ready for import and then maintaining the system. On the other hand, a district with a vision for a data warehouse and data use may not find the vendor to match its vision; such a district might need to create its own warehouse solution. A school district must balance what it wants from its data with what vendors say it needs or what they can provide. Whether you decide to build your own warehouse or buy one from a vendor, you need to be very clear on your vision. Remember, the primary function of the data warehouse is to improve teaching and learning.

*Whether you decide to build your own warehouse or buy one from a vendor, you need to be very clear on your vision.*

CHAPTER 9

# CREATING THE CULTURE TO USE DATA AND DATA TOOLS

School and school district personnel ask me all the time to help them create a culture for data and data warehouse use in their learning organizations. They look at me expectantly, as if I could give them the definitive steps that overnight would establish a culture to effectively use data and a data warehouse every day. I wish I did know the magical steps that could quickly establish a data culture. I wish it were so easy. There are no magical steps; there are some necessary and logical steps, however. It is the culture of the organization (which includes leadership) that will ultimately determine the use of data. Let's look at some of the issues involved in creating a data culture.

## Organizational Culture

Who or what determines or creates the culture of a school? Depending upon the current culture, the answer could include: the principal, the educators, the interaction of the principal with the educators, the interaction of the educators with each other, the interaction of educators and the principal with students and district administrators, and the superintendent. Also, the accepted behaviors of the community (e.g., regarding race or gender relations, religion, etc.) are part of the culture.

The word *culture* in the context of an educational organization can be defined as the shared assumptions, beliefs, and accepted normal behaviors (norms) of a group. These are powerful influences on the way people live, act, and work. Culture defines actions that are expected and accepted and how to sanction those actions that are not acceptable. How people act and work within any organization is greatly influenced by the culture of the organization.

> *The word "culture" in the context of an educational organization can be defined as the shared assumptions, beliefs, and normal behaviors (norms) of a group.*

*Steps in Creating
a Vision for Data Use*

1. *Secure commitment from
   the top.*

2. *Obtain professional learning
   about what data and how
   data can improve teaching
   and learning.*

3. *Create a shared vision of what
   it would look like, sound like,
   and feel like if all staff
   members were using data
   to improve teaching
   and learning.*

4. *Detail when, how, and why
   data will be used to improve
   teaching and learning.*

5. *Determine the social
   structures of teachers working
   together to use data to improve
   teaching and learning.*

6. *Leaders must model, enforce,
   and lead the way using
   data to improve teaching
   and learning.*

*Changing the culture*

*means changing the*

*way work is done.*

## Changing the Culture and Changing the Culture to Use Data

The social structure and culture of an organization consists of many dimensions. To change the social structure and culture in order to encourage everyone to perform more effectively, more constructively, and to the same end means changing the way work is done or, as some might say, "changing the business rules by which the school operates." So, how do we do this? It all starts with the top leader getting everyone on the same page with respect to where the organization wants to go. In other words, the first step is to create and lead a shared vision for the organization that is based on shared values and beliefs and on the purpose of the school and school district. To change the culture to include consistent data use, there have to be core understandings among all staff of how data and a data warehouse can help the organization implement and live that shared vision.

To change the way work is done to include the effective use of data, we have to change our collective thinking about what we are trying to accomplish and how data can help us get to that end. Before discussing these issues, staff might need professional learning about how data can improve teaching and learning. To change a culture and the actions it supports, we need to change the thinking of those who participate in the culture by creating a shared picture (vision) of what the school would look like, sound like, and feel like if we were working differently, with data. The when, how, and why we would use data must be detailed. The social structures of the school that will support the use of data, including the collaborative working arrangements for teachers need to be described, and the time to use data and collaborate must be provided. Finally, and most importantly, school and school district leaders must consistently model and lead the work with data, as well as reinforce the expectations of how others will use data. Once the culture changes, an effort must be made to sustain the change and not just drop it when times get tough—especially when dollars get scarce.

### A Note about Data Teams

Many schools establish data teams to gather, analyze, use, and get others to use data. The use of data is often effective with those teams; however, data use does not always permeate to the entire staff if there is no structure for implementing the use throughout the staff. Establishing a data team does not lead to cultural change—only changing the way work is done by everyone will change a culture.

A couple of strong educators can spearhead cultural changes; however, it takes leadership consistently reinforcing and modeling the way to get all educators working to the same end. This does not mean that data use is mandated from the top down. The best results seem to be achieved when there is a firm commitment from the top, which is communicated directly to each and every person in the school, and followed through. In addition, educator collaboration is a key ingredient of the new culture.

## Take a Measure of Culture

There are many ways to measure the culture of an educational organization. The Education for the Future staff, student, administrator, and parent questionnaires are highly effective in measuring the culture of the school and school districts from the perspectives of these groups, as briefly described in the Little River example at the end of this chapter. The results of these questionnaires help schools and school districts know where the culture is currently and allow for the discussion of what the school wants the culture to become. (See *http://eff.csuchico.edu* for Questionnaire Resources and Services.)

The *Continuous Improvement Continuums* (Appendix) can help schools and school districts know where they are with respect to data knowledge and usage, if they share a vision about using data, if their continuous improvement plan will help them get to the vision, and if the leadership structure and professional learning opportunities provided to all staff can support the implementation of the vision. The *Continuous Improvement Continuums* also assess the degree to which partnerships with parents, community, and businesses provide win-win opportunities for everyone to contribute to students' learning and how well the learning organization evaluates its continuous improvement efforts.

## What District Leadership Can Do to Help Schools Create a Culture for Data and Data Warehouse Use

Strong district leadership and operations are "essential to advancing equitable and sustainable reform." (McLaughlin and Talbert, 2003, p.3.) Districts must engage in continuous improvement with a plan to improve the entire system, including all the parts that make up the system. (A *system* is a group of interacting, interrelated, or interdependent elements forming a complex whole.) To do this, the district must know the system and how its parts interrelate.

*A couple of strong educators can spearhead cultural changes; however, it takes leadership consistently reinforcing and modeling the way to get all educators working to the same end.*

*The best results seem to be achieved when there is a firm commitment from the top, which is communicated directly to each and every person in the school, and followed through.*

*Strong district leadership and operations are "essential to advancing equitable and sustainable reform."*
*McLaughlin and Talbert*

Comprehensive data analyses show these interrelationships and the impact of the system and its processes on the students. These analyses also indicate where leadership and support are needed to improve the system and, thus, improve learning for all students.

One of the first and most important things district leaders can do for schools is to *encourage schools to commit to a continuous improvement framework* that is congruent with, or the same as, the district's framework and to stick with it. District leaders need to help schools embrace and implement a framework (support structure) for continuous improvement, monitor the results, and maintain a consistent process. Too many districts keep schools from improving by asking them to change their focus after the schools have committed to a framework. Without a framework, schools tend to lose focus and become inefficient and ineffective with their continuous improvement work, repeating things already done and not doing the things that matter. The framework keeps schools doing the work when the work gets hard. It is a structure for them to rely on so they can avoid just spinning their wheels.

Figure 9.1 shows the elements included in an effective framework for continuous improvement.

> *One of the first and most important things district leaders can do for schools is to encourage schools to commit to a continuous improvement framework that is congruent with, or the same as, the district's framework and to stick with it. District leaders need to help schools embrace and implement a framework (support structure) for continuous improvement, monitor the results, and maintain a consistent process.*

## Figure 9.1
# CONTINUOUS IMPROVEMENT FRAMEWORK

### Data: *Information and Analysis*

A framework for continuous improvement must have a strong data analysis component that requires looking at the entire system through different lenses. Student learning data are extremely important. However, these data, by themselves, do not provide enough information to know how to improve a system.

We find schools that use only student learning measures adding on to their days with "before school programs" and "after school programs." What they are telling their students is that we know you are not learning math during the day with our current processes, so just sit there all day; we will use processes that get to your learning needs before or after school. (Of course, some of these programs are very effective for special needs students, ESL, students with high mobility, etc.)

Certainly teachers must have ongoing student learning measures available to them at all times to know how their processes are helping students get to the desired outcomes.

In a perfect world, all teachers would be clear about what they want students to know and be able to do by the end of the year. They would conduct assessments that would tell them what their students know and do not know at the beginning of the year. They would have short-cycle assessments that would help students learn the content and provide information about how student learning is progressing throughout the year. That way, teachers would know how to adjust their teaching strategies throughout the year to ensure continuous student learning. The assessment information would be shared with students and parents.

### A Vision: *Student Achievement*

The vision clarifies what it will look like, sound like, feel like when the school is carrying out its mission. A vision must be understandable to everyone in the organization in the same way. It should cement commitments, not just compliance. A vision helps a system achieve *Focused Acts of Improvement*. Without a vision, a system could produce *Random Acts of Improvement*. The vision of the school—created from what it expects students to know and be able to do, the values and beliefs of the staff, and the purpose and mission of the school must be at the center of everything that the school does. When the vision is shared and clear, everything that is planned will focus on implementing the vision. Everyone will be working in the same direction. All parts of the organization are evaluated in terms of the degree of implementation to get the school to its vision, and how everything can be improved to better implement the vision.

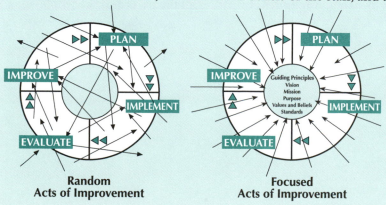

**Figure 9.1** *(Continued)*

# CONTINUOUS IMPROVEMENT FRAMEWORK

## A Plan: *Quality Planning*

A plan, one aligned to the vision, is a quality plan. A quality plan has goals, strategies, and activities to implement the vision and to eliminate student learning gaps. Each strategy and activity has a person or persons responsible, measurement, resources required, due date, and timelines so the plan and all of its elements can be evaluated on a regular basis and changed if there are data to support the change.

## Leadership

Leadership structures are necessary so everyone knows who is making what decisions, when decisions will be made, and when staff will meet to calibrate the implementation of the vision.

Education for the Future believes the job of leaders is to help everyone in the organization implement the vision and the plan. Teachers must become strong supporters and leaders of each other to implement the vision in the organization. Without strong and supportive leadership from administration to "shepherd" the vision, even the best plans will not result in continuous improvement throughout the district.

## Professional Learning

A major component of the plan and a continuously improving school is the professional learning of all staff to implement the vision. Professional learning is about professionals communicating and collaborating about student work and student data to improve student learning. Just as strategies to improve student learning should be implemented throughout the regular school day, professional learning should be embedded throughout the work week.

## Partnership Development

Schools are an important part of any community, and they cannot be successful if they exist in isolation. Starting with what we expect students to know and be able to do, conversations with parents, community, and businesses can lead to win-win partnerships and to improved student learning.

## Evaluation

Continuous improvement is about systems thinking. It requires evaluating all the parts and the whole on a regular basis.

Additional actions district leadership can take to help schools create a culture of data and data warehouse use include:

## Help the Schools with Data

School staffs get very busy with their day-to-day work with students. If the schools and their staffs do not get the support for data from the district, there is a chance that they will not get the data in a timely fashion (or at all) to be able to use them to improve teaching and learning. Following are ways the district can help schools with data:

▼ Student information system—get a good district-integrated system, provide district staff to help the schools clean the data, train personnel in how to input the data consistently and correctly, and establish systems to monitor data integrity.

▼ Establish data protocols, or data entry requirements, to ensure common data across the district.

▼ Help schools study root/contributing causes of their undesirable results, so they can make real changes, not just eliminate the symptoms.

▼ Help schools look at all their data, so they *see* the results of their systems and implement systemic changes, as opposed to making reactive changes.

▼ Create pre-determined data reports that are appropriate to the vision and get them to the schools to use. We want teachers and principals spending their time using the data, not gathering and organizing the data they receive. Do not overwhelm them with too many data reports. Clarify what is important for them to have and provide them with the complete story of their school, with more detailed data in problematic areas.

▼ Go beyond—at the district level, look across the data to understand the relationship of the data elements to each other and the impact of processes on student outcomes. Present data to the schools in meaningful ways so they can use them immediately.

▼ Get good ongoing assessments into the hands of the teachers. Looking for, or creating, formative assessments that predict the high stakes assessments is difficult and time-consuming. Check with test publishers for sample and practice items for the interim. The district needs to lead the way on this.

▼ Help teachers and school administrators understand what the high stakes tests are testing and how the results should be used appropriately.

▼ Make sure all technology equipment and software stay up to date and operational.

▼ Provide leadership for the numbers. Help schools understand what the numbers mean, what they should look like, and how to achieve the desired results.

▼ Model the use of data. When requiring schools to gather and use data, district leadership should use the schools' data for talking points during staff meetings, board meetings, and in-service days.

## Create Incentives for Schools to Do the Work

We want schools to stay committed to continuous improvement and data use. When schools are using a good framework for continuous improvement which includes a strong data-use component, they will make progress. Reward the schools for committing to continuous improvement and for making progress. Perhaps fewer district regulations would be reward enough.

## Help Create a School Vision

It is important for the district to have a vision and for each school in the district to have its own vision that reflects the district's vision. District leadership can help schools create a vision and understand how important a vision is to continuous improvement and data use.

## Help Schools Align Assessment/Benchmarks to Curriculum/Instruction

Aligning curriculum, instruction, and formative assessments to what you want students to know and be able to do (as well as to the high stakes tests, as long as the high stakes tests are testing what you want students to know and be able to do) prevents a curriculum from becoming merely a document for complying with state paperwork requirements. Help teachers know what it would look like if they were teaching in a totally aligned classroom and school, and then help them measure and reinforce the alignment.

*When schools are using a good framework for continuous improvement which includes a strong data-use component, they will make progress.*

*It is important for the district to have a vision and for each school in the district to have its own vision that reflects the district's vision.*

## Reinforce One Plan

School staffs routinely have to adjust their practices and procedures to accommodate changing state and federal laws and regulations, emerging trends in technology and pedagogy, and the shifting needs and expectations of parents and children. A continuous improvement plan, to be effective, must be continuous, consistent, and adaptable to changing theories of management. Reinforce one plan, aligned to the vision, that will get implemented, monitored, and evaluated on a regular basis.

## Establish Leadership

A school's leadership structure helps all staff know who is making what decisions and when. That leadership structure will require teachers to collaborate and communicate to continuously improve teaching and learning for all students, ensure that the system is set up for success, and help all staff to keep going when the work gets difficult. Schools need to help establish leadership structures that implement the school vision and, thus, reflect the district vision.

## Support Professional Learning

When sponsoring districtwide professional development, the district must make sure all activities will help with the implementation of the district vision and use of data. Provide coaches, modeling, demonstration lessons, and observations to support the classroom teachers in knowing what it will look like, sound like, feel like, when they are implementing the vision. Develop protocols to structure and encourage professional conversations and collaboration. Support teachers as they implement new strategies and provide guidance as teachers confront obstacles during the implementation of new strategies.

Never require all schools to do the same special program-related professional development just because one school was successful, without enlisting each school's support for the initiative. Do not think that you can take that successful professional development and "water it down" for entire district implementation and get positive results—the strategies that made it successful may require use of the "whole package." Additionally, no program will be implemented consistently without procedures to monitor and measure its implementation.

Help schools create the time to communicate and collaborate with the use of data to improve teaching and learning for all students. Give all staffs the motivation, inspiration, and courage to *implement* the vision.

> *A continuous improvement plan, to be effective, must be continuous, consistent, and adaptable to changing theories of management.*

> *Help schools create the time to communicate and collaborate with the use of data to improve teaching and learning for all students.*

## Develop Partnerships

District offices should set the tone for constructively including parents, community, and businesses in the learning mission of the school. Beginning with a discussion of what each partner expects students to know and be able to do will help all parties to contribute and benefit. These win-win partnerships will advance student learning.

## Assist with Evaluation

Continuous improvement is about systemic thinking and about evaluating the system on a continuous basis from preschool through grade 12. Schools need help from the district office in the evaluation of programs and processes. The district should model the way by evaluating its processes on a regular basis.

## Model the Way

*The best thing a school district can do to help schools create a culture that uses data effectively is to demonstrate that it values and uses data in all of its decision making.*

The best thing a school district can do to help schools create a culture that uses data effectively is to demonstrate that it values and uses data in all of its decision making. Too often district leaders say that they are data driven, but they do not provide good examples to indicate this is the case. When districts are planning for classes for the next year, they need accurate demographic data to determine how many teachers will be needed at each grade level or how many sections of Algebra II will be needed. When new programs are being considered for adoption, an evaluation of the successes or failures of previous programs needs to be conducted. When policies are under consideration for revision or replacement, the perceptions of students, parents, and staff about present policies need to be considered. When student achievement is being discussed, disaggregated data must be used to show how all students are really achieving. When budgets are being discussed, budgetary trends will show if the district is using its funds in an efficient and effective manner. When striving to close achievement gaps, the district must model looking at all data, not just student achievement results for the student group in question. When requests for new courses or programs are brought forth, the district must insist that such requests be accompanied with relevant and reliable data. Sometimes clues to making the most effective changes are found in other parts of the environment. Study all current processes to understand what is working and what is not, and reinforce the processes that are working and stop doing the things that are not working. Adding a quick "fix" hardly ever makes the difference needed.

*Study all current processes to understand what is working and what is not, then reinforce the processes that are working and stop doing the things that are not working.*

Reliance on data must be the way of doing business for all district administrators as well as for members of the Board of Education. Of course, in order to develop this culture, those making the decisions must have easy accessibility to the data and the data must be accurate. This calls for the use of a data warehouse that houses all the district data that are needed for true data-driven decision making.

## Example of Creating a Data Culture

*Little River Elementary School wanted to improve teaching and learning. The current school culture consisted primarily of individual teachers working independently in their own classrooms. The educators found themselves in trouble with the district and No Child Left Behind (NCLB). The school student achievement results were not improving, and not enough minorities and students with disabilities were reaching proficiency levels on the state assessment.*

*With a little help from an outside consultant, staff members determined that data were needed to create a sense of urgency to improve. The first thing they did was administer student, staff, and parent questionnaires about the learning environment. From these questionnaires, they realized several things:*

▼ *The staff had no shared vision for the school.*

▼ *Not all staff believed that student achievement could increase by using data.*

▼ *The morale of the staff was about as low as it could get.*

▼ *Staff agreed that communication with each other needed to improve to make student learning consistent across grade levels.*

▼ *Staff members did not believe that the principal communicated well with them, that she helped them implement a shared vision, or that she supported them in their work with students.*

▼ *Staff agreed that the school did not provide an atmosphere in which every student can succeed.*

▼ *One of the biggest staff issues that came out of the staff open-ended responses was that staff was upset that students do not behave well, and they believed the principal needed to fix the behavior problems.*

▼ *Students stated in the questionnaire that they did not like the discipline program.*

▼ *Students wanted all students to be more respectful.*

▼ *A significant number of students in fifth grade believed that they were not listened to, nor treated fairly, by teachers.*

▼ *Parents wanted improved discipline and better supervision.*

▼ *Parents also did not believe the school met the social needs of the students.*

*These questionnaires, in conjunction with the school's assessment on the* Education for the Future Continuous Improvement Continuums *(Appendix), helped all staff see, first of all, that they needed a vision for the school, a framework and structure for implementing the school vision, and also to incorporate the use of data into their daily work.*

*Because the data provided information that was consistent and compelling, all staff collectively agreed that they needed a vision to improve. The vision would not be a "pie in the sky" statement, but would consist of very specific commitments for the use of data to implement and improve the curriculum, instructional and assessment strategies, and the learning environment.*

## The Vision

*Little River began creating their school vision by surveying the staff to determine the individual values and beliefs of the staff with respect to the use of data to continuously improve.*

*Staff members discovered that their personal values and beliefs displayed many areas of agreement regarding what curriculum, instruction, assessment, and the school environment should include. After they came to consensus on core beliefs, they determined how data could be used to impact the identified areas of agreement. From these discussions, the Little River staff members agreed that the mission of Little River Elementary School is "to prepare students to be anything they want to be in the future." The vision became how staff planned to carry out the mission in curriculum, instruction, assessment, and environment, which were congruent with the staff's core values and beliefs. Staff agreed that they must develop a plan that focuses on the mission and that contains strategies from their core values and beliefs and vision to help them all work toward implementing the mission.*

## Values and Beliefs

*The following are the curriculum, instruction, assessment, and environmental factors that all staff members agree support effective learning for Little River students, along with how data will support these factors:*

### CURRICULUM

*Must—*

- Use student content standards to reach common outcomes
- Use up-to-date instructional materials, technology, and enrichment activities
- Spiral and be integrated
- Keep expectations high
- Be student-centered
- Be based on the level of students in the classroom
- Be relevant
- Be fun
- Have the community actively participating
- Include life-learning skills
- Build a continuum of learning that makes sense for all students
- Integrate cultural materials
- Be clearly defined – easy to follow and understand
- Be implemented with a means of accountability

### INSTRUCTION

*Must include the following elements—*

- Multiple intelligence strategies
- Differentiated instruction
- Research-based strategies
- Self-reflection by instructors
- Driven by student needs
- Teaching to students' strengths
- Attached to prior knowledge
- Make connections
- Flexibility and creativity
- Foster risk-taking
- Professional
- Fun
- Relate to lifelong learning
- Active learning
- Innovative—motivating
- Multifaceted
- Effective modeling
- Peer coaching and demonstration lessons
- Hands on
- Teachers knowledgeable about their subject areas

### ASSESSMENT

*Must—*

- Be ongoing
- Test how students are taught
- Test what students are learning
- Be used for improvement
- Include timely feedback
- Use a variety of assessments

### ASSESSMENT (*Continued*)

*Must—*

- Include classroom assessments that look like and predict the state tests
- Have high expectations
- Be about teaching above and beyond benchmarks and standards
- Include reflection (teacher) "what did I miss?"
- Support student feedback
- Include periodic assessments to track progress and determine instructional needs
- Include timely feedback
- Include teacher observations

### ENVIRONMENT

*Shall include—*

- Opportunities for all students to learn
- Awareness of cultural beliefs
- Teamwork
- Alternative instruction and even location to motivate all to learn
- Being safe/secure
- Reliable/structured flexibility
- Reflection of individuality
- Comfortable, emotionally and physically safe, appealing classrooms
- Honest and open communication
- Respect: teacher-to-teacher, student-to-student, teacher-to-student, student-to-teacher, teacher-to-parent, parent-to-teacher, teacher-to-administrator, administrator-to-teacher, administrator to student, administrator to parent

### DATA USE

*Will include—*

- Schoolwide data to show how we can improve the system
- Evaluations that will show us what programs/strategies are working and what programs/strategies are not working
- Monitoring of the degree to which the vision is being implemented to help everyone stay focused and committed to the vision
- Teachers working together in collegial groups to regularly review student work and student data to improve instruction and help each teacher reach all students
- Student, staff, and parent questionnaires completed each year, with recommendations implemented to show how the system can be improved
- Decisions based on data

> ## MISSION:
>
> *The mission of Little River Elementary School is to prepare*
>
> *students to be anything they want to be in the future.*

## Shared Vision

*A shared vision must include what curriculum, instruction, assessment, and environment will look like, sound like, and feel like when the mission of Little River School is implemented.*

### CURRICULUM

- State and national standards and benchmarks will be used to reach common outcomes (standards-based)
- Will be comprehensive K-6
- Effectiveness will be measured
- Will address all learning styles
- Relevant to needs of today and tomorrow
- Up-to-date and global
- Teachers actively teaching to curriculum standards and benchmarks
- Will be comfortable enough to the students that they are not afraid to try for fear they might fail, yet it is challenging—no leveling—all heterogeneous grouping
- Use up-to-date instructional materials, technology, and enrichment activities
- Needs to spiral and be integrated
- Keep expectations high
- Student-centered
- Based on the level of students in the classroom
- Fun
- Community actively participates
- Life-learning skills
- Integrate multicultural materials
- Clearly defined—easy to follow and understand
- Coordinated
- Sequential
- Career awareness
- Investigative
- Challenging
- Engaging

### INSTRUCTION

- Multiple intelligence/differentiated instructional strategies
- Research-based
- Self-reflection by instructors
- Driven by student needs

### INSTRUCTION (*Continued*)

- Teaching to students' strengths
- Attached to prior knowledge
- Make connections
- Teach for a purpose
- Flexible and creative
- Foster risk-taking
- Fun
- Relate to lifelong learning
- Active learning
- Innovative—motivating
- Peer coaching and demonstration lessons
- Inquiry-based
- Hands on
- Teachers knowledgeable about their subject areas
- Instruction based on active involvement, cooperative learning, hands-on and noisy, with lot of engaged time on task
- The teacher as "a guide on the side, not a sage on the stage"
- Investigative versus lecture/teacher-centered
- Cooperative learning
- Student responsibility and ownership of learning
- Teach to different learning styles
- Non-interrupted learning time

### ASSESSMENT

- Ongoing
- Used for improvement
- Teach above and beyond benchmarks and standards
- Reflection (teacher) "what did I miss?"
- Timely student feedback
- Test how students are taught
- Test what students are learning
- Journals to show students' understanding
- Periodic assessments to track progress and determine instructional needs
- Teacher observations

## Shared Vision *(Continued)*

*A shared vision must include what curriculum, instruction, assessment, and environment will look like, sound like, and feel like when the mission of Little River School is implemented.*

**ASSESSMENT** *(Continued)*

- Students are tested so their teachers can design learning opportunities appropriate to meet their needs
- Involve students in goal setting
- Build on student performance
- Application of skills and knowledge
- Different forms/varieties of assessments
- Varied and beyond standardized tests
- Student involvement in the whole process
- Inquiry and performance

**ENVIRONMENT**

- Opportunity for all students to learn
- Awareness of cultural beliefs
- Teamwork—willingness to work together
- Motivating
- Safe/secure
- Reliable/structured flexibility
- Comfortable, emotionally and physically safe, appealing classrooms
- Warm, homey classrooms
- Create and maintain rapport
- Honest and open communication
- Respect: teacher-to-teacher, student-to-student, teacher-to-student, student-to-teacher
- Relaxed, flexible
- Fun

**ENVIRONMENT** *(Continued)*

- Inspire students to want to be successful
- Strong leadership
- All student participation
- Ongoing parental communication
- Teachers working and listening to each other and to students
- Students working and listening to each other and to teacher

**DATA USE**

*Will include—*

- Schoolwide data to show how we can improve the system
- Evaluations that will show us what programs/strategies are working and what ones are not working
- The degree to which the vision is being implemented to help everyone stay focused and committed to the vision
- Teachers working together in collegial groups to regularly review student work and student data to improve instruction and help each teacher reach all students
- Student, staff, and parent questionnaires completed each year, with recommendations implemented to show how we can improve the system
- Decisions based on data

### Vision Narrative

*When the Little River Elementary School vision is implemented, all students will be proficient in all learning standards. Students will be learning, in context, in meaningful ways through hands-on and real-world experiences. Teachers will reach out to meet the diverse needs of students through a variety of instructional strategies and partnerships with parents, businesses, and the community. All students will feel safe, physically and emotionally. All students will be encouraged to do their best, and they will know what they are supposed to be learning. Teachers will work together, using student data and student work to communicate often about improving student learning. Teachers will implement a continuum of learning that makes sense for all students.*

### Little River Plan

*Little River staff created a plan to implement their vision. A vision implementation tool, based on the specifics of the vision, was created to measure staff implementation. The implementation of the vision was also supported by a leadership structure that committed collaborative working time, specifically the review of the impact of instructional strategies on student work and student data. Leadership ensured that teachers used student data and student work to continuously improve their instruction. All parts of the system were evaluated for continuous improvement.*

### Little River Results

*As a result of developing school-level data to help them understand the factors affecting the achievement of their students, Little River staff realized that they needed to improve their teaching and learning culture. Staff created and committed to a new vision for their school that included the continuous use of data to know what students learn throughout the course of the year and to know the impact of programs, curriculum, and instructional strategies. The improvement plan of the vision consisted of strategies to ensure its consistent implementation, such as collaboration time of teachers in their professional learning communities, a self-assessment provided by a vision implementation tool, professional learning as needed, and the overall evaluation of the system through comprehensive data analysis. The end result for teachers and administrators was instructional coherence, the implementation of a shared vision, and true data-driven decision making. For students, it meant overall and individual student achievement increases, multiple opportunities and strategies to learn content, and an overall feeling of an improved and caring learning environment.*

## Summary

*The only way to change a culture is to change the way work is done.*

To create a culture for data and data warehouse use, schools and school districts must create a vision for how their organizations will use data and a data warehouse. They must establish a plan, provide leadership and professional development structures to relentlessly implement that vision, and model the use of data in every decision they make. The only way to change a culture is to change the way work is done.

CHAPTER **10**

# REPORTING AND USING DATA RESULTS TO IMPROVE TEACHING AND LEARNING

Reporting the results of data analysis is critical if the analyses are going to affect decisions and if solutions are going to be implemented to improve teaching and learning. We can perform the most complex analyses in the world with our data tools; but if we want others to use the data, they must be able to understand the analyses, results, and uses.

## Reporting Data Analysis Results

Considerations in reporting data analysis results must include determining the audience, the level of detail needed to communicate the results, when to report results, the purpose for the report, and the appropriate method to communicate the results—the *who, what, when, why,* and *how:*

▼ Determine who the audience is for the report of your data analysis.

▼ Determine the message you want to convey about your data analysis results.

▼ Determine the timing for the report.

▼ Present the data as simply and clearly as possible to convey the message.

▼ Develop graphs with clear titles, legends, and numbers to convey the message.

▼ Write a narrative interpretation of the graphs to prevent misinterpretations.

▼ Compare your data to national, state, or other school and district data, when available and appropriate.

▼ Never display or provide data that will allow individuals to
be identified.

▼ Always state what your school is doing, or plans to do, with
the results.

▼ State how parents and the community can continue to help to
ensure student proficiency.

Chapter 3 described different analyses that can be created at different
educational organization levels. What follows are descriptions and examples of
what would be included in reports based on those analyses and how these
reports might look at each level. The information is then summarized in tables
shown as Figures 10.1, 10.8, 10.14, 10.19, and 10.20. Many possibilities exist for
reporting data results; these are just a few ideas.

## Reporting for Classroom Teachers

Teaching staffs are the most important recipients of data analysis results created
with analytical data tools. These reports tell the faculty how they are doing and
how they can improve teaching and learning. We want teachers to utilize the
analyses to understand how students learn, how to implement new ways of doing
business, if needed, and how to lead others in implementing systems that will
lead to all students becoming proficient learners. Sometimes teachers fear data
will be used against them in some way. Building trust with faculty is critical in
order for them to "buy-in" to using data. If trust is not built sufficiently, using
data may be seen as a negative.

Classroom teachers need to understand the achievement of their students and to
reflect on their own instructional strategies. The purpose and contents of the
reports they receive will vary by time of year, by what assessments are used, and
by how many times the assessments are administered during the year. A
discussion and example that summarize the types of reports classroom teachers
need follow the table in Figure 10.1.

> *Building trust with staffs
> is critical in order for them
> to "buy-in" to using data.*

**Figure 10.1**

# REPORTING RESULTS OF DATA ANALYSIS: CLASSROOM TEACHERS

| Timing | Report | Purpose for the Report | Level of Detail | Method of Communication |
|---|---|---|---|---|
| **Beginning of the school year** | Historical and/or diagnostic data on each student—including student achievement results, demographics, learning styles, and perceptions. | To understand what each student knows and does not know with respect to Grade-level Expectations (GLE) and Content Standards, and the context for her/his learning over time. | Highly detailed for each student, with color indicators for Standards and GLE attainment. See Figure 10.2. | Graph and data tables. Website or dashboard so teachers can access information at any time. Needs to be printable. |
| **Beginning of the school year** | Historical data on all students in the class—including student achievement results, demographics, learning styles, perceptions, and whom they had as teachers. | To understand what the students collectively know and what they do not know with respect to GLE and *Content Standards*, and the context for her/his learning over time. | Detailed for each class, with color indicators for Standards and GLE attainment. Figure 10.3 shows a demographic analysis for a class. | Graph and data tables. Website or dashboard so teachers can access information at any time. Exportable to Excel for resorting. Needs to be printable. |
| **Ongoing throughout the year** | Student achievement results and any other assessments at reporting periods—at least four times during the year. | To understand what the students are learning, with respect to what we want them to know at the end of the year; allows for mid-course corrections. | Detailed for each student and collectively by class. See Figure 10.4. | Graph and data tables. Website or dashboard so teachers can access information at any time. Needs to be printable. |
| **Prior to the high stakes assessment** | Up-to-date and itemized assessments of content that are similar to what will be covered on the high-stakes assessment. | To understand if there is some content that needs to be retaught before the high-stakes assessment. | Detailed for each item or content area, for each student, and for the entire class. See Figure 10.5. | Graph and data tables. Website or dashboard so teachers can access information at any time. Needs to be printable. |
| **End of the school year** | Student achievement results on the high-stakes tests, with item analyses, individual results, and group results disaggregated by student groups. | To know which students achieved during the year and which ones did not. To know what the students did know and did not know. | Highly detailed by item, for each student, and for the class. See Figure 10.6. | Graph and data tables. Website or dashboard so teachers can access information at any time and dig deeper into the data. Needs to be printable. |
| **End of the school year** | Student achievement results on the high stakes tests, compared to the ongoing assessments. | To understand the degree to which the ongoing assessments predicted the high-stakes test results. | Detailed for each student and collectively by class. See Figure 10.7 for an example of benchmark proficiency compared to the state assessment for a class. | Graph and data tables. Website or dashboard so teachers can access information at any time and dig deeper into the data. Needs to be printable. |

### *Beginning of the School Year*

At the beginning of the school year, each teacher needs to be clear on expectations for the content and grade level coverage. Most schools use Grade Level Expectations (GLE) and State Content Standards to guide what is being taught at every grade level. Each teacher will benefit from receiving an indication of what the new classes of students know and do not know with respect to the GLE and Standards. In addition, the classroom teacher will be able to guide the learning of each student if the teacher has an overview of each child's history—whom the child had as teachers, number of days absent, and other demographic and perceptions data over time. A good data warehouse solution will be able to provide this type of report quickly and effectively. In addition to the historical individual student report, teachers need to see data results aggregated for all students in their class(es). That way, teachers will know what they need to cover for the class as a whole. Figure 10.2 shows an example diagnostic student achievement report summary for one kindergarten student.

## Figure 10.2

# EXAMPLE BEGINNING-OF-THE-YEAR STUDENT ACHIEVEMENT REPORT

**Karen Johnson: Beginning-of-the-Year Summary**

*School:* **V Elementary School**
*Grade:* **Kindergarten**
*Teacher:* **Teacher A**

| ID # | Student Name | | English/Language Arts | | | | Math | Social Science | Science |
|------|------|-------|---------------|---------------|---------|---------------|------|----------------|---------|
| | Last | First | Word Analysis | Comprehensive | Writing | Oral Language | | | |
| 11167 | Johnson | Karen | *Basic* Needs to identify letters Reads own name | *Below Basic* Comprehends at grade level Practice relating stories | *Basic* Writes own name Beginning to write Writes some letters | *Basic* Knows rhyming words Follows directions Listens well | *Proficient* Applies Math to real life | *Below Basic* Practice respect for others Expresses choices | *Proficient* Sees likes/differences Describes objects |

| Level | Descriptors |
|-------|-------------|
| **Advanced 5** | ◆ Consistently uses major skills or processes with ease and confidence in completing grade level and above academic performance tasks.<br>◆ Consistently demonstrates a thorough understanding of grade-level appropriate curriculum strands and objectives taught during this reporting period.<br>◆ Consistently uses knowledge to skillfully communicate complicated ideas and concepts.<br>◆ Consistently completes and turns in quality, accurate class work and homework. |
| **Proficient 4** | ◆ Uses major skills or processes with ease and confidence in completing grade-level appropriate academic performance tasks.<br>◆ Consistently demonstrates a thorough understanding of grade-level appropriate curriculum strands and objectives taught during this reporting period.<br>◆ Demonstrates the ability to use knowledge to effectively communicate difficult ideas and concepts.<br>◆ Completes and turns in quality, accurate class work and homework. |
| **Basic 3** | ◆ Demonstrates partial use of major skills or processes with some errors in completing required grade level and appropriate academic performance tasks.<br>◆ Demonstrates some understanding of grade-level appropriate curriculum strands and objectives taught during this reporting period.<br>◆ Usually accomplishes basic purposes of academic tasks.<br>◆ Completes and turns in satisfactory class work and homework. |
| **Below Basic 2** | ◆ Makes a number of errors when using major skills or processes required to complete grade-level academic performance tasks.<br>◆ Demonstrates below-basic understanding of grade-level appropriate curriculum strands and objectives taught during this reporting period.<br>◆ Class work and homework often have errors and/or are incomplete. |
| **Far Below Basic 1** | ◆ Makes many errors when using major skills or processes required to complete grade-level academic performance tasks.<br>◆ Demonstrates an incomplete understanding of grade-level appropriate curriculum strands and objectives taught during this reporting period.<br>◆ Performance is markedly below grade level.<br>◆ Class work and homework fail to meet teacher criteria. |

Figure 10.3 shows another example of a beginning-of-the-year report for all students in an eighth-grade class. The complete report (not shown here) would show performance scores of every student in each teacher's class, along with meaningful demographic data.

## Figure 10.3
### EXAMPLE BEGINNING-OF-THE-YEAR STUDENT ACHIEVEMENT REPORT SUMMARY FOR TEACHER B'S CLASS, AUGUST 2007

**Roster of Students with Reading and Writing Assessment History**

School: **V Elementary School**
Grade: **Eight**

| SUMMARY TOTALS | | | |
|---|---|---|---|
| **Gender**<br>Female 11<br>Male 8 | **Ethnicity**<br>Caucasian 65%<br>African-American 25%<br>Hispanic 10%<br>Other | **Language Fluency**<br>English 90%<br>Spanish 10%<br>Other 0% | **Disabilities**<br>English 90%<br>Spanish 10%<br>Other 0% |

| ID # | Last | First | Gender | # of Days Absent June 07 | Recent GPA | Grade 5 Reading | Grade 6 Reading | Grade 7 Reading | Grade 5 Writing | Grade 6 Language NPR | Grade 7 Writing |
|---|---|---|---|---|---|---|---|---|---|---|---|
| | | | | | | **Reading Assessment** | | | **Writing Assessment** | | |
| 11029 | Mite | Micky | Female | 6 | 3.03 | | Well Below Standard | Well Below Standard | | 12 | Below Standard |
| 11082 | Brown | Allison | Female | 4 | 3.18 | | Not Tested | Met Standard | | 50 | Met Standard |
| 11099 | Martin | Sue | Female | 9 | 1.91 | | | Below Standard | | | Met Standard |
| 11102 | Gonzalez | Maria | Female | 17 | 2.13 | Below Standard | Below Standard | Met Standard | Below Standard | 33 | Not Tested |
| 11103 | Martinez | Juan | Male | 7 | 3.60 | Below Standard | Well Below Standard | Exempt/ NLE | Met Standard | 31 | Below Standard |
| 11111 | Perez | Bill | Male | 4 | 1.51 | | | Exceeded Standard | | | Met Standard |
| 11114 | Blanco | Carlos | Male | 2 | 3.82 | Exceeded Standard | Met Standard | Met Standard | Met Standard | 57 | Met Standard |
| 11129 | Ford | Makayla | Female | 13 | 2.21 | Met Standard | | Exceeded Standard | Below Standard | | Met Standard |
| 11177 | King | Patty | Female | 45 | 2.09 | Met Standard | Met Standard | Met Standard | Below Standard | 69 | Met Standard |
| 11180 | Myer | Tina | Female | 11 | 2.96 | Exceeded Standard | Met Standard | Exceeded Standard | Met Standard | 62 | Met Standard |
| 11200 | Thomas | Jayden | Male | 17 | 2.37 | Met Standard | Well Below Standard | Below Standard | Met Standard | 29 | Met Standard |
| 11227 | Smith | James | Male | 11 | 2.58 | | | Below Standard | | | Met Standard |
| 11239 | Thomas | Jesse | Male | 8 | 2.27 | | Not Tested | Well Below Standard | | 1 | Below Standard |
| 11270 | Maez | Lena | Female | 3 | 2.90 | Met Standard | Met Standard | Met Standard | Met Standard | 86 | Met Standard |
| 12101 | Deer | Jane | Female | 7 | 3.41 | | | Met Standard | | | Below Standard |
| 12119 | Ward | Briana | Female | 10 | 2.41 | Met Standard | Below Standard | Below Standard | Below Standard | 18 | Met Standard |
| 12149 | Jenkins | Sam | Male | 10 | 3.82 | | | Exceeded Standard | | | Met Standard |
| 12191 | Blake | Jasmine | Female | 3 | 3.67 | Met Standard | Met Standard | Met Standard | Met Standard | 44 | Exceeded Standard |
| 12195 | Victor | Jerry | Male | 10 | 2.85 | Below Standard | Below Standard | Below Standard | Below Standard | 14 | Met Standard |

## Throughout the School Year

Throughout the school year, teachers need quick turn around of their students' results on short-cycle and ongoing assessments. These reports need to show individual student and classroom growth on student achievement tests, state content standards, and GLE. From these reports, teachers will be able to alter instructional strategies and curriculum coverage in order to ensure that all students will be proficient by the end of the year. With a data warehouse that refreshes daily, this type of reporting will be easy to accomplish. Figure 10.4 shows a periodic report, over time, for one student. A report such as this would be produced for every student and then collectively for the class.

### Figure 10.4
### EXAMPLE ONGOING STUDENT ASSESSMENT REPORT

**Individual Student Assessment Report, May 2007**

*Student:* **Cindy Walker**
*Grade:* **Three**
*Teacher:* **Teacher C**

| Content Areas | Term | | | Comments |
|---|---|---|---|---|
| | First | Second | Third | |
| **READING – Word Analysis** (*Concepts of print, phonemic awareness, phonics, and word recognition*) | 3 Basic | 3 Basic | 3 Basic | Identifies all letters<br>Needs to practice sight words |
| **READING – Comprehension** (*Literary response and analysis*) | 3 Basic | 4 Proficient | 3 Basic | Answers questions about text<br>Needs to practice retelling stories |
| **WRITING** (*Writing developmental level*) | 3 Basic | 2 Below Basic | 3 Basic | Uses informal spelling<br>Uses formal spelling<br>Needs to use some punctuations |
| **ORAL LANGUAGE** (*Listening and speaking*) | 3 Basic | 3 Basic | 3 Basic | Knows rhyming words<br>Follows directions<br>Listens well |
| **MATHEMATICS** (*Number sense, measurement and geometry, mathematical reasoning, algebra and functions, and statistics, data analysis, and probability*) | 3 Basic | 4 Proficient | 3 Basic | Extends patterns<br>Follows patterns<br>Needs to recognize shapes |
| **SOCIAL SCIENCE** (*History, geography, and civics*) | | 3 Basic | 4 Proficient | Respects others<br>Expresses choices |
| **SCIENCE** (*Life science, environmental science, earth science, and physical science*) | | 3 Basic | 4 Proficient | Describes objects<br>Sees likes/difference |
| **WELLNESS** (*Physical education and strategies for healthy living*) | 3 Basic | 3 Basic | 4 Proficient | Has good hygiene habits |
| **VISUAL/PERFORMING ARTS** (*Visual arts, music, dance, and theatre*) | 3 Basic | 3 Basic | 4 Proficient | Draws simple pictures<br>Enjoys music<br>Follows music directions |
| **CITIZENSHIP AND STUDY HABITS** (*Independent and collaborative work, homework, follow direction, rules and procedure, respect authority and peers, and takes responsibility*) | *No achievement score* | | | Good citizen<br>Shows a positive attitude<br>Works well in groups |

| STATE ASSESSMENTS | DISTRICT ASSESSMENTS | | | ATTENDANCE | | | |
|---|---|---|---|---|---|---|---|
| **Standards Tests:** | **Criterion Reference Tests (CRT):** | *Fall* | *Winter* | | *1st Term* | *2nd Term* | *3rd Term* |
| *English Language Arts:* | *English Language Arts:* | | | Absence: | 1 | 1 | 0 |
| *Mathematics:* | *Mathematics:* | | | Tardy: | 0 | 0 | 0 |
| *Listening/Speaking:* | *Writing Assessment – English:* | | | | | | |
| *Reading:* | *Writing Assessment – Spanish:* | | | | | | |
| *Writing:* | | | | | | | |
| *Overall:* | | | | | | | |

### Prior to the High-Stakes Assessment

Prior to the high-stakes testing, it is good for teachers to check the itemized proficiency levels of their students' benchmark assessment results to clarify if specific content needs to be revisited. (These are similar to the reports that could be produced throughout the course of the year and used in conjunction with reports like Figure 10.4.) Figure 10.5, below, is an example of an item analysis report provided to teachers well before the high-stakes test is administered.

### Figure 10.5
## EXAMPLE BENCHMARK CLASS ASSESSMENT RESULTS

*School:* **V Elementary School**
*Grade:* **Four**
*Gender:* **All**

| STUDENT PERFORMANCE, May 2007 | | | | | | | | |
|---|---|---|---|---|---|---|---|---|
| **Student** | **Grade Four Language Conventions 1.1** (10 points possible) | | **Grade Four Language Conventions 1.2** (4 points possible) | | **Grade Four Writing** (1 point possible) | | **Grade Four Reading** (5 points possible) | |
| *Group Average:* | *Proficient* | 7.8 (78%) | *Basic* | 2.5 (63%) | *Proficient* | 0.8 (81%) | *Advanced* | 4.7 (94%) |
| Student A | Below Basic | 5 (50%) | Below Basic | 2 (50%) | Advanced | 1 (100%) | Proficient | 4 (80%) |
| Student B | Basic | 7 (70%) | Below Basic | 1 (25%) | Advanced | 1 (100%) | Advanced | 5 (100%) |
| Student C | Below Basic | 5 (50%) | Proficient | 3 (75%) | Advanced | 1 (100%) | Proficient | 4 (80%) |
| Student D | Advanced | 10 (100%) | Advanced | 4 (100%) | Advanced | 1 (100%) | Advanced | 5 (100%) |
| Student E | Proficient | 8 (80%) | Below Basic | 1 (25%) | Far Below Basic 0 (0%) | | Advanced | 5 (100%) |
| Student F | Advanced | 9 (90%) | Below Basic | 2 (50%) | Advanced | 1 (100%) | Advanced | 5 (100%) |
| Student G | Advanced | 9 (90%) | Advanced | 4 (100%) | Advanced | 1 (100%) | Advanced | 5 (100%) |
| Student H | Advanced | 10 (100%) | Advanced | 4 (100%) | Advanced | 1 (100%) | Advanced | 5 (100%) |
| Student I | Proficient | 8 (80%) | Below Basic | 2 (50%) | Advanced | 1 (100%) | Proficient | 4 (80%) |
| Student J | Advanced | 10 (100%) | Advanced | 4 (100%) | Advanced | 1 (100%) | Advanced | 5 (100%) |
| Student K | Basic | 6 (60%) | Proficient | 3 (75%) | Advanced | 1 (100%) | Advanced | 5 (100%) |
| Student L | Advanced | 10 (100%) | Below Basic | 2 (50%) | Far Below Basic 0 (0%) | | Advanced | 5 (100%) |
| Student M | Advanced | 9 (90%) | Below Basic | 2 (50%) | Far Below Basic 0 (0%) | | Advanced | 5 (100%) |
| Student N | Advanced | 10 (100%) | Proficient | 3 (75%) | Advanced | 1 (100%) | Advanced | 5 (100%) |
| Student O | Advanced | 10 (100%) | Advanced | 4 (100%) | Advanced | 1 (100%) | Advanced | 5 (100%) |
| Student P | Advanced | 10 (100%) | Proficient | 3 (75%) | Advanced | 1 (100%) | Advanced | 5 (100%) |
| Student Q | Proficient | 8 (80%) | Below Basic | 1 (25%) | Advanced | 1 (100%) | Advanced | 5 (100%) |
| Student R | Advanced | 9 (90%) | Below Basic | 1 (25%) | Advanced | 1 (100%) | Advanced | 5 (100%) |
| Student S | Proficient | 8 (80%) | Proficient | 3 (75%) | Advanced | 1 (100%) | Advanced | 5 (100%) |
| Student T | Basic | 7 (70%) | Proficient | 3 (75%) | Advanced | 1 (100%) | Advanced | 5 (100%) |
| Student U | Far Below Basic 0 (0%) | | Advanced | 4 (100%) | Advanced | 1 (100%) | Advanced | 5 (100%) |
| Student V | Below Basic | 5 (50%) | Below Basic | 1 (25%) | Advanced | 1 (100%) | Advanced | 5 (100%) |
| Student W | Below Basic | 5 (50%) | Below Basic | 2 (50%) | Far Below Basic 0 (0%) | | Far Below Basic1 (20%) | |
| Student X | Advanced | 9 (90%) | Below Basic | 2 (50%) | Advanced | 1 (100%) | Advanced | 5 (100%) |
| Student Y | Advanced | 9 (90%) | Advanced | 4 (100%) | Advanced | 1 (100%) | Proficient | 4 (80%) |
| Student Z | Basic | 6 (60%) | Below Basic | 1 (25%) | Far Below Basic 0 (0%) | | Advanced | 5 (100%) |

## *End of the School Year*

At the end of the year, teachers will want to know how all their students performed on the high-stakes assessment and if the ongoing assessments were good predictors of the high-stakes assessments. Teachers will also want to know which students achieved proficiency during the year, which ones did not, and what the students did and did not know on the assessment. Figure 10.6 displays an example report for end-of-the-school-year results for a student on the state assessment. Each teacher would get a report similar to this one for each of her or his students.

## Figure 10.6
## EXAMPLE STUDENT ACHIEVEMENT REPORT FOR END-OF-SCHOOL-YEAR RESULTS

*Student Number:* **45867**
*Grade:* **Three**
*School:* **V Elementary School**
*Exam:* **State Assessment 2006-07**

**Subject Area Scores**

| | Performance Level | Number Items Possible | Raw Score | Percent Score | Scale Score | 200 250 300 350 400 450 500 550 |
|---|---|---|---|---|---|---|
| English-Language Arts | Proficient | 65 | 51 | 78 | 367 | |
| Mathematics | Advanced | 65 | 56 | 86 | 415 | |

**Test and Reporting Cluster Scores: Grade 3**

| | Points Possible | Raw Score | Percent Score | 20 40 60 80 | State Average | State Minimally Proficient | State Minimally Advanced |
|---|---|---|---|---|---|---|---|
| **English Language Arts** | **65** | **51** | **78%** | | — | — | — |
| Word Analysis and Vocabulary | 20 | 17 | 85% | | 68% | 79% | 89% |
| Reading Comprehension | 15 | 9 | 60% | | 58% | 69% | 88% |
| Literary Response and Analysis | 8 | 7 | 88% | | 63% | 73% | 87% |
| Written and Oral Conventions | 13 | 10 | 77% | | 67% | 76% | 87% |
| Writing Strategies | 9 | 8 | 89% | | 57% | 69% | 85% |
| **Mathematics** | **65** | **56** | **86%** | | — | — | — |
| Place Value, Fractions, and Decimals | 16 | 12 | 75% | | 72% | 73% | 87% |
| Addition, Subtraction, Multiplication, and Division | 16 | 12 | 75% | | 62% | 58% | 81% |
| Algebra and Functions | 12 | 12 | 100% | | 69% | 68% | 86% |
| Measurement and Geometry | 16 | 15 | 94% | | 77% | 78% | 87% |
| Statistics, Data Analysis, and Probability | 5 | 5 | 100% | | 84% | 89% | 95% |

Figure 10.7 shows an example report that compares the results of English/Language Arts (ELA) benchmark assessments to state assessment results.

## Figure 10.7

## EXAMPLE OF COMPARISON OF ELA BENCHMARK TO STATE ASSESSMENT RESULTS REPORT

*School:* **A Elementary School**
*Grade:* **Four**
*Gender:* **All**

**Student Performance**

| Student | Overall Performance | | Score Better (+), Same (•), or Worse (–) than Benchmark |
|---|---|---|---|
| | Benchmark Proficiency | State Assessment Scaled Score | |
| Student A | Basic 50 (71%) | Basic 335 | • |
| Student B | Basic 51 (73%) | Proficient 373 | + |
| Student C | Below Basic 41 (59%) | Basic 319 | + |
| Student D | Advanced 69 (99%) | Advanced 435 | • |
| Student E | Basic 44 (63%) | Basic 307 | • |
| Student F | Proficient 57 (81%) | Proficient 362 | • |
| Student G | Advanced 64 (91%) | Advanced 449 | • |
| Student H | Advanced 63 (90%) | Proficient 379 | – |
| Student I | Basic 51 (73%) | Basic 343 | • |
| Student J | Proficient 55 (79%) | Basic 348 | – |
| Student K | Proficient 58 (83%) | Basic 315 | – |
| Student L | Proficient 58 (83%) | Far Below Basic 254 | ⊖ |
| Student M | Proficient 53 (76%) | Proficient 373 | • |
| Student N | Advanced 65 (93%) | Proficient 373 | – |
| Student O | Advanced 64 (91%) | Basic 311 | – |
| Student P | Advanced 65 (93%) | Advanced 435 | • |
| Student Q | Proficient 54 (77%) | Proficient 379 | • |
| Student R | Proficient 58 (83%) | Advanced 424 | + |
| Student S | Basic 52 (74%) | Below Basic 281 | – |
| Student T | Proficient 58 (83%) | Proficient 367 | • |
| Student U | Basic 43 (61%) | Advanced 406 | ⊕ |
| Student V | Basic 51 (73%) | Basic 335 | • |
| Student W | Below Basic 21 (30%) | Proficient 379 | ⊕ |
| Student X | Proficient 55 (79%) | Proficient 353 | ⊙ |
| Student Y | Advanced 63 (90%) | Basic 301 | ⊖ |
| Student Z | Proficient 55 (79%) | Far Below Basic 246 | ⊖ |

Note: Circled score ◯ = moved more than one level.

## Reporting for Schools

Schoolwide data can tell staffs how they are doing as a whole and how they can improve teaching and learning. We want staffs to utilize schoolwide analyses to understand how students learn, how to improve teaching and learning to ensure a continuum of learning for all students, and how to lead others in implementing systems that will lead to all students becoming proficient learners.

Schoolwide data analyses can be used to understand program and process effectiveness, to predict and prevent student failure, and to ensure student successes. Figure 10.8 summarizes ideas for reporting data analysis results for schools. A discussion and example reports follow.

### Figure 10.8
### REPORTING RESULTS OF DATA ANALYSIS: SCHOOLS

| Timing | Report | Purpose for the Report | Level of Detail | Method of Communication |
|---|---|---|---|---|
| *Beginning of the school year* | Historical data on each student, by grade level—including student achievement results, demographics, learning styles, and perceptions. | To understand what each student knows and does not know with respect to GLE and Content Standards, and the context for her/his learning over time. | Highly detailed for each grade level, with color indicators for Standards and GLE attainment, by student. | Graph and data tables. Website or dashboard so teachers can access information at any time. Needs to be printable. |
| *Beginning of the school year* | Student achievement results by grade level, over time, disaggregated, by demographics. | To understand the degree to which there is a continuum of learning for all student groups. | Detailed over time. See Figure 10.9. | Graph and data tables. Website or dashboard so teachers can access information at any time. Needs to be printable. |
| *Elementary —twice a day* *Middle and High—every class period* | Attendance and absences. | To allow staff to know who is absent immediately and to be able to track absences over time, by day of the week, time of day, month, and grade level. | Highly detailed. See Figure 10.10. | Website or dashboard so teachers and administrators can access information at any time. |
| *Daily* | Discipline (and similar demographics). | To allow teachers and administrators to know who is misbehaving, when, and where, and to be able to track over time, by day of the week, time of day, month, and grade level. | Highly detailed. | Website or dashboard so teachers and administrators can access information at any time. |

**Figure 10.8** *(Continued)*

## REPORTING RESULTS OF DATA ANALYSIS: SCHOOLS

| Timing | Report | Purpose for the Report | Level of Detail | Method of Communication |
|---|---|---|---|---|
| *Once a year* | Staff perceptions. Implementation measurement (school processes). | To understand if there is a continuum of learning in place from the perspective of the staff, if staff know the standards, if there is a shared vision, where staff is with the implementation of a vision, etc. | Group results, disaggregated. See Figure 10.11. | Graphs. |
| *Once a year, or when studying data results* | Staff and student perceptions, school processes, student achievement results, and student and staff demographics. | To understand if there is a continuum of learning from staffs' perspective. To understand which implemented processes lead to the best results for *all* students. | Detailed by teacher and grade level. | Graphs. Website or dashboard so teachers and administrators can access information at any time. |
| *Once a year, or when studying data results* | Prediction studies. Staff perceptions, school processes, student achievement results, and student and staff demographics. | To understand how to predict and prevent student failures, and to predict and ensure student successes | Detailed. See Figure 10.12. | Graphs. Website or dashboard so teachers and administrators can access information at any time. |
| *Once a year, or when studying data results* | Program effectiveness. School processes, student perceptions, and student achievement, by program/teacher. Program enrollment by student demographics, and by cohort. | To determine program/ process/teacher effectiveness. To understand program enrollment by gender and ethnicity. | Detailed program data disaggregated by student achievement results and demographics, over time. See Figure 10.13; shows a cohort analysis. | Graphs. Website or dashboard so teachers and administrators can access information at any time. |
| *Once a year data results* | Program cost effectiveness. | To understand the impact of the program by costs. | Detailed program and cost data. | Graphs. Website or dashboard. |

## Beginning of the School Year

At the beginning of the school year, schools need to ensure that all teachers and other appropriate staff members (guidance counselors, psychologists, interventions specialists, etc.) are aware of students' historical data and achievement results to understand what students know and do not know with respect to GLE and Content Standards. Students new to the school need to be identified since complete data might not yet be available for them.

A longitudinal look at student achievement will allow schools to see if there is a continuum of learning being implemented at the school. That longitudinal look would resemble Figures 10.2 and 10.3 for the classroom teacher. A school leadership team would be reviewing these data to identify students who need assistance, to plan interventions, and to ensure a continuum of learning that makes sense for students is in place. Figure 10.9 gives an example look at a historical school report by student groups within a school (typical disaggregations shown would include gender, ethnicity, SES, Special Education, Gifted, and Language Proficiency). Percentages below 50% are highlighted. For each category of scoring, e.g., "Far Below Basic," one could dig deeper to uncover which students are included in that category and why.

## Figure 10.9
# EXAMPLE MIDDLE SCHOOL REPORT

### Summary of English/Language Arts (ELA) State Achievement Test
### Number and Percentage Proficient, 2002-03 to 2006-07

| | | | ELA Proficiency | | | | | | | |
|---|---|---|---|---|---|---|---|---|---|---|
| | | | Grade 6 | | Grade 7 | | Grade 8 | | School | |
| | | | Number | Percent | Number | Percent | Number | Percent | Number | Percent |
| **Overall** | All Students | 2002-03 | 219 | 87% | 226 | 83% | 223 | 82% | 668 | 84% |
| | | 2003-04 | 233 | 72% | 238 | 87% | 214 | 85% | 685 | 81% |
| | | 2004-05 | 240 | 80% | 218 | 83% | 243 | 87% | 701 | 83% |
| | | 2005-06 | 244 | 84% | 242 | 88% | 224 | 84% | 710 | 86% |
| | | 2006-07 | 249 | 82% | 232 | 86% | 246 | 86% | 727 | 85% |
| **By Gender** | Female | 2002-03 | 129 | 92% | 133 | 88% | 132 | 88% | 394 | 89% |
| | | 2003-04 | 132 | 73% | 137 | 93% | 121 | 88% | 390 | 84% |
| | | 2004-05 | 130 | 83% | 122 | 88% | 140 | 91% | 392 | 88% |
| | | 2005-06 | 144 | 90% | 132 | 93% | 123 | 87% | 399 | 90% |
| | | 2006-07 | 140 | 84% | 140 | 87% | 132 | 87% | 412 | 86% |
| | Male | 2002-03 | 90 | 79% | 93 | 76% | 91 | 74% | 274 | 76% |
| | | 2003-04 | 101 | 70% | 101 | 80% | 93 | 82% | 295 | 77% |
| | | 2004-05 | 110 | 77% | 96 | 77% | 103 | 81% | 309 | 78% |
| | | 2005-06 | 94 | 84% | 106 | 84% | 96 | 82% | 296 | 83% |
| | | 2006-07 | 108 | 72% | 92 | 82% | 112 | 80% | 312 | 78% |
| **By Socio-Economic Status** | Free/Reduced Lunch | 2002-03 | 42 | 60% | 46 | 61% | 49 | 59% | 137 | 60% |
| | | 2003-04 | 68 | 37% | 40 | 65% | 44 | 61% | 152 | 51% |
| | | 2004-05 | 62 | 56% | 49 | 57% | 44 | 52% | 155 | 55% |
| | | 2005-06 | 64 | 58% | 55 | 71% | 49 | 53% | 168 | 61% |
| | | 2006-07 | 74 | 46% | 63 | 63% | 56 | 68% | 193 | 58% |
| | Non Free/Reduced Lunch | 2002-03 | 177 | 93% | 180 | 89% | 174 | 89% | 531 | 90% |
| | | 2003-04 | 165 | 86% | 198 | 92% | 170 | 91% | 533 | 90% |
| | | 2004-05 | 178 | 89% | 169 | 91% | 199 | 94% | 535 | 93% |
| | | 2005-06 | 180 | 94% | 187 | 94% | 175 | 93% | 542 | 93% |
| | | 2006-07 | 174 | 93% | 169 | 93% | 188 | 89% | 531 | 92% |
| **By Special Education Disability** | Special Education Identified | 2002-03 | 12 | 42% | 17 | 35% | 21 | 29% | 50 | 34% |
| | | 2003-04 | 27 | 44% | 30 | 23% | 24 | 42% | 81 | 36% |
| | | 2004-05 | 35 | 43% | 24 | 33% | 33 | 39% | 92 | 39% |
| | | 2005-06 | 14 | 36% | 27 | 52% | 22 | 23% | 63 | 38% |
| | | 2006-07 | 30 | 23% | 17 | 59% | 36 | 47% | 83 | 41% |
| | No Disability | 2002-03 | 207 | 89% | 209 | 87% | 202 | 88% | 618 | 88% |
| | | 2003-04 | 206 | 78% | 210 | 96% | 190 | 91% | 606 | 88% |
| | | 2004-05 | 205 | 87% | 194 | 89% | 210 | 94% | 609 | 90% |
| | | 2005-06 | 221 | 88% | 209 | 95% | 195 | 92% | 625 | 92% |
| | | 2006-07 | 215 | 87% | 215 | 87% | 208 | 90% | 638 | 88% |

*(Note:* Number=the number of students taking the test in that student group and grade level. Also note that members are small [less than 30] for some student groups, which means these analyses will be used very carefully and only inhouse.)

## Every Grade/Class Period

For every grade or class period, absences need to be tracked so teachers know who will need to make-up class work, especially assessments, and to understand when students are absent and to begin to determine why. This type of report would show up on a web portal or dashboard of a student information system. Figure 10.10 gives a close-up view of one week's student absences by day of the week, subject, and class period. Further analyses would allow the school to sort by student, by course, by period, subject, day of the week, week of the month, etc.

### Figure 10.10
## EXAMPLE STUDENT ABSENCES REPORT

**Week at a Glance: Class Schedule for Grade 9**

*School:* **B High School**

| | | Monday<br>March 5, 2007 | Tuesday<br>March 6, 2007 | Wednesday<br>March 7, 2007 | Thursday<br>March 8, 2007 | Friday<br>March 9, 2007 |
|---|---|---|---|---|---|---|
| **Period 1** | *Algebra I:*<br>*English I:* | Blanco, Carly<br>Mendoza, Bill<br>Thomas, Jaden<br>Victor, Teryl | *Algebra I:* Blanco, Carly<br>Ford, Makayla | *Algebra I:* Blanco, Carly<br>*English I:* Hernandez, Will | *Algebra I:* Brown, Susan | *Algebra I:* Brown, Susan<br>*History:* Munez, Carlos<br>Davila, Juan<br>*English I:* Green, Sara |
| **Period 2** | *Music:*<br>*History:*<br>*Art II:* | Blanco, Carly<br>Mendoza, Bill<br>Jones, Sally | *Algebra I:* Blanco, Carly<br>*Art II:* Jones, Sally | *Music:* Blanco, Carly<br>*Art II:* Jones, Sally<br>*History:* Hernandez, Will | *Music:* Brown, Susan<br>*Art II:* Jones, Sally | *Art II:* Jones, Sally<br>*Algebra I:* Brown, Susan<br>*History:* Munez, Carlos<br>Davila, Juan<br>*English I:* Green, Sara |
| **Period 3** | *Sociology:* | Blanco, Carly | *Sociology:* Blanco, Carly | *Sociology:* Blanco, Carly<br>*Geometry:* Hernandez, Will | *Sociology:* Brown, Susan | *Sociology:* Brown, Susan |
| **Period 4** | *Art I:* | Blanco, Carly | *Art I:* Blanco, Carly | *Art I:* Blanco, Carly | *Art I:* Brown, Susan | *Art I:* Brown, Susan |
| **Period 5** | *History:*<br>*Music:* | Blanco, Carly<br>Davila, Juan | *History:* Blanco, Carly | *History:* Blanco, Carly | *History:* Brown, Susan | *History:* Brown, Susan |
| **Period 6** | *English I:* | Blanco, Carly<br>Davila, Juan | *English I:* Blanco, Carly<br>Davila, Juan | *English I:* Blanco, Carly | *English I:* Brown, Susan | *English I:* Brown, Susan |

### Daily

Discipline and similar demographics need to be reported daily so all staff members know which students are misbehaving, along with when and where the misbehavior has occurred. These data will help staff know which students may need intervention to address discipline issues.

### Once a Year

A questionnaire should be administered once a year to assess staff and student perceptions and to measure the implementation of processes that are aligned to the standards. These questionnaires can show where staff members are in relation to the knowledge and the implementation of a shared vision. Figure 10.11 shows a middle school staff's questionnaire results, disaggregated by number of years of teaching experience. The results show that the newest staff members are having a difficult time fitting in. The results also indicate that the school needs to revisit its vision and plan and put a shared decision-making structure in place.

# Figure 10.11
# EXAMPLE QUESTIONNAIRE

## Example Middle School Staff Responses by Number of Years Teaching
## May 2007

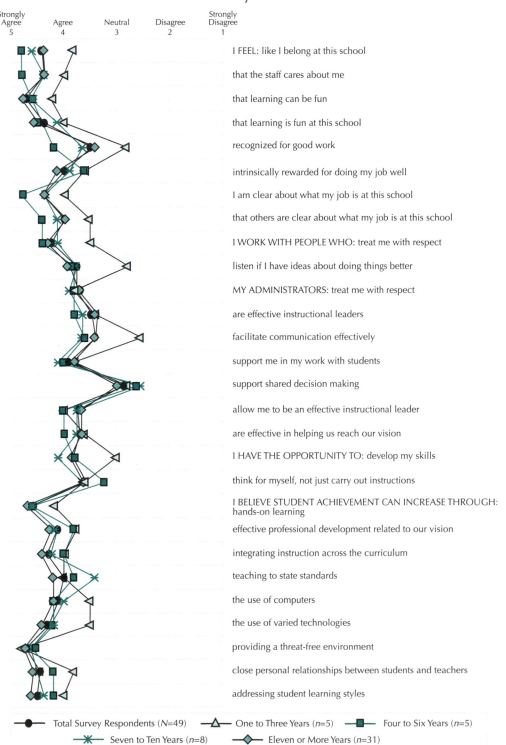

| Strongly Agree 5 | Agree 4 | Neutral 3 | Disagree 2 | Strongly Disagree 1 |

I FEEL: like I belong at this school

that the staff cares about me

that learning can be fun

that learning is fun at this school

recognized for good work

intrinsically rewarded for doing my job well

I am clear about what my job is at this school

that others are clear about what my job is at this school

I WORK WITH PEOPLE WHO: treat me with respect

listen if I have ideas about doing things better

MY ADMINISTRATORS: treat me with respect

are effective instructional leaders

facilitate communication effectively

support me in my work with students

support shared decision making

allow me to be an effective instructional leader

are effective in helping us reach our vision

I HAVE THE OPPORTUNITY TO: develop my skills

think for myself, not just carry out instructions

I BELIEVE STUDENT ACHIEVEMENT CAN INCREASE THROUGH: hands-on learning

effective professional development related to our vision

integrating instruction across the curriculum

teaching to state standards

the use of computers

the use of varied technologies

providing a threat-free environment

close personal relationships between students and teachers

addressing student learning styles

Total Survey Respondents (N=49)  One to Three Years (n=5)  Four to Six Years (n=5)
Seven to Ten Years (n=8)  Eleven or More Years (n=31)

**Figure 10.11** *(Continued)*
# EXAMPLE QUESTIONNAIRE

### Example Middle School Staff Responses by Number of Years Teaching
### May 2007

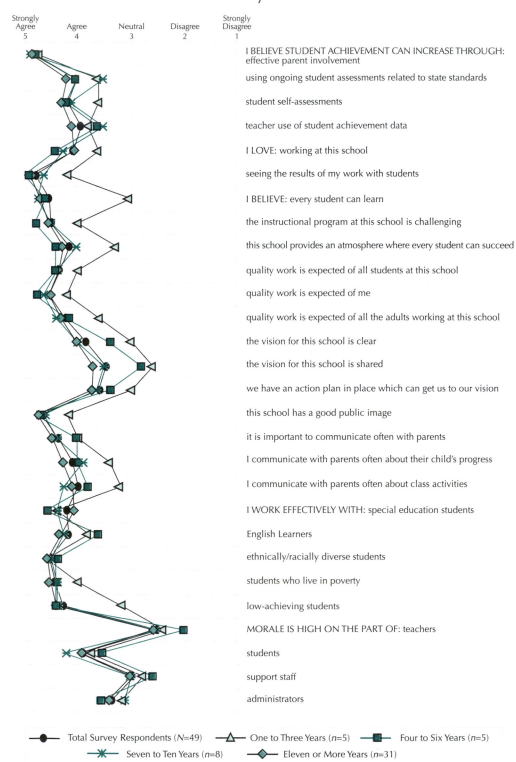

**Figure 10.11** *(Continued)*
# EXAMPLE QUESTIONNAIRE

## Example Middle School Staff Responses by Number of Years Teaching
## May 2007

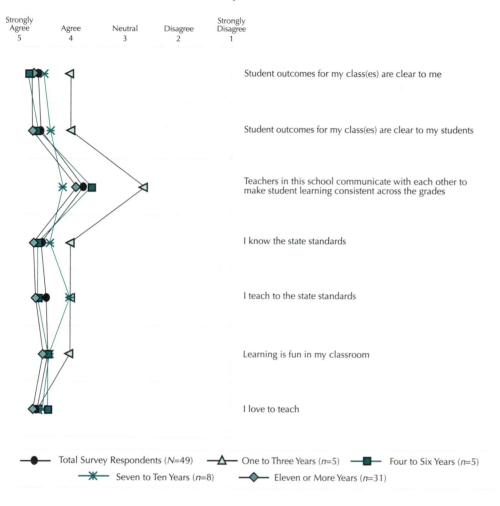

Strongly Agree 5    Agree 4    Neutral 3    Disagree 2    Strongly Disagree 1

Student outcomes for my class(es) are clear to me

Student outcomes for my class(es) are clear to my students

Teachers in this school communicate with each other to make student learning consistent across the grades

I know the state standards

I teach to the state standards

Learning is fun in my classroom

I love to teach

— ● — Total Survey Respondents (*N*=49)    —△— One to Three Years (*n*=5)    —■— Four to Six Years (*n*=5)

— ✳ — Seven to Ten Years (*n*=8)    —◆— Eleven or More Years (*n*=31)

### Once a Year, or When Studying Data Results

The results of staff, student, and parent perceptions questionnaires, the implementation of school processes, student achievement, and student and staff demographics need to be reviewed at least yearly. Studying data results will inform administrators and staff members about which processes are working with which students and which are not and also the cost effectiveness of different processes. A report of all four categories of data would consist of a complete school profile (see examples in *Using Data to Improve Student Learning* [Bernhardt, 2004, 2005, 2006, 2007] series). Figure 10.12 shows an example report that identifies students at risk of failing the state assessment, as measured by a district benchmark assessment. This school disaggregated its scores by the three student groups that were most at risk of not meeting proficiency on the state exam. This is a first-level analysis. *Going deeper, the school could see which students that score below 50 were in two or three of these student groups, determine what they know and do not know, and provide interventions for them.*

## Figure 10.12
## EXAMPLE SCHOOL BENCHMARK REPORT

■ 75–100
□ 50–75
□ Below 50

### C Elementary School

| Benchmark Test Title: English/Language Arts | Student Ethnicity: Hispanic | | Student Language Proficiency: LEP | | Student Socioeconomic Status: Low SES | |
|---|---|---|---|---|---|---|
| **Grade 1** Grade 1 Benchmark 1 | *n*=10 | 86.27 | *n*=9 | 84.68 | *n*=7 | 87.36 |
| Grade 1 Benchmark 2 | *n*=10 | 90.40 | *n*=9 | 84.38 | *n*=7 | 91.36 |
| Grade 1 Benchmark 3 | *n*=10 | 92.52 | *n*=9 | 87.42 | *n*=7 | 91.08 |
| **Grade 2** Grade 2 Benchmark 1 | *n*=15 | 57.80 | *n*=8 | 71.22 | *n*=10 | 59.70 |
| Grade 2 Benchmark 2 | *n*=16 | 59.97 | *n*=10 | 65.86 | *n*=11 | 64.89 |
| Grade 2 Benchmark 3 | *n*=15 | 73.38 | *n*=7 | 79.56 | *n*=9 | 75.91 |
| **Grade 3** Grade 3 Benchmark 1 | *n*=17 | 49.49 | *n*=16 | 48.03 | *n*=12 | 51.15 |
| Grade 3 Benchmark 2 | *n*=14 | 63.03 | *n*=12 | 60.00 | *n*=13 | 61.04 |
| Grade 3 Benchmark 3 | *n*=15 | 56.39 | *n*=15 | 47.57 | *n*=12 | 56.68 |
| **Grade 4** Grade 4 Benchmark 1 | *n*=19 | 47.53 | *n*=14 | 42.95 | *n*=14 | 45.91 |
| Grade 4 Benchmark 2 | *n*=17 | 50.30 | *n*=13 | 45.29 | *n*=13 | 47.83 |
| Grade 4 Benchmark 3 | *n*=15 | 44.92 | *n*=15 | 40.79 | *n*=15 | 44.14 |
| **Grade 5** Grade 5 Benchmark 1 | *n*=18 | 53.74 | *n*=19 | 46.71 | *n*=16 | 54.18 |
| Grade 5 Benchmark 2 | *n*=20 | 52.81 | *n*=18 | 43.84 | *n*=19 | 52.54 |
| Grade 5 Benchmark 3 | *n*=15 | 62.87 | *n*=16 | 54.03 | *n*=14 | 63.38 |

Additionally, at least once a year, schools should perform comprehensive data analyses that intersect program, process, teacher effectiveness, and student cohort data to determine which programs, processes, and teachers are getting the results the school needs and wants. Figure 10.13 is a specialized graph that looks at how matched cohorts of students scored on two years of state assessments as the state proficiency levels were increased each year. The student cohort from grade seven to grade eight, "Below Basic," made some of the greatest gains in the two years, although the gains were not enough to advance a level to "approaching Proficiency." The only cohorts to cross positively into another proficiency level were grades four to five and grades five to six from "Approaching Proficiency" to "Proficient." One cohort in grade eight to nine went from "Advanced" to "Proficient" the second year.

Follow-up analysis could show these same cohorts, by teachers and even by students, to see which individuals are achieving the highest results and why.

## Figure 10.13
# EXAMPLE SCHOOL MATCHED COHORTS GRAPH

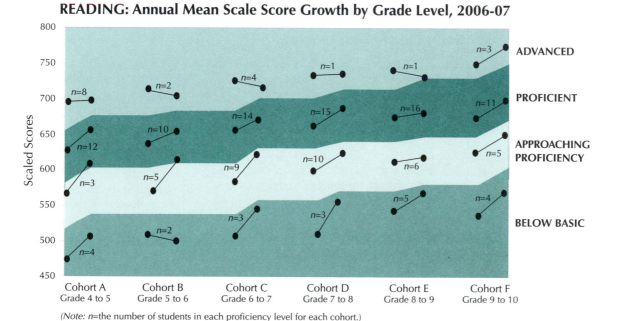

READING: Annual Mean Scale Score Growth by Grade Level, 2006-07

(Note: n=the number of students in each proficiency level for each cohort.)

## Reporting for School Districts

Districtwide data analyses show how all schools are doing on multiple measures, allowing district leadership the opportunity to lead schools to new results. District leadership must know how the numbers "should look" in order to guide schools to improved results. District reports need to show how the district is doing with respect to similar districts, NCLB, and district goals.

Figure 10.14 summarizes reporting data analysis results for school districts. A discussion follows the table.

**Figure 10.14**

## REPORTING RESULTS OF DATA ANALYSIS: SCHOOL DISTRICTS

| Timing | Report | Purpose for the Report | Level of Detail | Method of Communication |
|---|---|---|---|---|
| *Beginning of the school year* | Historical achievement data of students by school, grade level, and demographics. | To understand what students know and do not know with respect to GLE and Content Standards, and the context for student learning over time, by grade level and school.<br><br>To understand where the district can provide leadership. | Highly detailed for each grade level within each school.<br>See Figure 10.15. | Graph and data tables.<br>Website or dashboard access at any time, with the ability to dig deeper.<br>Needs to be printable. |
| *Beginning of the school year* | Demographic data by school, grade level, gender, and ethnicity, over time. | To plan for change.<br>To understand where the district can provide leadership. | School data, disaggregated by most demographic data.<br>See Figure 10.16. | Graph and data tables.<br>Website or dashboard access at any time, with the ability to dig deeper.<br>Needs to be printable. |
| *After student achievement results are released* | Student learning: percentage of students proficient by demographics by school, over time. | To know how the schools and school district are doing with respect to NCLB.<br>To ensure a continuum of learning.<br>To know where professional learning and leadership are necessary. | School data, disaggregated by school.<br>See Figure 10.17. | Graph and data tables.<br>Website or dashboard access at any time, with the ability to dig deeper.<br>Needs to be printable. |
| *After student achievement results are released* | Student learning: percentage of students proficient by demographics by school, compared to similar schools and school districts. | To know how the schools and school district are doing with respect to NCLB, compared to other districts and schools. (Usually available through a state or federal website.)<br>To know where professional learning and leadership are necessary. | School data, disaggregated by school and most demographic data, compared to like schools. | Graph and data tables.<br>Website or dashboard access at any time, with the ability to dig deeper.<br>Needs to be printable. |

**Figure 10.14** *(Continued)*

## REPORTING RESULTS OF DATA ANALYSIS: SCHOOL DISTRICTS

| Timing | Report | Purpose for the Report | Level of Detail | Method of Communication |
|---|---|---|---|---|
| *Once a year, or when studying data results* | Staff and student perceptions, school processes, student achievement results, and student and staff demographics. | To understand if there is a continuum of learning in each school, from staffs' perspectives.<br><br>To understand which implemented processes lead to the best results for all students. | Detailed by school and teacher. | Graphs.<br><br>Website or dashboard so teachers and administrators can access information at any time. |
| *Once a year, or when studying data results* | Prediction studies.<br><br>Staff and student perceptions, school processes, student achievement results, and student and staff demographics. | To understand how to predict and prevent student failures, and to predict and ensure student successes. | Detailed historical data.<br><br>See Figure 10.18. | Graphs.<br><br>Website or dashboard so teachers and administrators can access information at any time. |
| *Once a year, or when studying data results* | Program effectiveness.<br><br>School processes, student perceptions, and student achievement by program/school.<br><br>Program enrollment by student demographics by school. | To determine program/process/school effectiveness.<br><br>To understand program enrollment by gender and ethnicity.<br><br>To understand if the school district meets the needs of *all* students. | Detailed program data disaggregated by student achievement results and demographics. | Graphs.<br><br>Website or dashboard so teachers and administrators can access information at any time. |
| *Once a year data results* | Program cost effectiveness. | To understand the impact of the program by costs. | Detailed program and cost data. | Graphs.<br>Website or dashboard. |

### Beginning of the School Year

Whether a district consists of just two or three buildings or dozens of buildings, it is important to have historical data of students by school, grade level, and demographics at the beginning of the school year. These data allow the district to make comparisons within the district and to plan for changes that need to occur to better meet student needs. It is through studying these data that the district can determine where district leadership is needed to support individual schools and staff members. Figure 10.15 shows an example proficiency data table for the elementary schools, grade four, in a district.

## Figure 10.15
# EXAMPLE DISTRICT READING PROFICIENCY REPORT
## Grade Four by School and Gender, 2003-04 to 2006-07

| School | Gender | Year | Novice | | Nearing Proficiency | | Proficient | | Advanced | | Total Proficient | |
|---|---|---|---|---|---|---|---|---|---|---|---|---|
| | | | Number | Percent | Number | Percent | Number | Percent | Number | Percent | Number | Percent |
| ELEMENTARY — Elementary 1 | Female | 2003-04 (n=22) | 1 | 5% | | | 14 | 64% | 7 | 32% | 21 | 95% |
| | | 2004-05 (n=27) | 1 | 5% | 4 | 20% | 11 | 55% | 4 | 20% | 15 | 75% |
| | | 2005-06 (n=14) | 1 | 7% | 2 | 14% | 10 | 71% | 1 | 7% | 11 | 79% |
| | | 2006-07 (n=27) | 3 | 11% | 4 | 15% | 14 | 52% | 6 | 22% | 20 | 74% |
| | Male | 2003-04 (n=13) | 2 | 15% | 2 | 15% | 9 | 69% | | | 9 | 69% |
| | | 2004-05 (n=29) | 2 | 7% | 4 | 14% | 18 | 62% | 5 | 17% | 23 | 79% |
| | | 2005-06 (n=22) | 1 | 5% | 1 | 5% | 13 | 59% | 7 | 32% | 20 | 91% |
| | | 2006-07 (n=19) | 3 | 16% | 3 | 16% | 10 | 53% | 3 | 16% | 13 | 68% |
| Elementary 2 | Female | 2003-04 (n=13) | 2 | 15% | | | 10 | 77% | 1 | 8% | 11 | 85% |
| | | 2004-05 (n=24) | 3 | 13% | 1 | 4% | 19 | 79% | 1 | 4% | 20 | 83% |
| | | 2005-06 (n=17) | 5 | 29% | 1 | 6% | 9 | 53% | 2 | 12% | 11 | 65% |
| | | 2006-07 (n=10) | | | 1 | 10% | 7 | 70% | 2 | 20% | 9 | 90% |
| | Male | 2003-04 (n=26) | 4 | 15% | 6 | 23% | 10 | 38% | 6 | 23% | 16 | 62% |
| | | 2004-05 (n=20) | 2 | 10% | 2 | 10% | 16 | 80% | | | 16 | 80% |
| | | 2005-06 (n=24) | 2 | 8% | 2 | 8% | 13 | 54% | 7 | 29% | 20 | 83% |
| | | 2006-07 (n=20) | 3 | 15% | 1 | 5% | 10 | 50% | 6 | 30% | 16 | 80% |
| Elementary 3 | Female | 2003-04 (n=27) | 5 | 19% | 1 | 4% | 12 | 44% | 9 | 33% | 21 | 78% |
| | | 2004-05 (n=20) | 1 | 5% | 1 | 5% | 10 | 50% | 8 | 40% | 18 | 90% |
| | | 2005-06 (n=26) | | | 1 | 4% | 18 | 69% | 7 | 27% | 25 | 96% |
| | | 2006-07 (n=22) | 1 | 5% | 1 | 5% | 14 | 64% | 6 | 27% | 20 | 91% |
| | Male | 2003-04 (n=21) | 2 | 10% | 1 | 5% | 12 | 57% | 6 | 29% | 18 | 86% |
| | | 2004-05 (n=22) | 1 | 5% | 1 | 5% | 16 | 73% | 4 | 18% | 20 | 91% |
| | | 2005-06 (n=23) | 2 | 9% | | | 12 | 52% | 9 | 39% | 21 | 91% |
| | | 2006-07 (n=24) | 1 | 4% | 3 | 13% | 13 | 54% | 7 | 29% | 20 | 83% |
| Elementary 4 | Female | 2003-04 (n=39) | 1 | 3% | 3 | 8% | 22 | 56% | 13 | 33% | 35 | 90% |
| | | 2004-05 (n=28) | | | 1 | 4% | 21 | 75% | 6 | 21% | 27 | 96% |
| | | 2005-06 (n=38) | | | 2 | 5% | 21 | 55% | 15 | 39% | 36 | 95% |
| | | 2006-07 (n=34) | 1 | 3% | 3 | 9% | 16 | 47% | 14 | 41% | 30 | 88% |
| | Male | 2003-04 (n=38) | | | 5 | 13% | 21 | 55% | 12 | 32% | 33 | 87% |
| | | 2004-05 (n=46) | 1 | 2% | 2 | 4% | 33 | 72% | 10 | 22% | 43 | 93% |
| | | 2005-06 (n=32) | | | 4 | 13% | 19 | 59% | 9 | 28% | 28 | 88% |
| | | 2006-07 (n=43) | 1 | 2% | 1 | 2% | 24 | 56% | 17 | 40% | 41 | 95% |
| Elementary 5 | Female | 2003-04 (n=20) | 1 | 5% | 2 | 10% | 8 | 40% | 9 | 45% | 17 | 85% |
| | | 2004-05 (n=25) | | | 1 | 4% | 17 | 68% | 7 | 28% | 24 | 96% |
| | | 2005-06 (n=18) | 1 | 6% | 2 | 11% | 10 | 56% | 5 | 28% | 15 | 83% |
| | | 2006-07 (n=26) | 1 | 4% | 3 | 12% | 15 | 58% | 7 | 27% | 22 | 85% |
| | Male | 2003-04 (n=21) | 1 | 5% | 2 | 10% | 12 | 57% | 6 | 29% | 18 | 86% |
| | | 2004-05 (n=21) | | | 2 | 10% | 12 | 57% | 7 | 33% | 19 | 90% |
| | | 2005-06 (n=25) | 4 | 16% | 1 | 4% | 12 | 48% | 8 | 32% | 20 | 80% |
| | | 2006-07 (n=16) | | | 3 | 19% | 9 | 56% | 4 | 25% | 13 | 81% |

(*Note:* Number=the number of students taking the test in that student group and grade level. Also note that members are small (less than 30) for some student groups, which means these analyses will be used very carefully and only inhouse.)

Figure 10.16 is an example district table showing student proficiency results by school by grade level (grade four shown in this example), over time.

### Figure 10.16
# EXAMPLE DISTRICT PROFICIENCY REPORT SUMMARY

### Reading and Math Test of State Basic Skills by School Number and Percentage Proficient, 2003-04 to 2006-07

| Elementary 1 | | Reading Proficiency | | | Math Proficiency | | |
|---|---|---|---|---|---|---|---|
| | | Grade 4 | | | Grade 4 | | |
| | | Number Tested | Proficient | | Number Tested | Proficient | |
| | | | Number | Percent | | Number | Percent |
| All | 2003-04 | 35 | 30 | 86% | 35 | 28 | 80% |
| | 2004-05 | 49 | 38 | 78% | 49 | 35 | 71% |
| | 2005-06 | 36 | 31 | 86% | 36 | 31 | 86% |
| | 2006-07 | 46 | 33 | 72% | 45 | 31 | 69% |
| Female | 2003-04 | 22 | 21 | 95% | 22 | 19 | 86% |
| | 2004-05 | 20 | 15 | 75% | 20 | 15 | 75% |
| | 2005-06 | 14 | 11 | 79% | 14 | 10 | 71% |
| | 2006-07 | 27 | 20 | 74% | 28 | 17 | 65% |
| Male | 2003-04 | 13 | 9 | 69% | 13 | 9 | 69% |
| | 2004-05 | 29 | 23 | 79% | 29 | 20 | 71% |
| | 2005-06 | 22 | 20 | 91% | 22 | 21 | 95% |
| | 2006-07 | 19 | 13 | 68% | 19 | 14 | 74% |
| White | 2003-04 | 29 | 25 | 87% | 29 | 24 | 83% |
| | 2004-05 | 43 | 33 | 77% | 43 | 30 | 71% |
| | 2005-06 | 31 | 26 | 84% | 31 | 26 | 84% |
| | 2006-07 | 36 | 28 | 78% | 35 | 28 | 80% |
| Paid Lunch | 2003-04 | 24 | 21 | 88% | 24 | 20 | 83% |
| | 2004-05 | 29 | 23 | 79% | 28 | 23 | 82% |
| | 2005-06 | 24 | 22 | 92% | 24 | 22 | 92% |
| | 2006-07 | 22 | 17 | 77% | 22 | 16 | 73% |
| Free/Reduced Lunch | 2003-04 | 11 | 9 | 82% | 11 | 8 | 73% |
| | 2004-05 | 20 | 15 | 75% | 16 | 12 | 75% |
| | 2005-06 | 12 | 9 | 75% | 12 | 9 | 75% |
| | 2006-07 | 20 | 12 | 60% | 19 | 11 | 58% |
| IEP | 2003-04 | 4 | 2 | 50% | 4 | 3 | 75% |
| | 2004-05 | 5 | 3 | 60% | 5 | 2 | 40% |
| | 2005-06 | 2 | 0 | 0% | 2 | 0 | 0% |
| | 2006-07 | 5 | 1 | 20% | 6 | 2 | 33% |

(Note: Number=the number of students taking the test in that student group and grade level. Also note that members are small (less than 30) for some student groups, which means these analyses will be used very carefully and only inhouse.)

### After Student Achievement Results are Released

After student achievement results are released, the school district will report results with respect to No Child Left Behind. This report will include student learning results disaggregated by percentage of students proficient, by demographics, by grade level, by schools, and compared to similar schools and school districts. While some people may look on these reports as simply complying with NCLB, districts can use these reports to ensure a continuum of learning for all students, to determine where professional learning is needed, and to determine how the district leadership can provide the resources for the professional learning. Figure 10.17 shows a table of symbols that indicate proficiency levels for Language Arts and Mathematics, with respect to the most recent student achievement results for District DEF's 27 elementary schools disaggregated by grade level.

With respect to districts comparing their results to other districts—these analyses are available on state and/or federal websites. Districts would neither be entering another school district's data in their warehouses nor have access to another district's data through their warehouse.

### Once a Year, or When Studying Data Results

As districts analyze their data results by school and by teachers, they are able to see which implemented processes lead to the best results for all students. Being able to compare schools with similar schools in other districts sheds another light on the effectiveness of instructional strategies and programs. Analyzing perceptions, school processes, student achievement results, and student and staff demographics helps everyone understand if the programs and processes offered by the district are leading to the best results for all students. *Using Data to Improve Student Learning in School Districts* (Bernhardt, 2006) is a resource that shows a district's complete, once-a-year data analysis (three more districts' data appear on the accompanying CD-ROM). Additionally, the National Center for Educational Accountability sponsors the Just for the Kids website *(http://www.just4kids.org)* that allows any district or school in the U.S. to obtain its district or school data profile and to compare its results to the results similar schools/districts are getting.

Prediction studies, along with demographics, perceptions, process, and student achievement results, are necessary so districts are able to plan for the future and to improve their results. Prediction studies can help school districts understand the processes that are working for students, which ones are not, and how to identify students at risk of failing.

## Figure 10.17
# EXAMPLE STUDENT ACHIEVEMENT PROFICIENCY REPORT

**DEF District Elementary Schools Profile 2007**

| | | | |
|---|---|---|---|
| *Number of Schools:* **27** | *African-American:* **3.2%** | *Native American:* **2.2%** | |
| *Number of Students:* **31,646** | *Hispanic:* **50.6%** | *Caucasian:* **28.1%** | |
| *Low Income:* **42.04%** | *Asian:* **12.3%** | | |

✳ **Proficient or Advanced**

● **Basic**

☐ **Needs Improvement**

**OPPORTUNITY GAP**

| School | | | Language Arts | | | | Mathematics | | | |
|---|---|---|---|---|---|---|---|---|---|---|
| Elementary School | AYP MET | % Low Income | Grade 2 | Grade 3 | Grade 4 | Grade 5 | Grade 2 | Grade 3 | Grade 4 | Grade 5 |
| Elementary 1 | Yes | 36.5% | ● | ● | ● | ● | ☐ | ☐ | ● | ☐ |
| Elementary 2 | Yes | 71.9% | ☐ | ● | ☐ | ● | ☐ | ☐ | ● | ● |
| Elementary 3 | No | 74.7% | ☐ | ● | ☐ | ● | ☐ | ☐ | ☐ | ☐ |
| Elementary 4 | Yes | 15.2% | ✳ | ● | ✳ | ● | ● | ✳ | ✳ | ● |
| Elementary 5 | Yes | 71.2% | ● | ✳ | ● | ● | ☐ | ● | ☐ | ☐ |
| Elementary 6 | Yes | 32.2% | ● | ● | ● | ● | ● | ● | ● | ☐ |
| Elementary 7 | No | 85.6% | ☐ | ● | ● | ● | ☐ | ● | ☐ | ☐ |
| Elementary 8 | No | 85.9% | ☐ | ● | ☐ | ● | ☐ | ☐ | ☐ | ☐ |
| Elementary 9 | No | 79.8% | ☐ | ● | ● | ● | ☐ | ☐ | ☐ | ☐ |
| Elementary 10 | No | 83.2% | ☐ | ● | ☐ | ● | ☐ | ☐ | ☐ | ☐ |
| Elementary 11 | Yes | 80.3% | ☐ | ● | ● | ✳ | ☐ | ● | ☐ | ☐ |
| Elementary 12 | Yes | 3.3% | ● | ● | ● | ✳ | ✳ | ● | ● | ✳ |
| Elementary 13 | Yes | 15.8% | ● | ● | ● | ● | ☐ | ☐ | ☐ | ● |
| Elementary 14 | Yes | 44.5% | ☐ | ● | ● | ● | ☐ | ☐ | ☐ | ☐ |
| Elementary 15 | Yes | 7.1% | ☐ | ● | ✳ | ● | ● | ☐ | ● | ☐ |
| Elementary 16 | No | 85.3% | ☐ | ● | ● | ● | ☐ | ☐ | ☐ | ☐ |
| Elementary 17 | Yes | 87.5% | ● | ● | ● | ● | ● | ☐ | ● | ● |
| Elementary 18 | Yes | 87.3% | ☐ | ● | ☐ | ● | ☐ | ☐ | ● | ☐ |
| Elementary 19 | Yes | 25.6% | ● | ● | ● | ● | ● | ☐ | ● | ☐ |
| Elementary 20 | Yes | 40.9% | ☐ | ✳ | ● | ● | ☐ | ✳ | ● | ☐ |
| Elementary 21 | Yes | 39.4% | ● | ● | ● | ● | ● | ☐ | ● | ☐ |
| Elementary 22 | Yes | 3.7% | ● | ● | ● | ● | ● | ● | ● | ☐ |
| Elementary 23 | Yes | 49.4% | ● | ● | ● | ● | ☐ | ● | ● | ☐ |
| Elementary 24 | Yes | 59.9% | ☐ | ● | ● | ● | ☐ | ☐ | ● | ☐ |
| Elementary 25 | Yes | 92.5% | ☐ | ● | ● | ● | ☐ | ☐ | ☐ | ☐ |
| Elementary 26 | Yes | 1.4% | ✳ | ✳ | ● | ✳ | ● | ✳ | ☐ | ✳ |
| Elementary 27 | Yes | 51.1% | ● | ● | ● | ● | ● | ☐ | ● | ☐ |

One school district used a predict and prevent strategy to learn more about the educational experiences of the class of 2005 and to use that learning to prevent failures and ensure successes in future graduates.

Sixty-four percent of the class of 2005 graduated in 2005. In understanding more about these students, the district assessment department reorganized the class of 2005's performance on the tenth-grade state assessment data by those students who—

▼ Met, or exceeded, the state standard in both Reading and Math (39%)

▼ Met, or exceeded, the state standard in Reading, but not Math (25%)

▼ Met, or exceeded, the state standard in Math, but not Reading (4%)

▼ Did not meet the state standard in either Reading and Math (32%)

For each of these categories, the assessment department looked back in time to determine how the students performed on the state assessment as seventh and fourth graders. Additionally, they looked at their National Percentile Rank in grades nine, eight, six, five, and three on other norm-referenced assessments. Figure 10.18 shows how the district displayed these data. The table should be read left to right, such as—the students in the class of 2005, who met or exceeded the standard for Reading and Math as 10th graders in 2002-03, scored at the 81st percentile in Reading and the 87th percentile in Math as ninth graders on a norm-referenced test in 2001-02. These same students scored at the 87th percentile in Reading and the 84th percentile in Math as eighth graders in 2000-01. Additionally, 74% of this group met the Reading standard, and 70% met the Math standard as 7th graders in 1999-00 on the state assessment. As fifth graders, these students scored in the 74th percentile in Reading and 70th percentile in Math in 1997-98. In 1996-97, when these students were in the fourth grade, 85% met the standard in Reading and 60% met the standard in Math on the state assessment. In their first norm-referenced assessment as third graders in 1995-96, these students scored in the 77th percentile in Reading and 74th percentile in Math.

In addition, the district studied the demographic characteristics of the students in each of these categories (not shown). With these analyses, the district was able to see the characteristics and the actions that led to success for the students who met the standards in Reading and Math. They were also able to identify the characteristics of the students who did not meet the standards in Reading and/or Math and/or did not graduate. This information helped the district identify students currently in the early grades with similar characteristics and create interventions to increase attendance and ensure proficiency.

### Figure 10.18
## EXAMPLE DISTRICT BENCHMARK REPORT

### Class of 2005 Student Achievement History
### Grouped by Grade 10 Reading and Math Performance

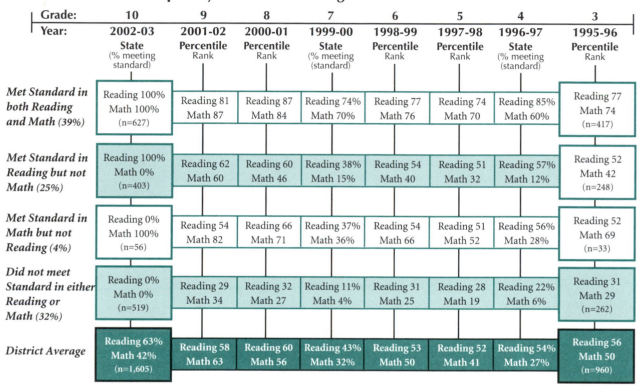

| Grade: | 10 | 9 | 8 | 7 | 6 | 5 | 4 | 3 |
|---|---|---|---|---|---|---|---|---|
| Year: | 2002-03<br>State<br>(% meeting standard) | 2001-02<br>Percentile Rank | 2000-01<br>Percentile Rank | 1999-00<br>State<br>(% meeting (standard) | 1998-99<br>Percentile Rank | 1997-98<br>Percentile Rank | 1996-97<br>State<br>(% meeting (standard) | 1995-96<br>Percentile Rank |
| Met Standard in both Reading and Math (39%) | Reading 100%<br>Math 100%<br>(n=627) | Reading 81<br>Math 87 | Reading 87<br>Math 84 | Reading 74%<br>Math 70% | Reading 77<br>Math 76 | Reading 74<br>Math 70 | Reading 85%<br>Math 60% | Reading 77<br>Math 74<br>(n=417) |
| Met Standard in Reading but not Math (25%) | Reading 100%<br>Math 0%<br>(n=403) | Reading 62<br>Math 60 | Reading 60<br>Math 46 | Reading 38%<br>Math 15% | Reading 54<br>Math 40 | Reading 51<br>Math 32 | Reading 57%<br>Math 12% | Reading 52<br>Math 42<br>(n=248) |
| Met Standard in Math but not Reading (4%) | Reading 0%<br>Math 100%<br>(n=56) | Reading 54<br>Math 82 | Reading 66<br>Math 71 | Reading 37%<br>Math 36% | Reading 54<br>Math 66 | Reading 51<br>Math 52 | Reading 56%<br>Math 28% | Reading 52<br>Math 69<br>(n=33) |
| Did not meet Standard in either Reading or Math (32%) | Reading 0%<br>Math 0%<br>(n=519) | Reading 29<br>Math 34 | Reading 32<br>Math 27 | Reading 11%<br>Math 4% | Reading 31<br>Math 25 | Reading 28<br>Math 19 | Reading 22%<br>Math 6% | Reading 31<br>Math 29<br>(n=262) |
| District Average | Reading 63%<br>Math 42%<br>(n=1,605) | Reading 58<br>Math 63 | Reading 60<br>Math 56 | Reading 43%<br>Math 32% | Reading 53<br>Math 50 | Reading 52<br>Math 41 | Reading 54%<br>Math 27% | Reading 56<br>Math 50<br>(n=960) |

State = State assessment
Percentile Rank = Average percentile rank on norm-referenced test

Schools districts must be able to show their communities that they are getting a good return on the dollars they invest in the schools. Comprehensively analyzing data results at least once a year gives districts the opportunity to showcase their successes and to realize where there are opportunities for improvement so they can be sure that plans, programs, and processes are in place to ensure a continuum of learning for all students in every classroom in every school throughout the district.

## Reporting for States

State reporting should show how schools and school districts are doing with respect to NCLB as compared to other schools, districts, and states. In addition, there might be other specific items that are required, by state.

Figure 10.19 summarizes possible data analysis reports for the state level. A discussion follows the table.

Figure 10.19
# REPORTING RESULTS OF DATA ANALYSIS: STATE LEVEL

| Timing | Report | Purpose for the Report | Level of Detail | Method of Communication |
|---|---|---|---|---|
| *After student achievement results are released* | Student learning: percentage of students proficient by demographics by school; by school district compared to similar schools, school districts, and states. | To know how the schools and school district are doing with respect to NCLB as compared to other schools, districts, and states. To know where professional learning and leadership are necessary. | School and school district data, disaggregated by most demographic data. | Graph and data tables. Web site or dashboard access at any time, with the ability to dig deeper. Needs to be printable. |
| *Once a year, or when studying data results* | Staff perceptions, school processes, student achievement results, and student and staff demographics. | To understand if there is a continuum of learning in each school, from staffs' perspectives. To understand which implemented processes lead to the best results for *all* students. | Detailed by district, school, and teacher. | Graphs. Web site or dashboard so teachers and administrators can access information at any time. |
| *Once a year data results* | Program cost effectiveness. | To understand the impact of the program by costs. | Detailed program and cost data. | Graphs. Web site or dashboard. |

### After Student Achievement Results are Released

States, usually through their Departments of Education, report student learning results on state mandated tests. The results should show percentage of students proficient by demographics, by district, and by school in a way that allows for comparisons to like districts, like schools, and other states. Analysis of these results helps states determine what types of professional learning are necessary to get all students to proficiency.

### Once a Year, or When Studying Data Results

States also need to study and report staff perceptions, school processes, and student and staff demographics, along with student achievement results, to understand which implemented processes are leading to the best results for all students. These results could be used as the basis for statewide professional learning that focuses on proven instructional strategies and best practices.

*Once-a-Year Data Results*

States should also report the return on investment that state residents receive for the dollars spent on education. Programs implemented in schools and districts need to be evaluated to determine their cost effectiveness.

## Reporting the Big Picture to the Public

When we conduct comprehensive data analyses for continuous school improvement, we need to communicate the results as widely as possible, since we want everyone to understand the results. The ideal report for general use is two-to-four pages long, or about 500 words, with high-quality graphics that convey the story. Every state has school and district report cards in place in order to communicate with the public.

Figure 10.20 summarizes reporting data analysis results to the public. A discussion of the table follows.

## Figure 10.20
## REPORTING RESULTS OF DATA ANALYSIS: THE PUBLIC

| *Timing* | *Report* | *Purpose for the Report* | *Level of Detail* | *Method of Communication* |
|---|---|---|---|---|
| *After student achievement results are released* | Student learning: percentage of students proficient by demographics by school, by school district compared to like schools, school districts, and states. | To know how the schools and school district are doing with respect to NCLB as compared to other schools, districts, and states. To know where professional learning and leadership are necessary. | School and school district data, disaggregated by most demographic data. | Local media. Web sites. Newsletters. |
| *Once a year, or when studying data results* | Staff perceptions, school processes, student achievement results, and student and staff demographics. | To understand if there is a continuum of learning in each school, from staffs' perspectives. To understand which implemented processes lead to the best results for *all* students. | Detailed by district, school, and teacher. | Local media. Web sites. Newsletters. |

### After Student Achievement Results are Released

The public is one of the most important audiences for the results of comprehensive data analyses. The public needs to know how the schools within the local district are doing with respect to No Child Left Behind and how the students are performing on district and state-mandated tests. Results should be communicated as widely as possible using school and district newsletters and web sites, and other local media.

### Once a Year, or When Studying Data Results

In addition to the results of student achievement tests, providing the public with information on perceptions, school processes, and student and staff demographics will help the public see changes that may be occurring in the schools and how the schools are using processes that will help students prepare to be anything they want to be in the future.

The support of the community is vital to the success of public schools. Publishing the results of comprehensive data analysis will enable schools and districts to share their results, both challenges and successes, and show the public how the schools are preparing to meet future challenges. This can be a step toward the engagement of the public as partners.

## Summary

Gathering data and putting together comprehensive data analysis reports are not easy tasks for schools and, often, school districts. Many schools have difficulty communicating data analysis results to their desired audiences largely because they do not get all of the pieces in one report. A data warehouse, with all the data in one location, will assist schools in getting reports for any audience. Brief, comprehensive reports can be very informative and useful for all stakeholders. This communication process must be well-planned and carefully written so it clearly conveys a true picture.

Determining what data analysis to make at different levels is only half the issue of reporting/communicating results. Determining how to display the results might be a harder job, but reporting the big picture to the desired audiences is vital so all stakeholders understand the challenges and successes of their local schools.

CHAPTER **11**

# WHO GETS TRAINED ON THE TOOLS: WHO GETS ACCESS?

After the data warehouse is in place, questions regarding its use must be answered. *Who should be trained on the data warehouse, and who should be expected to use it? When is the training most useful and appropriate? When are the most appropriate times to get all staff using the data warehouse?*

## Who Gets Trained on the Data Warehouse and When?

A school district that is going to use a data warehouse effectively and efficiently will have a vision for its use. The district will let all staff know that a data warehouse is in place, what it can do, and how it will be used. The district will establish training strategies that are well-defined and planned systematically to eventually include all decision-makers and all teachers. These training strategies will be developed to coincide with existing infrastructure and dissemination points and customized for job functions. Most often the vendor will provide the training. However, since not everyone will be, or needs to be, trained at the same time, a training plan should be developed with the vendor.

Stated a little differently, everyone on staff needs to know the vision for the data warehouse. However, not everyone needs to learn how to use the warehouse at the same time—or maybe at all. There are logical times to get individuals with different job functions trained and using, or helping to build or grow, the warehouse. In a perfect world, a district data person would support and help the curriculum/assessment personnel get the reports they need to use with teachers. The curriculum/assessment personnel can then spend their time analyzing and using the data with them. These personnel would work together to create standard district, school, and classroom level reports that are pushed out to teachers. School staffs need to learn to use the warehouse when they are ready to

*Everyone on staff needs to know the vision for the data warehouse.*

go deeper into the data. When taking the data warehouse to the school level, I highly recommend having teams of individuals at each school become the trainers of the other staff members, with the most technologically advanced member becoming the ultimate data warehouse go-to person. This will keep a level of expertise at the school level, with less reliance on the district warehouse team or person. Additionally, during training, I would pair teachers. Having a training partner will get teachers using the data warehouse more often because they can ask questions of each other and share concerns and ideas.

Figure 11.1 and the discussion below spell out when you might get different staff trained and involved in the data warehouse work.

## During the Design of the Warehouse

It is not too soon to get key administrators and appropriate staff members, such as clerical staffs who input data and IT staffs, trained on the data warehouse while you are in Data Discovery—that time when you are considering what data need to be included in the data warehouse. Think about what data are gathered on a regular basis, what reports need to be produced for the school board, state and federal departments of education, and how you want to evaluate the effectiveness of your programs, processes, and schools. These people need to make sure the warehouse will easily produce and/or automate the reports they have to pull together. The training will let them know how the warehouse works and allow them to think about what they need to have in the warehouse to make it most useful for the needs and work of the district. It will also impress upon them the need to have clean data and why someone must own each piece of data to ensure the gathering, analysis, and use of clean data. Procedures for cleaning data need to be created, monitored, and enforced. *Note:* If the warehouse is redesigned, initial training will need to be offered again.

*Procedures for cleaning data need to be created, monitored, and enforced.*

## First Iteration of Your Warehouse

When the first version of the data warehouse is ready to be released to the district, the individuals who are responsible for reports and who will be responsible for the data rollout should have the first opportunity to use the warehouse and to view the quality and integrity of the data. These individuals will look at their own data in the warehouse and determine how clean the data are. If the data are clean, other people can be trained. If the data are not clean, they must be cleaned before others are trained. Training with dirty data is not a good use of anybody's time, could sabotage the feelings that the warehouse will be useful, and will make it very difficult to get the trainees back to the training sessions later. Again, procedures for assuring that data are clean as they are

## Figure 11.1
# DATA WAREHOUSE STAFF TRAINING

| Timing / Overview | Who | Considerations |
|---|---|---|
| **Design of your warehouse:**<br>• *Data Discovery*<br>• *How data work in the warehouse*<br>• *How to ensure clean data in your warehouse* | School and district administrators and staff who know what data exist in the district and what data need to be gathered for different purposes. This includes clerical staff who input data, administrators, the Information Technology staff, and other data personnel. | Think about what data are gathered on a regular basis, what reports need to be produced for the school board, and state and federal departments of education, and how you want to evaluate the effectiveness of your programs and schools. The people determining what data to include in the warehouse need to make sure the warehouse will easily produce and/or automate the reports they have to pull together. The training will let them know how the data work in the warehouse and what data they need to have in the warehouse to make it most useful for the needs and work of the district. Somebody at the district level *must own* each piece of data. |
| **First iteration of your warehouse:**<br>• *How the data warehouse works*<br>• *Determine roll-out of warehouse throughout the district* | The same people as above who can check the warehouse for clean data, and who can make immediate corrections to clean the data. | These individuals would be looking at their own data in the warehouse and determining how clean the data are. If the data are clean, other people can be trained. If the data are not clean, it must be cleaned before others are trained. Training with dirty data will not be a good use of anybody's time and could sabotage the feelings that the warehouse will be useful. Additionally, procedures for assuring that data are clean as they are being entered in the student information system and, ultimately, the data warehouse, need to be created, disseminated, and monitored. |
| **Clean version of your warehouse:**<br>• *Learn warehouse functionality*<br>• *Develop a product such as a school or district profile to learn how to use the warehouse* | School administrators and key teachers who will become the trainers in the schools, with supportive district administrators. | These individuals can learn about the warehouse's functionality while creating analyses they will use for their own schools or departments. The training is most effective if it includes developing a product, such as a data profile for the district or school or a historical profile of data of all students for the classroom teacher. We recommend doing a district profile first to ensure the cleanliness of the data and to do some of the hard work for all schools, and then putting together school profiles from the district profile. |
| **Advanced training:**<br>• *How to do complex querying*<br>• *How to use the data warehouse to dig deeper into the data*<br>• *How to create and automate common or standard reports* | School administrators, district administrators—testing, curriculum, data personnel— and key teachers who become the trainers in the schools. | Advanced training could include learning to create reports to automate the data work of the district and schools or learning how to create complex and deeper analyses.<br>After data profiles have been created, this advanced training could follow the analyses and help users dig deeper into the data to uncover root causes of their "undesirable results" and to follow student histories backward through previous educational experiences to predict and ensure student successes and to predict and prevent student failures. |
| **Growing the warehouse:**<br>• *How to use the warehouse to its fullest by evaluating progress and automating* | Administrators and the key teachers who have used the warehouse and who will train others in their schools. | After having used the warehouse for initial purposes, users get ideas about other things they wish the warehouse could and would do. What questions can you not answer with the warehouse? What data do you need to add to the warehouse to answer these questions? |
| **New user training:**<br>• *Learn to use the warehouse* | New administrators and teachers. | Districts need to create a plan and budget for the training of new staff. |

entered into their respective systems, especially the student information system, need to be created, disseminated, and monitored. Examples of procedures to ensure clean data are discussed in Chapter 4.

## Clean Version of Your Warehouse

District and school administrators and key teachers can learn about the warehouse's functionality while creating analyses that they will use for the district or their own schools or departments. *The training is most effective if it includes developing a product, such as a data profile for a school or district.* (See the *Using Data to Improve Student Learning* series [Bernhardt, 2004, 2005, 2006, 2007] for models of profiles and graphing templates.) For teachers, creating a historical profile of data for all the students in their classrooms would be a great learning exercise that they would appreciate. Make sure that teachers are paired as they are trained to use the warehouse, so they have someone they can ask questions of when they work with the warehouse later on.

> *The training is most effective if it includes developing a product, such as a data profile for a school or district.*

## Advanced Training

Advanced training should be offered to just about anyone who will be using the data warehouse. In the first year or so, it might be appropriate to limit advanced training to school and district administrators, especially assessment, curriculum, and data specialists, and the key trainers from each school. The advanced training should cover how to create reports to automate the data work of the district and school and learning how to create complex and deeper analyses. After data profiles have been created, advanced training should include how to do analyses to help users dig deeper into the data. Staff should learn how deeper analysis of the data can uncover contributing causes of "undesirable results" and enable users to follow student histories backward through previous educational experiences; using this information, they can better predict and ensure student successes and better predict and prevent student failures.

## Growing the Warehouse

After having successfully used the warehouse for initial purposes, users get ideas about other things they wish the warehouse could do. Deciding how to expand the usefulness of the warehouse emerges from the answers to questions such as: *What questions can we not answer with the current warehouse? Can we evaluate all parts of our system with what is in the warehouse? What data do we need to add to the warehouse to answer these questions? What additional reports should we be generating and automating?*

Growing the warehouse might not involve training as much as budgeting time periodically for power users and administrators to talk about what questions the warehouse needs to answer that it is not currently capable of answering and what data elements are necessary to generate those answers. It could be that there are more or different reports required of the warehouse. This would also be a time for warehouse users to compare notes on the most common queries and on reports that can be made into standard reports.

### New-User Training

During the course of data warehouse creation, implementation, and use, new staff members will be joining your district and schools. The district must have a plan for bringing on new users. The plan might be budget-focused for periodically bringing the vendor back or train-the-trainer focused, providing time for in-house staff to train new staff. No matter which procedure is used, new employees must be brought on board with data warehouse use as soon as possible.

## Who gets Access to the Warehouse?

Providing access to the data warehouse means developing secure arrangements for individuals to use parts or all of the warehouse. Access to the warehouse has to include everyone that should be using data to improve teaching and learning. Basically, that would mean all teachers and administrators. Typically, data warehouse administrators must set up and manage the security arrangements. Policies and procedures must be established to determine how access is allocated and how security of the data will be assured.

*Access to the warehouse has to include everyone that should be using data to improve teaching and learning.*

Security considerations that warehouse administrators must come to grips with include:

▼ *Should school staffs be able to see only their current student data?* If so, it would limit the ultimate value of the warehouse, which includes enabling the retrieval of historic data and following feeder patterns forward.

▼ *Should teachers be able to see records of only their students or team members' students as well?*

▼ *Should everyone with access see student names or just identification numbers?* Some districts believe identification numbers, in lieu of actual names, add privacy for their students.

▼ *Who should be allowed to modify the data?* A very limited number of people should be allowed to modify the data. Most users will need access that is read only.

▼ *Will there be some people who should get aggregate data access only?* There might be other locations for accessing aggregate data, such as your state department of education website.

▼ *Who, besides teachers, should have access to all student data?*

▼ *Who should see lunch status, IEP information, small sample sizes?*

▼ *What does FERPA say about all this access?*

These are questions that must be answered by each district as it determines how it will create and implement a culture of data use.

## Family Educational Rights and Privacy Act (FERPA)

The Family Educational Rights and Privacy Act (FERPA) is a federal law that was enacted in 1974, and has been amended several times, that applies to schools and educational agencies that receive funding under a program administered by the U.S. Department of Education. The law gives parents and "eligible students" (those over 18 or who attend a school beyond the high school level) access to their education records in order to inspect and review them.

Schools are not required by FERPA to maintain education records, to provide a student with notices or information that does not generally contain information directly related to the student, or to respond to questions from the public about students.

A school must have consent from the student or parent prior to the public disclosure of personally identifiable education records and must ensure that the consent is signed, dated, and describes the purpose of the disclosure. FERPA allows schools to disclose personally identifiable education records, without consent, to:

1. School officials with legitimate educational interest;

2. Other schools to which a student is transferring;

3. Specified officials for audit or evaluation purposes;

4. Appropriate parties in conjunction with financial aid to a student;

5. Organizations conducting certain studies on behalf of the school;

6. Accrediting organizations;

7. Appropriate officials in cases of health and safety emergencies; and

8. To comply with a lawfully issued court order or subpoena.

Schools may disclose, without signed consent, "directory" information such as student name, address, telephone number, date and place of birth, honors and awards, and dates of attendance. However, schools must first notify parents and eligible students about directory information and allow them a reasonable time to request that the school not disclose directory information about them.

In terms of who has access to the information in the data warehouse, FERPA mandates that teachers and other school officials must have a legitimate educational interest. Therefore, FERPA would not limit the access of teachers and administrators as they establish strategies to improve student learning. It is, however, important that all those with access to the data warehouse be educated about the provisions of FERPA and the protections it affords students and parents.

According to the Data Quality Campaign (August 2006), sharing student data that are not personally identifiable is permissible. State longitudinal data systems can obtain and disclose anonymous student information provided there are safeguards against sharing data that are traceable to individual students. Even in instances in which personally identifiable information on students is shared, there are several purposes for which disclosures are permitted under FERPA:

▼ Evaluating/auditing state and local programs and implementing school and district accountability

▼ Monitoring and analyzing assessment, enrollment, and graduation data

▼ Performing studies to improve instruction

▼ Sharing student records among schools (as in prior and prospective schools)

▼ Maintaining a teacher identification system that links teachers and students

## Summary

Some of the most critical issues a school district has to address about the use of a comprehensive analytical tool, or data warehouse, include who will get trained to use it and when, and who will have access to what parts of the warehouse. Decisions need to be consistent with the warehouse vision and desired uses of the data.

*Some of the most critical issues a school district has to address about the use of a comprehensive analytical tool, or data warehouse, include who will get trained to use it and when, and who will have access to what parts of the warehouse.*

# CHAPTER 12

# MANAGING THE DATA WAREHOUSE

The smooth, efficient, and secure management of the data warehouse requires careful planning and time considerations. Districts need to plan for long-term dedication of resources to focus on the continuous growth and improvement of the data warehouse. Remember, a data warehouse is a process, not a product. Even after the warehouse is initially loaded and operational, there are components that need continuous attention, especially managing the data items that comprise the warehouse, as well as the updating process.

> *Districts need to plan for long-term dedication of resources to focus on the continuous growth and improvement of the data warehouse.*

How many people are needed to manage the warehouse depends upon who is hosting the server on which the warehouse resides, how often the warehouse is updated or refreshed, the tools that are available to the district to refresh and clean the data, and the tools available to analyze the data, create desired reports, and grow the warehouse. A data warehouse administrator who manages the overall project from inception to full implementation to maintenance is highly recommended. Not having someone who knows the entire system could spell disaster. Most districts have at least one IT person and someone with an education background working together to maintain their data warehouses.

Some of the jobs related to managing a data warehouse include:

▼ Server management, including monitoring data warehouse data, operations, security, and performance

▼ Data warehouse refresh

▼ Managing the data items that comprise the warehouse, including identifying all items, monitoring data input, and overseeing the addition of new data

▼ Data quality and the continuous improvement of business processes

▼ Data warehouse growth

▼ Creating and generating reports

▼ Managing the training—scheduling, identifying appropriate participants

▼ User support

▼ Managing the vendor

## Server Management

School districts purchasing data warehouse systems can host the data warehouse server or pay the vendor to host their warehouse at the vendor's server center. If a district chooses to manage its own server onsite, the job of managing the data warehouse server can often be added to the job description of the same person who manages other servers onsite.

Automated extract, transform, and load (ETL) tools that can collect and clean data nightly can make managing a data warehouse server similar to managing a student information system. The work involved with managing a server includes making sure that it is operational and securely performing periodic checks, updating the virus protection and version of the operating system software, and backing up the warehouse.

If the vendor houses the warehouse at its site, the vendor can take care of the virus protection and updating. Most vendors would prefer to host the servers, as it is easier to access when problems arise or when software updates are needed. Some vendors maintain that most of the problems with district warehouses are district-server related. When they host the server, the vendors can take care of problems very quickly.

## Managing the Data Refreshing Process

Creating the warehouse involves a lot of work to set up the warehouse correctly and to ensure that the data are clean. At least one full-time person will be needed to check that all data are clean and establish data-entry protocols to organize how data will be gathered consistently and accurately. Even with good protocols, consistent monitoring, and continuous improvement of practices, a full-time person might still be required on an ongoing basis.

> *Creating the warehouse involves a lot of work to set up the warehouse correctly and to ensure that the data are clean.*

If an automated ETL tool is used to refresh the warehouse, and if the data do not change much from year to year, it is reasonable to estimate that one full-time person would suffice for total data warehouse management. That person must know the ETL inside and out. If the district refreshes the data only once every month, or four times a year, the percentage of a person's job could be reduced if her/his job is only data refreshing—although, some districts say, in reality, knowledge is lost because of infrequent uses, and refreshing the warehouse might take even more time. Most districts are rapidly moving toward refreshing their data on a nightly basis. Even when the ETL tool is automated, there needs to be someone on staff who is familiar with how to modify or write the automated scripts to respond to and correct data when changes or repairs are needed. Someone also needs to monitor the data transformation exceptions or issues discovered while loading. Additionally, warehouse companies offer an annual maintenance contract, which provides the district with a higher level of expertise to fall back on when needed.

If a manual ETL or no ETL tool is used to refresh the warehouse, districts will need two people for this process. Managing the extracting, cleaning, and loading of educational data is not easy and, even when automatic ETL tools are used, there should always be at least two people within the district who are familiar with this process. This provides redundancy in case one person leaves the district.

## Managing the Data Items that Comprise the Warehouse

The manager of the data items in a data warehouse has to understand all of the data systems used within the district and how they all work together. This component of managing a warehouse requires a person to have a grasp of what and where data are kept, who enters the data, why certain fields are entered, and what fields could/should be added to what database. This person also needs to understand the operation of a school district. The data warehouse manager also needs to know what data need to be loaded at what times throughout the school year to make all the data relevant and timely for teachers. The manager of the data warehouse has to understand the *big picture* of organizational management of a school district and their vision for the warehouse.

Adding data items (both entities and attributes) to a warehouse requires the knowledge and understanding of how data items relate to other data items in the warehouse. New items can have a one-to-one, one-to-many, or many-to-many relationships to other new or existing data items. Understanding these relationships is necessary in order for items to be properly connected to each other to support queries and reporting. Experience with relational databases is needed to do this properly. Many districts have found that a person with knowledge of the education elements of the data needs to manage the data items or at least work very closely with the technology person.

*The Data Warehouse Manager:*

♦ *Has to understand all of the data systems used within the district and how they all work together*

♦ *Needs to understand the operation of a school district*

♦ *Needs to know what data need to be loaded at what times throughout the school year to make all the data relevant and timely for teachers*

♦ *Has to understand the "big picture" of organizational management of a school district and their vision for the warehouse*

## Data Quality and the Continuous Improvement of Education Processes

Monitoring the quality of data is a huge job for the data warehouse manager. It requires putting into place protocols for entering data correctly and consistently in the first place, training data clerks, and monitoring their data entries to ensure that the protocols are being adhered to. These protocols could change the way the district has been gathering data for a long time. Monitoring the quality of data also means being able to spot missing, incorrect, and misaligned student and staff identification codes and being able to write scripts to correct problematic data identified in exception reports.

## Managing Data Warehouse Growth

Managing data warehouse growth involves designing new entities, cleaning new data, developing new reports, and continuously working with users to make sure the data they want are in the warehouse. This work should never stop. If you have a viable warehouse solution, users will always be asking for new data elements and for new reports so they can work smarter, not harder.

## Creating and Managing the Reports

The amount of time and work required to create and manage data warehouse reports depends on the analysis tools used with the warehouse, how many people get trained to use the warehouse, and/or the access capabilities of the end-users. It would be nice if the data warehouse managers and the district administrators could establish standard reports that they want everyone to use and provide quality training to allow school data teams to learn how to dig deeper into the data. Some district data warehouse managers hope that after a couple of years of end-user access to the warehouse, the managers would provide 80% of the reports and query templates that school districts need, relying on the users to develop the other 20% through ad hoc tools.

## Managing the Training

Chapter 11 discusses who gets trained to build and use the warehouse. This should include training for those who will be doing the data entry. Data entry people throughout the district need to know how important their jobs are and that they are being depended upon to enter data accurately and consistently.

Data-entry protocols must be established so all those entering data know how to do their jobs. The data entry must then be monitored regularly to limit, or eliminate, mistakes.

## User Support

User support provides onsite technical support for the use of the data warehouse. The vision of the warehouse and data use, along with how people are trained to use the warehouse, will determine how much time is required to support end-users. Many school districts provide Leaders' Training to "data coaches" in each school building. These coaches really understand the data, the warehouse, and the analysis tools, and they are able to help others see the value of the data warehouse as a tool to help improve teaching and learning.

The person(s) providing user support must understand the data analysis tools, how the data items relate to each other in the warehouse, and enough about education to understand the types of reports being requested.

*The vision of the warehouse and data use, along with how people are trained to use the warehouse, will determine how much time is required to support end-users.*

## Managing the Vendor

Someone needs to be the point person to communicate with the vendor. That person will discuss data issues, data refreshes, contract and training issues, and how the warehouse operates. Some districts have a person who speaks with their data warehouse vendor every week to keep both sides up-to-date.

## Summary

In order to effectively manage a data warehouse, we advise that a district have at least two trained people available. Supplementing the data warehouse contract with a maintenance agreement from the warehouse vendor can reduce the number of full-time people needed. It is highly recommended that at least two people know all parts of the data warehouse and how it operates so users of the warehouse have confidence in the reliability and timeliness of the data and in their ability to access and use the data.

CHAPTER 13

# STORIES OF SCHOOL DISTRICTS BUILDING DATA WAREHOUSES

School districts all over the world are coming online with data warehousing. This chapter relates the stories of five real school districts—Chilton Public Schools, Chilton, Wisconsin (Enrollment=1,350); Columbia Public Schools, Columbia, Missouri (Enrollment=17,200); Northview Public Schools, Grand Rapids, Michigan (Enrollment=3,340); San Jose Unified School District, San Jose, California (Enrollment=32,000); and Tyler Independent School District, Tyler, Texas (Enrollment=17,480). The stories of two multi-district consortiums, in Connecticut and Vermont, are shared for insight into what it takes to pull together a data warehouse and use it to improve teaching and learning. Also, note that a different type of solution (zone integration) is described in Chapter 8 for Western Heights Public School District in Oklahoma City, Oklahoma. The names of specific data warehouse, assessment, and student information system companies have been removed to remain vendor neutral.

# The Chilton Data Warehouse Story

*"Even cute, little districts can use data for instructional decision making."*

**Dr. Rebecca J. Blink (bblink5381@aol.com)**

**Director of Curriculum and Instruction**

**District Assessment Coordinator**

**District Data Manager**

*Chilton is in the center of east-central Wisconsin, about one-half hour from Green Bay. It is the county seat of Calumet County and has a population of approximately 3,700. The Chilton School District has three schools—one elementary, one middle, and one high school—with a total student population of about 1,350 students.*

In January of 1999, the Chilton School District (in Wisconsin) adopted an assessment tool. We began to administer that tool and enter the data from those assessments into our student information system (SIS). As the database of assessment scores grew (we assess a minimum of twice a year), we wanted to start to analyze the data that were in our SIS. The SIS allows only four fields to be selected at one time for a query, so we quickly realized that we could not accomplish what we had set out to do using the SIS as the tool. We did not have the capacity to analyze data or look at the information longitudinally. We wanted to be able to use the information we were gathering to make informed decisions about the instructional programs for students in our District and also for program evaluation.

Coincidentally, during this same time, our regional educational services office was offering an opportunity for individuals to participate in the review of several data-warehouse tools because it wanted to move forward in our region with a consortium warehousing project. Four companies were reviewed by a committee and eventually one corporation was selected as the company with which to move forward. When I saw the possibilities of the data-warehouse tools, I knew these were the tools that we needed to move the District forward. These tools allowed us to place all of our data into one system and actually analyze them so we could use the data to help facilitate change.

*Why they got into data warehousing—Chilton discovered that their student information system could not help them with instructional program evaluation, and instructional improvement.*

As is sometimes typical in education, we had been basing decisions on "gut feelings" rather than on cold, hard facts. We continued to do things and fund programs because we "thought" they were working well, but we had no proof of that. We made some changes in curriculum because we "thought" that was what we needed to do, but we had no proof. We had implemented a reading program almost ten years ago, but we had absolutely no proof that the program was valuable. We had no idea if the things that were put in place were actually accomplishing what we wanted them to do.

The Assistant Director of Technology and the Director of Curriculum and Instruction (me) were the only two people on the selection committee for our data warehouse. We were selected by the superintendent and told that we were going to be the two people evaluating what was available. We went to meetings and evaluated solutions from four different vendors. After seeing all the possibilities, we brought a recommendation forward to the Superintendent.

When selecting a data-warehouse solution, we had certain things that we were looking for in a tool. First, we wanted the warehouse to be able to store and retrieve all of our data. Chilton is a bit unusual in that we have a countywide special education program. We needed a system that would allow us to track information on not only our own students, but also on students who were attending schools in Chilton and were residents of a neighboring district. We needed a tool that would allow us to look at data longitudinally and provide us with the ability to analyze program effectiveness, how staff development affected student learning, how our NCLB subgroups were performing on state assessments, how all students were doing (trends) on local assessments, etc. We selected a vendor based on a rubric that we designed for CESA 7 (Cooperative Educational Service Agency), our regional educational service office. Cost and user friendliness were the two most important categories for selection.

After the original loading of the data warehouse, our District went through a period of data clean up. We had a tremendous amount of inaccurate or incomplete data that needed to be corrected. We had no idea that the data we currently had in our District were so erroneous. It literally took us a couple of years to clean up what data we had and develop a system to reduce the number of data-entry errors. I designed a *Data Entry Protocol* for all of our data-entry personnel to follow to standardize the data that are entered. This protocol is shown in Chapter 4 (Figure 4.5).

Currently, the data warehouse is utilized mainly by me at the district level. Teachers send their data requests to me: I run the queries in the warehouse and provide teachers with the information they need. We have not released the full warehouse to the staff because of its complexity. We need a tool for teachers that will enable them to wrap their arms around the data with ease. They really don't need to understand the intricacies of a statistical database and its underlying functions; they need a tool that will simply provide them with information quickly. However, there are a few district-level specialists who have been trained (K-12 District Reading Specialist and Math Specialist) who do have access to the entire warehouse.

*Chilton wanted the warehouse to store and retrieve all of its data; to track information on special education students who were attending schools in Chilton, but were residents of a neighboring district; to look at data longitudinally; and to provide the District with the ability to analyze program effectiveness, how staff development affected student learning, how NCLB subgroups were performing on state assessments, and how all students were doing (trends) on local assessments.*

*It took a couple of years to clean the data. A Data Entry Protocol, for all data-entry personnel to follow to standardize the data that are entered, was developed.*

> *The key to the success of implementing a data warehouse in a school district, in my opinion, is having a person in the district who will "champion" the cause.*

The key to the success of implementing a data warehouse in a school district, in my opinion, is having a person in the district who will "champion" the cause. There has to be one person in the district who oversees the entire implementation process and assures the sustainability of such an effort. For Chilton, that person is me. Everyone in the district who deals with data and enters data into our multiple data sources knows that that they should call me if they have any questions about how and/or when something should be entered. From there, I constantly check the validity of the data that resides in the warehouse because the data have to be accurate if we are basing our decisions on what we see. Then, it is my job to get the data into the hands of teachers so they utilize the data to make instructional decisions. Data are never left out of a discussion related to student learning. We have implemented "Data Days" solely for the purpose of providing teachers with time to analyze and interpret their classroom level data.

*Leading an effort to implement a data warehouse in a school district requires strong leadership and a never-ending commitment to continuous improvement.* Someone in the district has to be responsible for leading the charge with data and the development and use of a data warehouse. School improvement planning has to become a part of the culture in the district. Proving the usefulness of the tool and its necessity in improving student learning is critical to all school and/or district stakeholders.

### The Chilton Data Warehouse Timeline

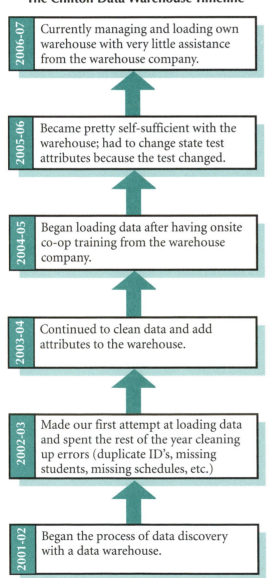

**2006-07** Currently managing and loading own warehouse with very little assistance from the warehouse company.

**2005-06** Became pretty self-sufficient with the warehouse; had to change state test attributes because the test changed.

**2004-05** Began loading data after having onsite co-op training from the warehouse company.

**2003-04** Continued to clean data and add attributes to the warehouse.

**2002-03** Made our first attempt at loading data and spent the rest of the year cleaning up errors (duplicate ID's, missing students, missing schedules, etc.)

**2001-02** Began the process of data discovery with a data warehouse.

## Columbia Public Schools' Experience with a Data Warehouse

**Dr. Cheryl Cozette (ccozette@columbia.k12.mo.us)**

**Assistant Superintendent for Curriculum and Instruction**

**and**

**Dr. Sally Beth Lyon (slyon@columbia.k12.mo.us)**

**Director of Research, Assessment, and Accountability**

In the spring of 1999, the Assistant Superintendent for Elementary Education of the Columbia School District, in Missouri, was invited to attend a Missouri Leadership Academy session on data analysis. At the session, Dr. Victoria Bernhardt presented information on the power of using multiple measures of data to improve student achievement. As a result of that presentation, Dr. Bernhardt's book, *Data Analysis for Continuous School Improvement* (Second Edition, 2004), became the new book-study material for principals in Columbia Public Schools (CPS).

At that time, CPS administered the Missouri Assessment Program (MAP) tests and other varied assessments throughout the system with no plan for the collection or analysis of longitudinal data. Therefore, student achievement data, which were kept in notebooks in the central office, were basically meaningless. Demographic data, which were housed in the student information system, were incomplete and inconsistent. Perceptual data were collected once every five years in conjunction with the Missouri School Improvement Program Five-year Review. The "data" about Columbia Public Schools processes were anecdotal and informal.

The journey from that point to the District's status in 2007 has been long and arduous. The need for a data warehouse became apparent as administrators began to collect student data that were available. Making any kind of meaningful analysis—even to use demographic data in conjunction with student achievement data—was impossible.

As the District Assessment Plan was updated in 2000, the consensus of the staff, after much discussion, was to give the same assessment to students in grades 3-5. Secondary schools were not ready to give up their instructional time for consistent assessments. The only standardized achievement data available for secondary schools continued to be the MAP data, which provided a grade-span assessment.

*Columbia, Missouri, has a population of approximately 90,590. Centrally located between Kansas City and St. Louis, Columbia is the home of the University of Missouri.*

*The public school enrollment is approximately 17,200 students in 19 elementary schools, three middle schools (grade 6-7), three junior high schools (grades 8-9), three high schools (grades 10-12), and four special needs centers.*

*Columbia needed a system to make data collection and analysis more factual and formal.*

However, even with the additional testing data available at the elementary grades, analysis continued to be an insurmountable challenge. A method of housing the data and analyzing the data was imperative. The District's leadership did not know what that tool was called, but they knew they needed something! At that time, one of the assistant superintendents read Dr. Bernhardt's book, *Designing and Using Databases for School Improvement* (2000, Eye on Education —out of print). This was the catalyst for Columbia Public School's quest for a data warehouse. It was also the guide for the journey through the change process that moved the District from the paper world to the electronic world of data analysis.

A data warehouse was first demonstrated to CPS by Dr. Bernhardt in 2000. It was in its infancy stages, but it seemed intuitive and easy to use. It appeared to be the answer to the District's data analysis needs. But the journey down the road toward the use of a data warehouse had just begun. What approach would inspire buy-in from staff members and the Board of Education? Who should be involved in the decision-making process? Should data be "in shape" before purchasing a warehouse? Or should the warehouse be purchased and used as the template for data preparation?

The first step was to determine which stakeholders should be involved in data analysis in the District. Principals were key players, and they had progressed to the point where they *wanted* the data. That was no longer the issue it had been earlier in the process. However, they wanted the data to be clean, and they wanted the data quickly. The data-processing folks became very important players. They could help us get the data into the format necessary for uploading into the warehouse. And they had to be committed to clean, accurate data entry.

*The data-warehouse selection committee included members of the data-processing department, central office administrators, representative principals, and instructional technology specialists.*

A small committee was formed to discuss data needs. The committee members were those who might be involved in the data-discovery and data-collection process: the members of the data processing department, central office administrators, representative principals, and instructional technology specialists. Many of the members were skeptical. Some did not believe in the need to analyze district data. Others believed that the internal development of a data warehouse would be preferable to working with an outside entity. This created challenging dynamics in the effort to get unbiased, objective input regarding a prospective process for data analysis.

After many meetings, much discussion, and with some trepidation, a recommendation was made to the Board of Education for the purchase of a data warehouse. The Board of Education, with its traditional forward-thinking, approved the purchase of a data warehouse in 2000, after examining various products on the market. It appeared the journey was about finished when, in actuality, the journey had just begun.

Implementing the data warehouse in Columbia Public Schools was both an enlightening and a discouraging process. The demographic data were seriously flawed. The first upload of data into the warehouse resulted in queries that revealed inaccuracies and inconsistencies across all grade levels. The first job was to further systematize the way student data were entered districtwide. That would help us in the future. It did not help with the data that had been previously entered. Therefore, the next job was to "cleanse" the data that were already in the warehouse. Working with the people from the data warehouse company, the quality of the data in the warehouse was improved. That process took many months.

*The first upload of data into the warehouse resulted in queries that revealed inaccuracies and inconsistencies across all grade levels.*

As school personnel began to see the possibilities of the data warehouse, principals became interested in acquiring additional data about their students. This precipitated yet another change in the District Assessment Plan. The secondary schools wanted to administer a standardized achievement test so they could gather longitudinal data, in addition to grade-span data, about their students. The District adopted a standardized achievement measure for grades 3-9, in addition to the mandated grade-span assessments.

As more data were added to the warehouse, the need for different types of queries became apparent. Principals were asking for information that had not been discussed during the data-discovery phase of implementation. The warehouse was in existence, but it was "anemic." Further, because the warehouse was being populated by data from the student information system periodically, the warehouse was seldom current. Principals would run a simple query to count students, get the results, and exclaim, "This thing isn't right! That's not how many students I have in my school!" And finally, the fact that end users—principals, coordinators, and central office administrators—used the warehouse sporadically meant that, in spite of ongoing training efforts, they were unable to use the product efficiently or effectively. Frustration mounted. Many thought the product was "a dog."

*As more data were added to the warehouse, the need for different types of queries became apparent.*

At about the time of this nadir, the District created a central office position called the Director of Research, Assessment, and Accountability. This person's responsibilities included using, and improving, the data warehouse. The first director was promoted from within the District and confessed:

> *I thought the data warehouse was "a dog," too. As a building administrator,*
> *I had been to those trainings where queries resulted in inaccurate results,*

*and I had been one of the people who attempted a query three weeks after a training meeting, only to be frustrated with my inability to tease the information I needed from the system. I spent a few months in my new position subtly trying to persuade my colleagues to "cut and run."*

*However, the potential of the product was obvious, and my job was to make it work. Herein lies the first "lesson" about data analysis in general, and about data warehouses specifically—these need a steward. An organization should not expect to realize a successful data warehouse operation without investing in the personnel to support it, and one or more of these persons must be educators with the experience doing the work about which the data reports, in order to understand their uses and applications and to advise about their analysis. Our District's information-technology folks had taken the warehouse as far as they could take it, and our District executives had championed the vision, but did not have the time to direct implementation. The warehouse needed an "end-user advocate."*

The 2004-05 school year was a turning point in Columbia Public Schools' ability to use the warehouse effectively because of three crucial steps:

1. The District invested in the programming necessary for uploading data nightly from the student information system. In a district as large and complex as CPS, with the degree of student mobility and the changeability of other data, it was unacceptable to update the warehouse from the student information system only occasionally.

2. The District added important data elements to its warehouse. This process began with a "database planning session" attended by end users, the District's information technology staff, and data-warehouse personnel, the results of which informed an enhanced warehouse design. The database was expanded to include, for instance, scores from district common assessments, course grades, and markers that documented student participation in various interventions. Much of that meeting was brainstorming and dreaming that even now is not fully implemented, but it charted a path and opened eyes to the analyses that were possible with the product.

3. The District's Director of Research, Assessment, and Accountability learned how to use the product! Through a three-day onsite training conducted by a data-warehouse representative from the vendor, key end users became facile enough at creating queries—from simply understanding how

to use measures to more sophisticated techniques such as time constraints and matching—to both appreciate the product's power and begin to proselytize its use.

One of the invaluable discoveries during training was the idea of documenting how to run a query inside the query itself, using the tool's "Notes" function. It had always been the District's vision that all end users—teachers, principals, coordinators—would use the data warehouse directly to answer their questions and inform their analyses; but many users are not trained to use the more powerful and, therefore, most informative, functions of the system. The technique of centrally creating shared queries for distributed use and documenting how to run them in the Notes accompanying each query provided the key to allowing novice users to retrieve expert results.

In the years that have followed, the District has continued to struggle with inevitable detours and occasional pitfalls (especially during a period of student information system conversion), but all of these have been in the context of a fully functional, well-used production system. End-user training in how to use shared queries is conducted through scheduled tutorials in district computer labs or as requested for an entire faculty at school locations. A training video has been produced and is accessible through the District intranet. And, frequently, principals, literacy coaches, teachers, or others with little time but a great need to know simply call the Office of Research, Assessment, and Accountability, which can run a quick query and return needed data within, literally, minutes.

Even though the journey toward acquiring a fully functional data warehouse that is used by people throughout the District had many bumps and turns, when we arrived at the destination, everyone believed it was worth the trip. Without question, the functionality of the data warehouse system has saved the District time and money and has resulted in better decision making about students and school and district processes.

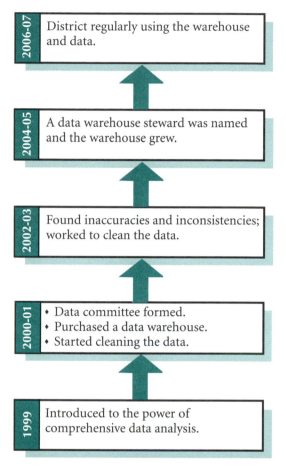

**The Columbia Public Schools Data Warehouse Timeline**

**2006-07** District regularly using the warehouse and data.

**2004-05** A data warehouse steward was named and the warehouse grew.

**2002-03** Found inaccuracies and inconsistencies; worked to clean the data.

**2000-01**
• Data committee formed.
• Purchased a data warehouse.
• Started cleaning the data.

**1999** Introduced to the power of comprehensive data analysis.

*Even though the journey toward acquiring a fully functional data warehouse that is used by people throughout the District had many bumps and turns, when we arrived at the destination, everyone believed it was worth the trip.*

# Northview Public Schools' Data Warehouse

Kathy Tokarek (ktokarek@nvps.net)
**Director of Technology**

*Located in Grand Rapids, Michigan, the Northview School District has a population of approximately 27,000 people. The District has a student enrollment of approximately 3,340 students in its seven schools—three elementary, two middle, and two high schools.*

In partnership with the Ball Foundation, a team comprised of teachers and administrators from Northview Public Schools visited Broward County School District in Florida in March, 2001, to begin learning about data warehousing. The Ball Foundation was interested in partnering with the District to research the questions, *How do we know students are learning (or not learning)? How will classroom accessibility to student data affect student achievement?* From that visit, Northview began looking at data-warehouse solutions. The evaluation team consisted of several teachers and administrators. In June, 2001, an agreement was signed with a vendor.

In August, the administrative staff, consisting of building principals, the superintendent, the curriculum director, and the technology director, met with the vendor staff for a Data Discovery meeting where decisions were made regarding the types of data to put in the warehouse. We were advised to keep it simple to start, and Northview chose some basic demographic, grading, and assessment information. From August to February, technology staff worked with the warehouse company to gather and upload data to the warehouse. It was much more difficult to gather historical data than was previously thought, especially in the student management program. Other problems were encountered: there were no common key fields such as student ID in the K-6 grading program, and the state standardized test kept changing formats on a yearly basis. When the warehouse was finally ready, there were a lot of "dirty data" to clean.

Between April 2002 and June 2003 staff training took place. Administrators were trained first, followed by key leaders in each building and, finally, all teachers. There were several obstacles: no one really seemed to understand the concept of a data warehouse; it seemed hard to use; no one knew what questions to ask; and there was not enough time to work with it. Some teachers did use it, but most just stayed away.

In the fall of 2003, North Central Association Commission on Accreditation and School Improvement (NCA CASI) accreditation was taking place, and Northview needed a way to credential students. Northview's programmer developed a program that pulled information from the data warehouse to easily show student history to teachers. The teachers thought it was easy to use and worked with it a lot. They began seeing the value of data. Their next request: bring historical as well as real-time data to each teacher in a simple program so each can see data on his or her own students. Teachers who want to dig further can go to the warehouse.

From those conversations, another inhouse program was developed called FLIGHTS *(First Look Information for Guiding, Helping, and Teaching Students)*. This program utilizes current data such as attendance and grading, as well as historical data, that are pulled from the data warehouse. This program is a tool used daily by teachers to gather the information they need to make instructional decisions for students with the ultimate goal of increasing student achievement.

Maureen Grey, former Director of Instruction, stated, "The data warehouse has been the catalyst tool for the professional learning community work in our District. It enables teachers, principals, and School Improvement Teams to answer the key question, *How do we know if students are learning?*"

FLIGHTS and the data warehouse pull relevant, meaningful, authentic data together for teachers at the classroom level. These spark teachers to:

▼ analyze demographic and outcome data;

▼ assess curriculum alignment;

▼ tailor interventions and classroom practices to impact student achievement; and

▼ engage in collaborative conversations about instruction.

Northview feels it has moved from being a good district to being a great district in terms of making data-driven instructional decisions that truly impact student achievement. Dr. Michael Stearns, Northview superintendent, states, "In the Northview Public Schools, there exists a commitment to use data to inform instructional practice and raise student achievement. The use of a data warehouse has enabled staff to achieve that goal. The more our teachers use data, the more data they request! Knowledge about their students makes teachers more able to deliver a customized instructional program."

Northview, along with the Ball Foundation, will continue to do research to measure the effectiveness of the use of data in making instructional decisions. Their vision to make the use of data drive instruction and solve problems has become second nature for teachers and administrators when making instructional changes.

**The Northview Public Schools
Data Warehouse Timeline**

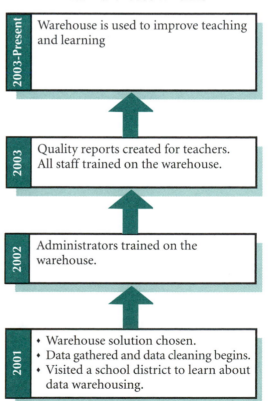

| 2003–Present | Warehouse is used to improve teaching and learning |

| 2003 | Quality reports created for teachers. All staff trained on the warehouse. |

| 2002 | Administrators trained on the warehouse. |

| 2001 | • Warehouse solution chosen. • Data gathered and data cleaning begins. • Visited a school district to learn about data warehousing. |

# San Jose Unified School District Warehouse

Marcy Lauck (marcy@lauckmail.com)

**Supervisor of the Continuous Improvement Program**

**Data Warehouse Manager**

*San Jose, California, the county seat of Santa Clara County, is the third largest city in California and the tenth largest city in the United States, with a population of approximately 894,950. Located 50 miles south of San Francisco, the city is in the heart of Silicon Valley. The San Jose Unified School District has an enrollment of approximately 32,000 students in its 52 schools—27 elementary schools (grades K-5), six middle schools (grades 6-8), eight high schools (grades 9-12), one alternative school, eight continuation schools, and two community day schools.*

In 1985, the San Jose Unified School District (SJUSD), in California, began implementing a comprehensive desegregation plan under a federal court order. The desegregation lawsuit, filed on behalf of Hispanic students, was based upon racial imbalance at schools in the north end of the District. Residential patterns, in conjunction with the unique geographical configuration of the District, had significantly contributed to the racial imbalance in the schools. SJUSD is 24 miles long and four miles wide, with the Hispanic population concentrated in the northern end of the District. In order to avoid mandatory busing desegregation plans, the District devised an innovative remedy—referred to as The Choice Plan—in which parents were granted a choice to select any school within the District. In order to assure that the choices had a positive desegregative impact, the District expended significant resources for strategic placement of educational enhancements (such as magnet programs), parent outreach, student recruitment, and staff training. With the advent of School Choice and the need to monitor progress on the desegregation order came an added emphasis on capturing more accurate and detailed information on students' demographic characteristics and academic performance. In 1986, for example, English learners comprised 14% of the District's enrollment. In 2005, they comprised 35% of the enrollment. Such changing demographics presented significant educational challenges. New enrollment processes helped the District identify and digitally capture critical characteristics such as students' ethnicity, language proficiency, and eligibility for participation in federally funded programs such as Title I. As a result, before accountability frameworks by the state Academic Performance Index (API) and federal Adequate Yearly Progress (AYP) became the norm, the District had done significant work to capture detailed, accurate information on students in its student information system. As the demographics of the District changed and schools began to implement innovative reforms, the need for comprehensive, site-based data analysis capabilities grew. Schools and teachers began requesting greater access and autonomy with respect to their data so that they could study the impact of their programs and processes on students' diverse needs.

A two-year data pilot with 16 volunteer schools began in 1998 and met with resounding success. In the post-pilot evaluation, 100% of participating schools said this kind of easy access to data was critical to their learning mission, and

100% said they needed more training on the technology tools and analysis skills to make effective use of data. The critical lesson learned from the pilot was that the District needed to centralize data sources and to standardize file formats so that all data could "talk" to other data. In 2000, data warehousing had moved into mainstream business practices, but it was not yet a significant part of the education landscape. A newly-entered company in the data warehouse market for education was introduced by Dr. Victoria L. Bernhardt of the Education for the Future Initiative. Its data-warehouse and data-analysis tools were a great match for the District's needs. Data needs and requirements had already been established during the pilot phase through extensive conversations with district and site administrators and teachers. In spring 2002, all district files were provided to the company and construction of the SJUSD data warehouse began. While extensive validation processes were occurring during the summer and fall with the District's technology services department, the District's cross-functional data-warehouse team was creating training and implementation plans and providing regular progress updates at monthly administrator meetings. Although the goal is to eventually provide desktop/dashboard access for the entire organization, initial training roll-out targeted administrators and site data teams. In spring 2003, training of 700 district administrators and site data teams was launched. Reviews were positive, but schools needed data refreshed more frequently than the planned six-week intervals. When the technology that would refresh core data every night became available, the District revised its contract and re-engineered its warehouse for the nightly uploading of data.

As uses of data grew and schools were identifying other data they needed to effectively assess and support their students, the District focused on several key vendors and data sources that would enable a more comprehensive picture of student learning. In 2003-04, the District added two products to provide benchmark testing capabilities. Both programs brought formative levels of assessments to augment the high stakes testing required by the California Department of Education and the U.S. Department of Education. Programs provide teachers with information on how students are progressing towards mastery of the standards they must meet to graduate to their next level of schooling. Although both formative assessment products have strong internal reporting capabilities on the data they each measure, the District wanted to have those data sources in the data warehouse to enable the kind of deep analyses regarding comparisons among state and formative assessments, assessments and students' grades, attendance patterns, program participation, course selection, teacher education, the impact of professional development on students' success rates, etc. Sophisticated "root cause" and cohort analyses that previously had

*The critical lesson learned from the pilot was that the District needed to centralize data sources and to standardize file formats so that all data could "talk" to other data.*

*SJUSD got into warehousing because with the advent of School Choice and the need to monitor progress on the desegration order came an added emphasis on capturing more accurate and detailed information on students' demographic characteristics and academic performance.*

been the domain of statisticians and researchers now became possible for schools to explore on their own with the use of the warehouse's data-analysis tools. The District's warehouse currently encompasses nine years of master schedules, attendance and discipline data, and information about every program in which students can be involved. Everything from gifted and talented programs to benchmark-test results and from state assessments of students' mastery of standards to their progress toward English-language proficiency is included. Other data in the warehouse include the number of community service hours high school students have completed toward their graduation requirement, data on students' grade level reading scores and numbers of books read, student progress by standard, and the California High School Exit Exam results. Even physical education data are included, as district physical education teachers look at the impact of students' overall physical fitness on their academic performance and engagement with school. The data warehouse now provides more than 300 SJUSD-specific standard queries that administrators and school data teams can click on to determine, for example, how students' Algebra I grades compared to the state's Algebra I test. Some standard queries help schools identify students who, with targeted support, are good candidates to become part of the AYP proficient band. With the confluence of all these data, site data teams are now able to know precisely with which standards students are struggling, what professional support teachers need to help them better meet students' needs, and how to determine which students need additional support.

With the upload of benchmark data into the warehouse in 2004-05, site leadership teams were able to look at how federal AYP student subgroups of Hispanic, low socio-economic status, and English learners were performing prior to the state test in May. At Horace Mann Elementary School, a Program Improvement School with 70% English learner, 70% Hispanic, and 70% low socio-economic status students, the school's leadership team was able to re-organize their instructional day based on never-before-possible data analyses. As a result, by the end of the last benchmark exam in English Language Arts, 100% of first graders, including those whose primary language was Spanish, scored proficient on the test. The school achieved a 63-point gain on the state's Academic Performance Index and ranked in the top 10 schools in Santa Clara County for greatest gains on the API. English learners at Horace Mann scored double the average of their peers at any other similar school in the District. As a result of its use of data, this school has now moved out of Program Improvement status. In the first months of 2005-06, teachers at Horace Mann had already identified each student's strengths and challenge areas and knew how to leverage existing resources to best support the school's continued progress to meet state and federal targets. Through the use of the data they pull from the warehouse, teachers are confident they can repeat and sustain the kinds of gains their students made in the past.

The District's Pioneer High School data team wanted to investigate the academic history of students getting Ds and Fs in Algebra I. Using the analysis tools of the data warehouse, the data team went back four and five years into students' academic records and found gaps. Analyses of these gaps led to some significant recommendations to supplement the middle school math curriculum. Use of the data warehouse in these ways puts power into the hands of schools and teachers to understand the impact of their work with students. Access to high-quality data and current work with continuous improvement strategies are bringing increased use of data districtwide. Several of the District's middle schools held "Data Days" in October 2005, during which staff used student achievement data from the warehouse to engage in thoughtful analyses of their overall academic program and to identify target students in each of their classes. As a "window" into the performance of all of their students, teachers gauge their target students' progress on district benchmarks to determine areas for reinstruction.

Since August 2005, hits on the data-warehouse site have averaged about 200,000 per month, with approximately 700 visitors. The warehouse currently holds nine years of longitudinal data and houses over 20 million records. With the advent of new human resources and financial systems in 2006-07 and a new student information system planned for 2008, the centralization of data has become increasingly important to measure progress toward the District's strategic goals. In 2004-05, SJUSD's Academic Performance Index grew by 23 points. The District narrowly missed its AYP targets for English learners and students with disabilities. In the case of SJUSD, early results prove how access to data can support systemic improvement and indicate that data warehousing and analysis technologies are showing great promise as the leverage this urban district needs to meet rigorous state and federal requirements.

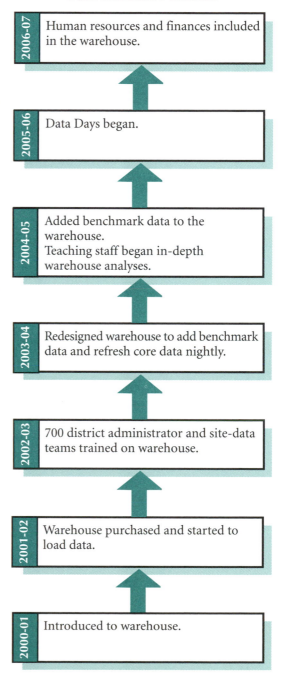

**The San Jose Unified School District Data Warehouse Timeline**

**2006-07** Human resources and finances included in the warehouse.

**2005-06** Data Days began.

**2004-05** Added benchmark data to the warehouse.
Teaching staff began in-depth warehouse analyses.

**2003-04** Redesigned warehouse to add benchmark data and refresh core data nightly.

**2002-03** 700 district administrator and site-data teams trained on warehouse.

**2001-02** Warehouse purchased and started to load data.

**2000-01** Introduced to warehouse.

# Tyler Independent School District Warehouse

**Dr. Karen Raney (karen.raney@tylerisd.org)**
**Director of Secondary Education**

In 2002, the Tyler Independent School District (TISD), in Texas, hired a new superintendent, and the District began implementing plans to improve community perceptions of the school district. A successful bond proposal had not been passed in the District since 1984, and that one was for maintenance only, with no new construction. A pervasive belief existed among community and business leaders that the school district was poorly managed financially and student achievement was average. A growing system of private schools in the area was changing district demographics as families moved from Tyler's changing urban district to small surrounding districts and private schools. The new superintendent quickly set two goals for Tyler ISD: exemplary student achievement and fiscal effectiveness and efficiency.

District leadership understood that accurate data, properly analyzed, evaluated, and reported in a continuous cycle, would enhance efficiency and effectiveness in school system operations. In an environment of limited resources, the state legislators talked about allocating school funds according to statistical effectiveness. In order to demonstrate their effectiveness, school districts would need to produce measurable results in terms of industry standards in all areas of operations. Very few districts in the state were measuring anything except student performance.

The state of Texas uses two established performance measures for schools: the Academic Excellence Indicator System (AEIS) and the Financial Integrity Rating System of Texas (FIRST). AEIS measures student performance on state assessments, attendance, completion rate, and passing rates for advanced placement tests and college entrance exams. FIRST measures the financial effectiveness of school districts.

During 2002-03, TISD established a district software evaluation committee to find a new student information management system. The committee did not find a system that could replicate the many custom reports that district programmers were currently writing. One committee member attended training on *The School Portfolio Toolkit* with Dr. Victoria Bernhardt, Executive Director of Education for the Future Initiative, and was introduced to the idea of a data warehouse. As a result, the committee turned its focus from student management systems to data-warehouse products. The committee found that

> *District leadership understood that accurate data, properly analyzed, evaluated, and reported in a continuous cycle, would enhance efficiency and effectiveness in school system operations.*

some warehouse products were limited in reporting, some were very expensive, and some had limited or no school experience. The evaluation committee eventually discovered a warehouse that had the most flexibility for the price, with a strong focus on what schools needed.

The 2003-04 school year was dedicated to building the first warehouse and to training the first users. Because of the District's need for data to support an aggressive campaign to change community perception, a decision was made to create a warehouse that would provide data on demand, updating every night from the district information management system. By spring, multiple training sessions were offered for principals and central office staff to be introduced to a data-analyzer-tool suite, the warehouse attributes, and how to perform basic queries.

Technical difficulties interrupted some sessions, and participants began to see "dirty data." The unlimited potential for the warehouse to provide data to help improve student achievement and fiscal accountability was immediately evident; but the realities of operating schools on a daily basis overwhelmed staff, and they were discouraged that the warehouse didn't provide quick and easy answers. The challenge would be to turn the data into information that could inform decisions.

By the summer of 2004, users were seeing the potential in the warehouse; but they still had limited time to learn how to use it. Most principals had been trained in the use of *The School Portfolio Toolkit* (Bernhardt, 2002), so Dr. Bernhardt returned to Tyler to help principals assimilate data in a framework that would help principals tell the stories of their schools. What was not anticipated was the difficulty that administrators experienced with the queries and the cut and paste skills required to create data profiles. Evenings were spent running standard queries to reduce the frustration level and move the project along. To provide continuity in the learning process, Dr. Bernhardt was invited to return to Tyler in the fall.

While principals worked on school portfolios and learned to look at student data, a financial task force was at work to improve the District's reputation in terms of financial accountability. The task force contracted with a firm to help the District establish performance measures for the non-instructional operations such as transportation, food service, human resources, accounting, and facilities operations. The consulting firm stressed to each central office director the importance of "owning the data." As data were compiled for these operations, district administrators learned that the data are only as accurate as

*Tyler, Texas, is the largest community in East Texas, with a population of approximately 101,000. Located 90 miles east of Dallas/Fort Worth and 90 miles west of Shreveport, Louisiana, Tyler is the home of Tyler Junior College and the University of Texas at Tyler. The Tyler Independent School District has a student enrollment of approximately 17,480 in its schools— 16 elementary schools, six middle schools, two high schools, one alternative school, one center for exceptional programs, one Head Start school, and one outdoor education program.*

*The consulting firm stressed to each central office director the importance of "owning the data." As data were compiled for these operations, district administrators learned that the data are only as accurate as the source.*

*District staff began to question processes for recording attendance, identifying special program students, and entering achievement data in the information management system. But even with all of the questions, administrators were experiencing the value of having data over time. For the first time, campus and district portfolio data were used to drive enrollment studies over time to better inform staffing projections.*

the source. Most directors had relied on technology department staff members to run data reports from the information management system. But data differed greatly depending on who ran what report and on which date the data were gathered.

As principals continued work on the school portfolios, the same questions arose: *Where did these data come from? What if the data are not correct? How do we fix the errors? Can we all agree on one source (place) to collect data at one standard time?* As answers to these questions were determined, it further became evident that there was a need for data elements or attributes in the warehouse that were currently not defined. Collection time was also determined to be a critical issue. So warehouse consultants returned in the fall of 2004 to identify new warehouse elements, and the role of "warehouse manager" began to be better defined.

As district administrators became more effective data users, more questions were raised. Presentations for the Board of Trustees on the performance measures for non-instructional operations uncovered more "data source" issues. Continuing portfolio training uncovered more "data integrity" issues. District staff began to question processes for recording attendance, identifying special program students, and entering achievement data in the information management system. But even with all of the questions, administrators were experiencing the value of having data over time. For the first time, campus and district portfolio data were used to drive enrollment studies over time to better inform staffing projections.

All of the data questions drove the District to begin to audit processes for attendance, scheduling, grading, and human resources. Central office staff and principals were asking the same kinds of questions about district data and their sources. Campus administration and human resources helped other departments to understand the Public Education Information Management System (PEIMS), the state's information management system. All required district data are submitted to the state at specified times during the year. Student achievement data and attendance data are aggregated and published in the AEIS report each fall reflecting school data from the previous year. Districts use these data to compare enrollment, staff ratios, attendance, and student performance year-to-year.

The root of the District's data questions seemed to be related to time. Using data on demand from the warehouse caused a replication problem. If PEIMS was the standard against which annual comparisons were made, "live" data from the warehouse did not provide accurate comparisons unless staff remembered to pull the next year's data on exactly the same date each year. That standard already existed in PEIMS. The need for an additional warehouse became apparent—one that was static and bound by time. February 2005 saw the development of the District's PEIMS warehouse.

Now the District would have the benefit of live data to monitor daily processes such as enrollment and attendance, as well as a warehouse that would preserve annual state data and make the data accessible for comparisons with other information within the District, especially financial data. Dr. Bernhardt returned to the District in the spring of 2005 to help the District design standard queries for the district portfolio based on the new PEIMS warehouse.

During the 2005-06 school year, the "warehouse manager" position continued to develop. This person now has loaded a multitude of standard queries that district staff can access. Program directors work with the warehouse manager to design queries for needed data. District technology trainers incorporate the data warehouse in leadership and capacity-building institutes to promote data-driven campus decisions.

The District's greatest challenge at present is how to increase warehouse usage, a problem that is being explored with the data warehouse company. A new "data dashboard" may provide daily access to relevant data to classroom teachers along with student profiles for each student enrolled.

Starting from a premise of using data to improve problematic perceptions of the school district, Tyler ISD created a data warehouse that has evolved into a data management system that has taken into account all aspects of data work and continues to expand in effectiveness and usefulness.

Making different district leaders "owners of the data" alleviated some of the challenges of clean data. Having the support of district instructional leadership contributed to the usefulness of the data warehouse to schools.

> *Program directors work with the warehouse manager to design queries for needed data. District technology trainers incorporate the data warehouse in leadership and capacity-building institutes to promote data-driven campus decisions.*

**The Tyler Independent School District Data Warehouse Timeline**

**2005-06**
- Warehouse manager creates standard queries for schools.
- Warehouse is used throughout the district.

**2004-05**
- New elements added to the warehouse.
- Warehouse manager role identified.
- Additional warehouse was developed.

**2003-04**
- First build of the warehouse and training.
- Trained all principals on the warehouse.
- "Dirty Data" discovered.

**2002-03**
- New Superintendent.
- Committee formed to look for a new student information system.
- Changed thinking to look for data warehouse.
- Purchased a data warehouse.

# The Connecticut Experience with Data Warehousing

Andrea Hartman (ahartman@aces.k12.ct.us)

Data Services Coordinator

Area Cooperative Educational Services (ACES)

*With a population of approximately 3,547,800, Connecticut ranks 29th among the states by population. Student enrollment is approximately 577,390 in its 1,103 elementary and secondary schools.*

The Connecticut Data Warehouse (CTDW) Initiative began in late 2002 as a project of the Connecticut Alliance of Regional Educational Service Center (RESC). RESCs are not-for-profit agencies that provide a variety of educational services to school districts. Connecticut has six RESCs, each covering a specific geographical area.

Once a decision was made by the RESCs to provide a statewide data warehouse to Connecticut districts, the first step in moving toward the availability of the warehouse involved a review of several data-warehouse vendors. The agreement with the selected vendor called for a Connecticut–specific data warehouse that would be hosted in Connecticut by the RESCs. The RESCs would also be responsible for performing data conversions and loading, training of district personnel, and management of individual district projects.

Once the vendor agreement was finalized, the RESCs held preliminary regional informational sessions with Connecticut districts designed to inform them about the initiative, inquire about possible offerings, and provide suggestions for the structure of the warehouse. The intention of these meetings was to engage the districts and to begin building a client base for the project. With over 40% of the Connecticut districts participating in these meetings, it was an exciting and productive time for everyone. The districts who attended were eager to get started on the project.

In order to build upon the preliminary meetings, districts participated in additional planning meetings that would actually define the Connecticut warehouse data model. In an effort to make these meetings possible, the RESCs and the vendor offered several regional sessions to which they invited administrators, technology coordinators, curriculum specialists, and other district personnel. The agenda for these meetings included details of the typical data structure and time to discuss specific Connecticut needs. These discussions included any data element that a district could potentially use, as we were building a single data model to fit all districts. Initially, there were 14 objects, 110 student attributes, 40 staff attributes, 2 tests, and more than 30 attributes with the remaining objects. Based upon the momentum from the regional sessions, districts were eager to begin their involvement in the project, with 13 districts signing contracts to begin immediately.

As the data model was being finalized with the districts, the RESCs were brainstorming and planning for implementation, training, and overall project management. This process involved defining a team of technicians who would do the actual data imports, conversions, and loading of the data; the trainers who would be offering professional development; and the project leaders who would manage the overall project.

The team of technicians attended a two-week training course at the vendor's headquarters to learn the tools needed to host the warehouse and perform the loading of the data independently. During this training, the technicians started building actual warehouses for the initial 13 districts.

The trainer team consisted of educational specialists from the 6 RESCs, each of which would be responsible for providing professional development services within its region.

*The Connecticut data warehouse now includes over 130 distinct objects, including over 100 district benchmarks and 10 standardized assessments; more than 120 student attributes; 50 staff attributes; and 40 attributes in the other non-test objects.*

During this planning stage, it was determined that one RESC (ACES) would be primarily responsible for technical project management while another RESC (EASTCONN) would be primarily responsible for overall project and professional-development management. The RESCs then formed a Steering Committee to guide the direction and implementation of the project. The Steering Committee consisted of the decision makers on the RESC level. This Committee also formed a District Advisory Board that consisted of district personnel ranging from data specialists to school administrators. The primary purpose of the Advisory Board was to help guide the direction of the project from the district perspective.

With the help of the vendor, the original 13 data warehouses were built and released to the participating districts in the spring of 2003. After the release of data warehouses to the first 13 districts, the RESCs were solely responsible for building, loading, and implementing of all other participating districts, with the vendor playing a supporting role. Over the course of the project, the RESCs have built over 70 data warehouses which include student, staff, course-grade, and assessment/benchmark data.

*Over the course of the project, the RESCs have built over 70 data warehouses, including student, staff, course-grade, and assessment/benchmark data.*

Funding for the project comes directly from district participation and requires a contract for services. During the first two years, numerous districts paid their participation costs with grant monies. These grants contributed up to 50% of the participation costs for two years. Districts who contract to participate in CTDW receive data services for loading of the data, limited professional development days, and user-group participation. Additional professional development services and user conferences are available at additional costs.

## Project Challenges

Since the project was implemented and managed on two levels (district and RESC), there were many challenges for this project. Some of these challenges are outlined below.

### District Resources

Once districts selected to participate in the CTDW Initiative, they were responsible for forming data teams, selecting the data for uploads, scheduling uploads, and implementing the project internally in the districts.

Typically, a technology coordinator or data specialist was in charge of the project and selected the data to be uploaded. Unfortunately, some districts began uploading data quickly, using a minimum set of student demographic data and some test scores, without doing some of the essential data team work, planning, and brainstorming. As a result, the technology staffs found it difficult to manage the project, upload the data, cleanse the data, and still continue to do their regular tasks, especially without clear and defined planning. In contrast, the districts that were successful had a champion within the district who helped coordinate, plan, and implement the CTDW project within a school improvement context and who worked closely with the technology team to move forward.

### Data

After districts uploaded data, the RESC Technology Team began processing the data for loading into the warehouse. During this processing, many data issues were found, such as duplicate student codes or teacher codes, and/or changing student codes over time and across schools within a district. During the data review, the RESC Technology Team often found invalid data, such as differences in value representation, inaccurate values, and/or missing values. As an example of differences in value representation, one school used "4" to represent "Asian" for ethnicity, and another school in the same district used "4" to represent "Caucasian." Inaccurate values included the use of "AAA" in the primary disability field, when "AAA" did not match a real disability within the district. And sometimes, data would actually be missing from the field.

In essence, many districts had "dirty data" and were required to perform data cleansing. Since the code issues and invalid values affected the data displayed for analysis, it was important to require districts to perform this data cleansing. The existence of dirty data requiring cleansing was unexpected by both the districts and the RESCs and required many resources to remedy.

### Pricing

Since district participation in the CTDW Initiative was not required, RESCs were required to offer a cost-effective package for all districts in Connecticut. In an effort to make the initiative affordable, the participation fee was kept very low. This, in effect, limited the number of RESC resources that were available for training and project management.

### Professional Development

Various training sessions, such as topics covering the upload process, the data-discovery process, tool usage, and data cleansing, were offered to districts. Many times these sessions were offered on demonstration data prior to a full implementation of district data. Although district participation in these trainings was high and included administrators, technology staff, and curriculum specialists, the skills learned while using demonstration data did not transfer well to a district implementation. In an effort to meet the district requests for using district data, the trainers began using actual district data to conduct trainings. While it was a common request of districts to move to a training model that used district data, trainers sometimes found it more difficult to implement. The RESCs found that the major weaknesses of conducting training on district data were twofold:

1. Trainees spent time reviewing the data rather than acquiring specific skills (focusing their time on review of data rather than the training).

2. District warehouses were minimally populated.

Districts had not uploaded enough data elements into the warehouse to make a training session meaningful. That is, a district may have only uploaded student demographic data, but not any standard assessments or district benchmarks. With limited data available in the warehouse, districts were unable to build effective queries during training.

We also found that districts did not always know how to analyze the data. Once they learned how to use the tool, they did not always know what questions to ask or what queries to build. As the warehouse tool allows users to ask almost any question, users can find it difficult to get started if they have no question in mind. Based on this knowledge, the RESCs began offering professional development sessions on data analysis to help build capacity within the districts.

### Overall Project

The amount of resources, training, and project management required to implement the project exceeded original expectations. We found that the RESCs fell short by not providing more specific guidance to districts. With the knowledge that the RESCs have now, a more structured approach is being offered that includes training and guidance from project initiation to implementation. This new model includes training on forming data teams, building essential questions, analyzing data, implementing the data warehouse, and tool training. It focuses more on the process of data-driven decision making than on using the tool.

## Project Successes

Project successes have occurred on both the RESC and district level as summarized below.

### RESCs

The RESCs offer a data conference to Connecticut districts and other regional schools on an annual basis. This conference has included well-known guest speakers, group forums, and breakout sessions on data analysis, data-warehouse planning, and tool usage. Over the course of the past three years, participation in the conference has doubled and includes participants from Massachusetts, Rhode Island, and Vermont.

Beginning in the fall of 2006, the RESCs offered the first two-day CTDW Academy to Connecticut districts. This Academy focused on providing specific skills necessary to utilize the school improvement process along with data warehousing. Participation in the event was greater than expected and helped build capacity within the districts by focusing on a process that uses data analysis techniques to answer essential questions, identify underlying causes, and select effective strategies for improvement.

### District

As one of the original 13 participants in the CTDW project, the East Haven School District has been through the planning sessions, the first data warehouse build, training, and "dirty" data. The District has seen it all and persisted through the difficulties and struggles to build success.

Initially, some of the struggles and/or difficulties East Haven encountered included "dirty" data, disparate data, and/or no data. After collaborating with the RESCs to locate dirty data, the East Haven technical staff members worked hard at cleansing the data at its source. This meant they had to write and implement data entry guidelines, alter the ways data were stored, and update incorrect data. Not only did they improve their data submissions for the warehouse, they improved their ability to analyze data accurately within the data warehouse and in their student management system.

After thoughtful planning and coordination, East Haven began evaluating data sources and where data were stored. Based upon its findings, the District changed the way it was tracking data, especially demographic data and, most importantly, test data. They developed spreadsheets and data-entry methods for teachers to get the data into a format that could be easily imported into their student information system and the data warehouse. This process also allowed East Haven to develop new sources of data, such as district benchmarks, that were previously stored on paper.

While working on all of the technical aspects of cleansing the data, implementing data-entry techniques, and adding data sources, East Haven was also building upon the data culture within the District. The District began holding regular data planning meetings with participants including technicians, teachers, and administrators. The meetings were held on a regular basis and included data-team updates and specific trainings by the RESCs on team building, analysis of data, and project planning.

Although the use of data from the data warehouse has not yet begun to directly impact instructional strategies and/or student learning on a regular basis, the districts continue to make strides toward this goal. They have been able to make these strides by building upon the data culture, planning for the use of data, and implementing changes within the districts.

## Connecticut Summary

Based upon the experience of the CTDW Initiative, I believe the following are keys to success:

- ▼ Identify a willing project champion
- ▼ Build a good foundation by forming district and school-level data teams
- ▼ Plan, brainstorm, and plan again
- ▼ Form and/or learn how to form questions for data queries
- ▼ Incorporate a data culture
- ▼ Provide project management

**The Connecticut Data Warehouse Timeline**

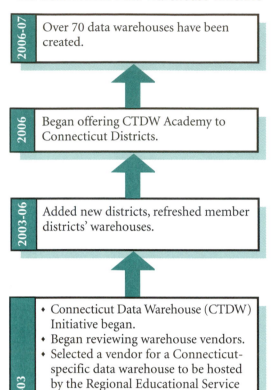

**2006-07** Over 70 data warehouses have been created.

**2006** Began offering CTDW Academy to Connecticut Districts.

**2003-06** Added new districts, refreshed member districts' warehouses.

**2002-03**
- Connecticut Data Warehouse (CTDW) Initiative began.
- Began reviewing warehouse vendors.
- Selected a vendor for a Connecticut-specific data warehouse to be hosted by the Regional Educational Service Centers.
- Held regional information sessions with 40% of Connecticut Districts.
- Vendor met with districts and RESCs to determine data model.
- Thirteen (13) initial district warehouses were created.

Without any one of these, the project can become dependent on one person and/or will not be utilized to its full potential. I believe setting valid and achievable goals and expectations early in the project will help districts find small successes along the way. These small successes should help facilitate further planning, questions, and involvement.

Even with the best technical staff, education specialists, and administrators, the implementation of a data warehouse will not be effective without commitment, collaboration, and planning.

*Note:* Information and feedback regarding the East Haven portion of this article was supplied by Randel Osborne (Districtwide Technology Specialist), Jim Pompano (Technology Consultant), Matt Ullring (Districtwide Technology Specialist), and Frank Meoli (Director of Technology and Curriculum).

# Vermont Data Consortium

Diane Lemieux (dhlemieux@yahoo.com)

Associate Principal, St. Albans Town Education Center

Technology Coordinator, Franklin Central Supervisory Union

Founding Member, Board Representative, and Past President of
Vermont Data Consortium

## History

In the fall of 2002, Franklin Central Supervisory Union (FCSU) in Vermont began investigating data warehousing as a means to improve student performance. At that time, FCSU had approximately 1,200 students. The SU had begun to realize that the increasing mountains of data accumulating could be used much more effectively if they could be accessed in an efficient manner. All schools in Vermont have been engaged in writing Action Plans based on a variety of data. Meaningful, timely, and accurate data that could be analyzed became a crucial part of this process. Data are used to understand student performance, set targets for improvement, and to assess the value of programs, initiatives, professional development, and interventions.

## Data Warehouse Review

FCSU began researching vendors that claimed to provide data warehouse capabilities. The research revealed significant differences between solutions. The SU was looking for a solution that would allow the user to define what data and fields could be used, as well as provide unlimited capacity and relational capability, along with numerous other criteria.

## Birth of the Vermont Data Consortium

After reviewing the results of the research, the FCSU selected one vendor to present a demonstration. An invitation was distributed to Vermont's collaborative, tight-knit technology community, and a group of twenty educators attended the session. Excitement spread, and additional demos were scheduled in different areas of the state. In May 2003, a dedicated group of fifteen supervisory unions formalized their intention to build a data warehouse together by forming the Vermont Data Consortium (VDC). The group's goal at that time was to have a membership that represented 20,000 students, or 20% of Vermont's students. The Consortium became a legal entity in the fall of 2003.

*With a population of approximately 623,000, Vermont ranks 49th among the states by population. Enrollment in the public schools is approximately 98,300 students among the 392 elementary and secondary schools in the state.*

*Data are used to understand student performance, to set targets for improvement, and to assess the value of programs, initiatives, professional development, and interventions.*

## VDC Takes on a Partner

The VDC worked for several months toward its goals. In the spring of 2004, a new Commissioner of Education came on board. He was both experienced in and supportive of data warehousing and approached the VDC about creating a partnership between the Vermont Department of Education (VT DOE) and the schools in the field to build a data warehouse together. The VDC and the VT DOE met to discuss the mutual goals of the partnership, which were efficiency, effectiveness, improving teaching and learning, and support of each other. The VT DOE also wanted to improve its own data collection and analysis processes.

A Memo of Understanding was developed in July 2004 that would guide our partnership and working relationship. The Commissioner made the data warehouse one of his top priorities. We were very pleased to embark upon this partnership that would enhance each partner's capacity to improve student performance through data collection and analysis. The Memo of Understanding covered issues such as cost sharing, minimum staffing requirements, viability of the VDC, communication, project planning, decision making, conflict resolution, policy development, and responsibilities of each organization. The VT DOE agreed to provide the infrastructure for the Educational Data Warehouse (EDW), including a project manager, other staff, hardware, a data dictionary for state data, support for state data to be loaded into the warehouse, and the purchase of the software license. The VDC agreed to provide a field advisory group (VDC Board of Directors), a minimum of two staff, responsibility for loading local data into the EDW, a data dictionary for local data, testing and pilot use of the initial EDW, contribution toward software licenses, professional development, policy development, and tech support to the field.

## Vendor Selection

While the advent of the partnership had many benefits, it also had some drawbacks. The size of the project grew, and the project was revised for 100,000 students. This meant that we had to formalize our bid process and meet state requirements for securing a contract with a software vendor. These new requirements ultimately resulted in a year's delay in our timeline. The VT DOE project manager led a thorough Request for Proposals (RFP) process that resulted in a signed contract with the selected vendor in January 2005, roughly two years after our initial contact. The process included two rounds of RFPs, a vendor showcase, and a hands-on trial period with broad-based field and VT DOE representation and rigorous rating scales, followed by an independent review and state approval process. The selection process allowed input from educators in the field such as teachers, curriculum coordinators, administrators, and technology staffs, and employees from the VT DOE such as human services, education, and information technology staff members. The VDC Board of Directors and VT DOE Project Manager asked for volunteers and recruited raters to round out the group by position. A broad-based selection process was central to VDC goals of including all of our stakeholders in this venture. The list of key indicators below outlines the direction of our first few years (many other resources can be found on our website: *http://vermontdata.org/*):

### Key Indicators for Our Goals:

1.1 Establishment of a centralized data warehouse containing members' federal, state, and local data including student demographics, student assessments, teacher, classroom, and other school information.

1.2 Development of an agreement with vendors in order to secure a data warehouse and analysis tools.

1.3 Collaborative work with the state of Vermont and other organizations to identify essential fields and federal and state data opportunities and reporting requirements.

1.4 Design of a data management system that allows users to investigate the smallest unit (the student or teacher), provides a global perspective, and allows for longitudinal study of information.

1.5 Data accessible via a client or browser to all stakeholders: district and school-level administration, teachers, students, and parents.

2.1 A train-the-trainer model to disseminate warehouse data-analysis methodology and best practices.

2.2 Opportunities for consortium members to enhance their knowledge of data collection and analysis as they apply to the school-improvement process.

3.1 Establishment of a model and building a core group of members.

3.2 Adoption of a multi-year plan for data design, development, installation, and training.

## Building Vermont's Data Warehouse

During 2005, data-warehouse engineers built our EDW with the help of our combined Project Team. The Project Team worked on building, testing, and maintaining the EDW. Dedication, communication, hard work, and problem solving from both sides of the partnership helped us resolve issues that arose during this complex and challenging year. Some of the challenges that we faced were delays to the timeline, product delivery, maintaining viability of the VDC, and communication. The VDC managed the creative tension of recruiting and pleasing sufficient members to meet its financial obligations while writing and implementing grants, providing professional development, and building the EDW. The biggest challenge was being responsive to the constantly changing needs of the growing organization, as well as to the newly created EDW. During this year, student membership passed 50,000. When misunderstandings occurred among the partners, they were addressed with increased face-to-face meetings and conference calls, clarification of roles and responsibilities, and the broadening of the decision-making group. The VDC staff responsibilities also changed during 2005. We designated some staff as local data-support staff to work on local data and professional development and other staff to work on building the EDW. We found that we needed to specialize in order to meet all of our needs.

## VDC Growth

The VDC Board was comprised of a representative from each member supervisory union or district. As the board grew, the Executive Committee of this board made decisions for the organization, while the Project Team made day-to-day EDW decisions. Throughout this process, the volunteer VDC Board functioned as a working board, doing whatever was needed to accomplish the mission. Since most of the Board members were already working full time, this proved challenging but ultimately successful, since members' superintendents all supported the goals of the VDC. In July of 2005, the VDC moved into its first office, close to the VT DOE offices.

## VDC Funding

The VDC is funded through partnership agreements with its members. The first year of operation was spent in research and development, with costs being paid for by the first-year members. Each ensuing member also pays this same fee when it joins, as its contribution towards these costs. Each year, projections are made, budgets are created, and per-student fees are set. While affordability was a factor in selecting a vendor, it was only one of several factors that were considered. One of the most important criteria that was considered, aside from the technical aspects of the software, was the ability of the vendor to be responsive to our needs, work with us, and be creatively flexible. We never wavered from our vision about our goals for the data warehouse. That being said, we did balance the costs that our members could or would bear, the

> *While affordability was a factor in selecting a vendor, it was only one of several factors that were considered. One of the most important criteria that was considered, aside from the technical aspects of the software, was the ability of the vendor to be responsive to our needs, work with us, and be creatively flexible. We never wavered from our vision about our goals for the data warehouse.*

staffing needed to accomplish the job, and the timeline for delivery of a functional warehouse. In that same vein, we also selected an initial common data model for each local warehouse to enable us to provide local data in a timely manner.

## Data Warehouse Goes Live!

After testing and acceptance, the VT EDW went live on October 13, 2005. After the initial glee and benefits of easy access to the state data about our students, we found ourselves thirsting for more local data about our students, our staffs, our programs, and our assessments. State assessments for recent years and student demographic information were in the warehouse. In addition to our state warehouse, we would all need to have a local warehouse so we could analyze the relationships between these data sets. This need raised the issue of clean data for all of us. What were clean data, how did you collect them, and how did you ensure that all data were clean? This learning process has taken additional time, but guaranteed that the data that get into the warehouse will be reliable.

## Professional Development

We selected a train-the-trainer implementation option. Each VDC Board member and selected VT DOE staff were trained by the warehouse company in July 2005. Our job as trainers was to go back to our SU/district and develop a training plan and timeline, deciding who would be trained, when, and at what level. After that, each school would have its own trainers, who would provide the training in its building. The SU trainer decides what level of access each user will have to the warehouse. Each user receives a password, which can be used to access the EDW from anywhere. VDC staff is responsible for maintaining user accounts and providing access. The VDC staff also provides ongoing professional development to VDC members and VT DOE staff as more users begin to fully access the EDW.

## Challenges

Continued challenges for the project are timelines for building the local data warehouse and data refreshes, simplifying use of the analysis tool through standard reports and tools, which we expect most teachers will use, and rolling out the professional development for using the EDW and for learning how to use data for school improvement. At the same time, we are still taking on new members, working toward our goal of representing all of Vermont's students.

## Current Status

By the summer of 2006, the VDC had added an additional data analyst to help build the local data warehouses and an Executive Director to manage the work of the organization. EDW use varies from SU to SU depending on the level of training they have had and the degree to which they are using state data versus local data. Action Planning Teams are accessing the warehouse to analyze their recent data and inform improvement plans and program decisions. Some supervisory unions are waiting until the New England Common Assessment Program (NECAP) data are available or until their local data are loaded. Some administrative teams are committing to bringing data to their meetings to discuss a common focus area.

## Successes

The Vermont Data Consortium and the Vermont Department of Education are very pleased with the progress of the Vermont Educational Data Warehouse to date. The EDW has the capacity and flexibility we planned for. We are able to perform complex statistical queries in seconds instead of hours and days. Our members can use their data more efficiently, relating numerous data sets over periods of time. The VDC Board and staff, VT DOE Project Manager, and combined Project Team have collaborated to make this a successful venture. To those of you considering going down this road, I offer this advice: *Get ready to learn and enjoy the ride!*

**The Vermont Data Consortium
Warehouse Timeline**

**2006-07**
4.0 staff, including Executive Director.

**2005-06**
- 50,000 students.
- 2.3 staff.
- Grant-funded professional development.
- First local warehouses built.

**2004-05**
- VDC grows.
- Memorandum of Understanding (MOU) signed with Vermont Department of Education (VT DOE); July.
- 1.3 staff.
- Grant-funded professional development.
- Educational Data Warehouse (EDW) goes live; October 13.

**2003-04**
- VDC grows.
- Commissioner buys in; May 2004.
- VT DOE hires Project Manager; June 2004.

**2002-03**
- Franklin Central Supervisory Union (FCSU) research.
- Data warehouse software demos.
- Grassroots support builds.
- VDC formed; May 2003.
- 15,000 students.

## Summary

As you can read from the examples in this chapter, each one of these entities had a very good reason for beginning the data-warehouse journey. Each had a vision that focused on improving teaching and learning, and each understood that such improvements needed to have data to support their findings. Each organization wanted to perform longitudinal analyses, disaggregate its data by student groups and processes, view ongoing assessment results, understand the relationship of ongoing assessments to the high-stakes assessments, and evaluate programs. *How can we improve if we don't know where we are?* is a common theme echoed throughout their experiences. From a small district with three schools, to a district in the tenth largest city in the United States, to a state consortium, each entity had to go through growing pains to make the effort work. It took each district/consortium anywhere from three to eight years to get its data warehouse fully operational. All entities struggled with "dirty data," which set their timing back. The successful use of the warehouse ultimately came from someone in the district office "owning" each piece of data to ensure the integrity of any results and a champion of the potential uses of the warehouse. The champions turned out to be the people with the biggest reasons to use and lead the data warehouse to improve teaching and learning—the curriculum/instruction/assessment directors.

> *"How can we improve if we don't know where we are?" is a common theme echoed throughout the experiences of all five school districts.*

CHAPTER **14**

# ISSUES AND RECOMMENDATIONS REGARDING SUCCESSFUL USE OF A DATA WAREHOUSE

Acquiring a data warehouse and establishing a data culture to use data to improve teaching and learning is hard work, sometimes taking multiple years to do it all right. One can decrease the challenges by thinking through all the elements up front. Many of the elements have been mentioned in the preceding chapters. Many of the main issues and recommendations about the data warehouse are described below.

## Issues and Recommendations: Setting Up the Data Warehouse

Many school districts are unhappy after they purchase their data warehouse because they think it should be easier than it is to set up. Again, a data warehouse is a complex tool that requires engineering and a deep understanding of all the data.

Once you commit to buying a data warehouse, the hard work begins. The work is hard whether or not you are prepared. The work will be a little easier if you start getting ready for the warehouse far in advance. Below are some of the issues that surface when school districts purchase their first data warehouse.

> **Issue #1:** *Most school districts are shocked by how long it takes to put a data warehouse together.* Yes, the importing of your disparate data files will take time because of the sheer volume of the data and the complexity of the system. Parts of most data warehouses end up being reprocessed more than once because of needed corrections. Additionally, testing the warehouse could take a couple of weeks. However, that is not what takes the longest time.

*Once you commit to buying a data warehouse, the hard work begins. The work is hard whether or not you are prepared.*

If you have not had to clean your data before, believe me, they are dirty! By dirty, I mean that there might not be a consistent and unique identification number for each student and teacher, and that names might have been entered into each data file in different fashions, which could count the same person as multiple people (e.g., Victoria L. Bernhardt, Victoria Bernhardt, Vickie Bernhardt, Vickie L. Bernhardt, V. L. Bernhardt, V. Bernhardt could show up as six different people). You might also find missing data, invalid codes, and no scheduling information that would allow for the linkage of students to teachers. These issues make the "cleaning up" of the data labor intensive and time consuming. If you are in a large school district, expect it to take a year to clean up your data—sometimes longer. There are programs that data warehouse companies can run to help you with the cleansing of your data; but, by and large, it comes down to someone checking the records in every file and developing a system of consistent data entry and monitoring.

> *There are programs that data warehouse companies can run to help you with the cleansing of your data; but, by and large, it comes down to someone checking the records in every file, and developing a system of consistent data entry and monitoring.*

**Issue #2:** *Many districts are disappointed at not being able to get the information they want out of their warehouse, in the format they want.* This is usually a result of missing data. Sometimes districts think they sent to the warehouse company lots of good clean data in usable formats, when, in reality, the data were incomplete and in hard-to-use formats. Corrupted backups and missing pieces of data are usually the culprits. Districts are also often disappointed to find that their student information systems may not permit the easy export of data they anticipated, or that they made poor choices years ago in deciding how their data were to be organized. Another reason districts are disappointed with not being able to get the information they want out of their warehouses is their lack of familiarity with the data in the warehouse and their status as beginning users of the data analysis tool.

**Issue #3:** *Some districts are disappointed and shocked to learn they have been using student information systems for years that delete the previous year's data when a new year is entered.* Many districts archive data from past years, but may lose track of the data in the process. There is nothing the data warehouse company can do for you on this one. Just make sure the necessary adjustments are made so it no longer happens this way.

**Issue #4:** *It is often hard to get data from some district departments—especially Human Resources.* For many and varied reasons, some departments will want to hold on to their data. Leadership cannot and should not allow this to happen. Leadership may need to acknowledge the barriers the different departments face, reinforce the benefits to be gained by integrating demographic and process data, and suggest safeguards to protect sensitive student and staff information.

**Issue #5:** *You are going to spend a lot of time extracting, cleaning, and loading data.* No matter how long you think it will take to do this work, it will take longer. Cleaning the data is complex; extracting and loading the data are even more complex. A data warehouse company will be extremely helpful with this piece. Make sure the warehouse company has quality extract, transform, and load (ETL) tools.

Your district can save some of the time and frustration it could take to put together a data warehouse. Below are recommendations for getting started and for working with a data warehouse company.

**Recommendation #1:** *Establish a vision for your warehouse and begin to create a culture for data use.* Clarifying with everyone in the organization why a warehouse is needed and how it will be used is a great beginning. A warehouse is needed to bring all data sources together to get a better handle on the system and areas that need improvement. During this visioning piece, the way work will be accomplished when the organization is using data begins to create a culture of data use. For example: Teachers will be given "just-in-time" reports of ongoing assessment results to understand what their classes know and do not know, and will then work with other teachers to learn how to differentiate instruction to better meet the needs of the students who are not learning.

*Clarifying with everyone in the organization why a warehouse is needed and how it will be used is a great beginning.*

**Recommendation #2:** *Check now to see that you have one unique identification number for* **each student and teacher,** *regardless of how many times she/he enters or leaves the district.* Never recycle a student or teacher identification number. This is the only way to accurately match data over time. Districts need a unified student information system, as well, so it can link a student's identification number as she/he moves from school to school. A unique identifier is essential. If you must assign new identification numbers, keep your old numbers in a field for reference, so they will not be reused.

**Recommendation #3:** *Start cleansing your data now. Set procedures, districtwide, for how data will be entered into each data file, and monitor the procedures.* Data warehouse companies have told me they have never experienced a school district submitting data that were 100% clean. Get all departments on board with the warehouse and the cleansing of data. *Set districtwide processes and procedures for entering data, and monitor their use.* Smart districts identify administrators to own different pieces of data. For example: The Director of Special Education may become the "owner" of all special education data, making sure every piece is entered accurately and is reliable, in all parts of the organization.

**Recommendation #4:** *Review all the data you would like to have in your data warehouse and list the numbers that should appear, including numbers of students and teachers in each building and grade level.* This will serve three important functions:

1. It will help you see what you have, what you don't have, and how accurate your data systems are.

2. It is extremely helpful to any data warehouse company with which you would contract. The company will see what you want and how the data ought to appear. It will be able to spot errors much more quickly and correct some of the errors without involving you and your time.

3. It will help you correctly identify all the fields you will want included—now and/or for the future.

**Recommendation #5:** *Do not expect your first data warehouse to be perfect.* The first warehouse build is often best at pointing out problems. A good data warehouse company will work with you on correcting the problems; most will correct the mistakes and provide multiple builds as a part of your contract.

**Recommendation #6:** *Know your student information system.* Make sure you know what data are in your student information system, where they are kept, and how to get the data out of the system. When buying a student information system, make sure it has easy import and export functionality. Also, make sure a new year's data will not overwrite historical data. You will never be able to retrieve these data. Proprietary databases (those developed by a privately-owned software companies) often limit a district's options.

**Recommendation #7:** *Before exporting your data, talk with the data warehouse company about what format would be the best and what is needed in the data.* This relates to the earlier issue of making sure you contract with a company that wants to work with you and one that knows educational data.

> *Make sure you know what data are in your student information system, where they are kept, and how to get the data out of the system.*

**Recommendation #8:** *Assign a local project director to work with the data warehouse company and champions to "own" the district data and data issues.* Districts that have a data leader, who knows all the data and can provide the data warehouse company the data it needs in the format they need to be in, decrease the overall time it takes to pull a data warehouse together. Assigning "owners" of all the data and creating procedures to get and keep the data in clean, useable form is a great idea.

**Recommendation #9:** *Follow, methodically, all directions and instructions given to you by the data warehouse company.* A data warehouse is a big investment, requiring much of your time and that of busy engineers. Everyone involved should work to be sure that time is well-spent. A good data warehouse company has lots of experience with many different educational organizations and knows what it takes to get the work done well the first time.

**Recommendation #10:** *When sending data to the data warehouse company, identify and document the information being sent.* It is better to document too much rather than too little. For example: For assessments, send all data layouts and data definitions. Data warehouse companies tell me all the time that districts send data files without column headers; therefore, the engineers have no idea what data they are working with. Worse yet, these same districts do not return the engineer's calls for weeks and then complain that loading of the warehouse is taking too long.

**Recommendation #11:** *Talk with the engineers who are loading your data to make sure you are going to get what you want.* In other words, communicate, communicate, communicate. And stay in touch.

> *A good data warehouse company has lots of experience with many different educational organizations and knows what it takes to get the work done well the first time.*

Overall, consider the far-reaching consequences of your decisions; make sure a decision isn't going to cause issues a few years down the road. For example: If you decide not to include an object or attribute because it is just too hard to get the data clean right now, consider how that lack of data will impact future analyses and decisions.

## Who Does the Data Analysis Work?

For the types of data analyses discussed in this book and described as comprehensive data analyses, it would be ideal if someone at the district level did the major analyses. With a data warehouse and a good strong data analyzer tool, the district person can do the analyses for all the schools, at all grade levels, and for all subtests in one query. A clerk can then copy and paste the individual results into graphing templates. (Graphing templates for basic organizational profiles are provided on CD-ROMs for all K-12 educational levels in the *Using Data to Improve Student Learning* [Bernhardt] series.)

Our passion with data analysis is getting the results into the hands of teachers and giving them the time to study the results of the analyses, instead of having them use their time performing the analyses. In our ideal world, at minimum, teachers would start the school year with historical data on each student in their class(es). They would know what the students know and what they need to know. Also in our ideal world, teachers would be using ongoing measurements in their classrooms (at least four times a year) to make sure all students are progressing and mastering the content.

Let's say your district does not have a data warehouse and provides only the state assessment results on paper; you can still use these data in meaningful ways. At minimum, schools can graph average scores over time—if there have been positive improvements in the school, you should see increases in scores. If the school is making a positive impact on students, student cohort scores should increase over time—they should never go backward. Don't forget the powerful demographic data gathered through your student information system.

Who does all this at the school level, if there is no district support for the analysis, depends on your school make-up. Often instructional coaches, assistant principals, teachers on special assignment, and/or the Leadership or Data Teams do this work.

A "champion" user of data will help ensure that the data are applied correctly. These champions most often are curriculum, instruction, and/or assessment directors.

## Summary

The discussions throughout this book have focused on getting a data warehouse set up for comprehensive data analyses with the right data and on establishing a data culture to improve teaching and learning.

There have been enough districts and states that have established data warehouses that we can learn from them—both from their missteps and their successes.

Do remember that you are building a *high-maintenance system.* If you go through all the work to think through a data warehouse to set it up, you will need to commit the resources to keep the warehouse clean, secure, up-to-date, growing, and well-used.

*If you go through all the work to think through a data warehouse to set it up, you will need to commit the resources to keep the warehouse clean, secure, up-to-date, growing, and well-used.*

# APPENDIX: CONTINUOUS IMPROVEMENT CONTINUUMS FOR DISTRICTS AND SCHOOLS

These *Education for the Future Continuous Improvement Continuums,* adapted from the *Malcolm Baldrige Award Program for Quality Business Management,* provide an authentic means for measuring organizational improvement and growth. Districts and schools use these Continuums as a vehicle for ongoing self-assessment. They use the results of the assessment to acknowledge their accomplishments, to set goals for improvement, and to keep staff and partners apprised of the progress they have made in their improvement efforts.

## Understanding the Continuums

These Continuums, extending from *one* to *five* horizontally, represent a continuum of expectations related to continuous improvement with respect to an *Approach* to the Continuum, *Implementation* of the approach, and the *Outcome* that results from the implementation. A *one* rating, located at the left of each Continuum, represents a district that has not yet begun to improve. *Five,* located at the right of each Continuum, represents a district that is one step removed from "world class quality." The elements between *one* and *five* describe how that Continuum is hypothesized to evolve in a continuously improving district. Each Continuum moves from a reactive mode to a proactive mode—from fire fighting to prevention. The *five* in *Outcome* in each Continuum is the target.

Vertically, the *Approach, Implementation,* and *Outcome* statements, for any number one through five, are hypotheses. In other words, the implementation statement describes how the approach might look when implemented, and the outcome is the "pay-off" for implementing the approach. If the hypotheses are accurate, the outcome will not be realized until the approach is actually implemented.

## Using the Continuums

Use the *Continuous Improvement Continuums* (CICs) to understand where your district or school is with respect to continuous improvement. The results will hopefully provide that sense of urgency needed to spark enthusiasm for your improvement efforts.

Start the assessment by stating or creating the ground rules, setting the tone for a safe and confidential assessment, and explaining why you are doing this. Provide a brief overview of the seven sections, taking each section one or two at a time, and having each staff member read the related Continuum and make independent assessments of where she/he believes the district is with respect to *Approach, Implementation,* and *Outcome.* We recommend using individual 8 1/2 x 11 copies of the Continuums for individual assessments.

Then, have each staff member note where she/he believes the district is with a colorful sticker or marker on a large poster of each Continuum. The markers allow all staff to see how much they are in agreement with one another. If only one color is used for the first assessment, another color can be used for the next assessment, and so forth, to help gauge growth over time, or you can plan to use two different charts for gauging progress over time such as in the photos that follow.

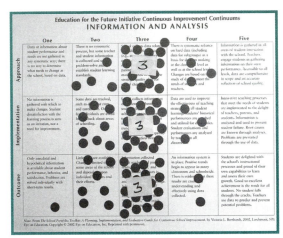

**Fall Assessment**

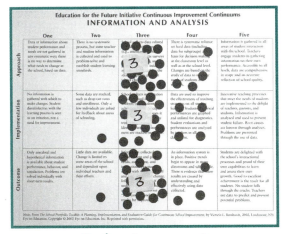

**Spring Assessment**

When all dots or marks have been placed on the enlarged Continuum, look at the agreement or disagreement of the ratings. Starting with *Approach*, have staff discuss why they believe the district is where they rated it. Keep discussing until the larger group comes to consensus on one number that reflects where the district is right now. You might need to make a quick check on where staff is with respect to coming to consensus, using a thumbs up, thumbs down "vote." Keep discussing the facts until consensus is reached. Do not average the results—it does not produce a sense of urgency for improvement. We cannot emphasize this enough! Keep discussing until agreement is reached by everyone on a number that represents where "we" are right now. When that consensus is reached, record the number and move to *Implementation* and then *Outcome*. Determine *Next Steps*. Proceed in the same way through the next six categories.

During the assessments, make sure someone records the discussions of the Continuum assessments. Districts and schools might want to exchange facilitators with a neighboring district/school to have someone external to the district/school facilitate the assessments. This will enable everyone in the district to participate and provide an unbiased and competent person to lead the consensus-building piece. Assessing over time will help staff see that they are making progress. The decision of how often to assess on the *Continuous Improvement Continuums* is certainly up to the district/school. We recommend twice a year—about mid-fall and mid-spring—when there is time (or has been time) to implement next steps. Over time, once a year might be sufficient.

Using these Continuums will enable you and your district to stay motivated, to shape and maintain your shared vision, and will assist with the continuous improvement of all elements. Take pictures of the resulting charts. Even if your consensus number does not increase, the dots will most probably come together over time showing shifts in whole staff thinking.

Remember that where your district/school is at any time is just where it is. The important thing is what you do with this information. Continuous improvement is a never-ending process which, when used effectively, will ultimately lead your district toward providing a quality program for all children.

## District Continuous Improvement Continuums
# INFORMATION AND ANALYSIS

| | One | Two | Three | Four | Five |
|---|---|---|---|---|---|
| **Approach** | Data or information about school student performance and needs are not gathered in any systematic way. The district does not provide assistance in helping schools understand what needs to change at the school and classroom levels, based on data. | There is no systematic process for data analysis across the district. Some school, teacher, and student information are collected and used to problem solve and establish student-learning standards across the district. | School district collects data related to school and student performance (e.g., attendance, enrollment, achievement), and surveys students, staff, and parents. The information is used to drive the strategic quality plan for district and school improvement. | There is systematic reliance on hard data (including data for subgroups) as a basis for decision making at the district, school, and classroom levels. Changes are based on the study of data to meet the educational needs of students and teachers. | Information is gathered in all areas of student interaction with the school. The district engages administrators and teachers in gathering information on their own performance. Accessible to all schools, data are comprehensive in scope and an accurate reflection of school and district quality. |
| **Implementation** | No information is gathered with which to make district or school changes. Student dissatisfaction with the learning process is seen as an irritation, not a need for improvement. | Some data are tracked, such as attendance, enrollment, and drop-out rates. Only a few individuals are asked for feedback about areas of schooling and district operations. | The district collects information on current and former students (e.g., student achievement and perceptions), analyzes and uses it in conjunction with future trends for planning. Identified areas for improvement are tracked over time. | Data are used to provide feedback to improve the effectiveness of teaching strategies on all student learning. Schools' historical performances are graphed and utilized for diagnosis by the district. | Innovative teaching processes that meet the needs of students are implemented across the district. Information is analyzed and used to prevent student failure. Root causes are known through analyses. Problems are prevented through the use of data. |
| **Outcome** | Only anecdotal and hypothetical information are available about student performance, behavior, and satisfaction. Problems are solved individually with short-term results. | Little data are available. Change is limited to some areas of the district and dependent upon individual administrators and their efforts. | Information collected about school needs, effective assessment, and instructional practices are shared with all school and district staff and used to plan for school and district improvement. Information helps staff understand pressing issues, analyze information for "root causes," and track results for improvement. | An information system is in place. Positive trends begin to appear in many schools and districtwide. There is evidence that these results are caused by understanding and effectively using the data collected. | Schools are delighted with their instructional processes and proud of their own capabilities to learn and assess their own growth. Good to excellent achievement is the result for all schools. Schools use data to predict and prevent potential problems. No student falls through the cracks. |

## District Continuous Improvement Continuums
## STUDENT ACHIEVEMENT

| | One | Two | Three | Four | Five |
|---|---|---|---|---|---|
| **Approach** | Instructional and organizational processes critical to student success are not identified. Little distinction of student learning differences is made. Some schools believe that not all students can achieve. | Some data are collected on student background and performance trends. Learning gaps are noted to direct improvement of instruction. It is known that student learning standards must be identified. | Student learning standards are identified, and a continuum of learning is created across the district. Student performance data are collected and compared to the standards in order to analyze how to improve learning for all students. | Data on student achievement are used throughout the district to pursue the improvement of student learning. The district ensures that teachers collaborate to implement appropriate instruction and assessment strategies for meeting student learning standards articulated across grade levels. All teachers believe that all students can learn. | The district makes an effort to exceed student achievement expectations. Innovative instructional changes are made to anticipate learning needs and improve student achievement. District makes sure that teachers are able to predict characteristics impacting student achievement and to know how to perform from a small set of internal quality measures. |
| **Implementation** | All students are taught the same way. There is no communication between the district and schools about students' academic needs or learning styles. There are no analyses of how to improve instruction. | Some effort is made to track and analyze student achievement trends on a districtwide basis. District begins to understand the needs and learning gaps within the schools. | Teachers across the district study effective instruction and assessment strategies to implement standards and to increase students' learning. Student feedback and analysis of achievement data are used in conjunction with implementation support strategies. | There is a systematic focus on implementing student learning standards and on the improvement of student learning districtwide. Effective instruction and assessment strategies are implemented in each school. District supports teachers supporting one another with peer coaching and/or action research focused on implementing strategies that lead to increased achievement. | All teachers correlate critical instructional and assessment strategies with objective indicators of quality student achievement. A comparative analysis of actual individual student performance to student learning standards is utilized to adjust teaching strategies to ensure a progression of learning for all students. |
| **Outcome** | There is wide variation in student attitudes and achievement with undesirable results. There is high dissatisfaction among students with learning. Student background is used as an excuse for low student achievement. | There is some evidence that student achievement trends are available to schools and are being used. There is much effort, but minimal observable results in improving student achievement. | There is an increase in communication among district and schools, students, and teachers regarding student learning. Teachers learn about effective instructional strategies that will implement the shared vision, student learning standards, and how to meet the needs of students. The schools make some gains. | Increased student achievement is evident districtwide. Student morale, attendance, and behavior are good. Teachers converse often with each other about preventing student failure. Areas for further attention are clear. | Schools and teachers conduct self-assessments to continuously improve performance. Improvements in student achievement are evident and clearly caused by teachers' and students' understandings of individual student learning standards, linked to appropriate and effective instructional and assessment strategies. A continuum of learning results. No students fall through the cracks. |

# District Continuous Improvement Continuums
## QUALITY PLANNING

| | One | Two | Three | Four | Five |
|---|---|---|---|---|---|
| **Approach** | No quality plan or process exists. Data are neither used nor considered important in planning. | The district realizes the importance of a mission, vision, and one comprehensive action plan. Teams develop goals and timelines, and dollars are allocated to begin the process. | A comprehensive plan to achieve the district vision is developed. Plan includes evaluation and continuous improvement. | One focused and integrated districtwide plan for implementing a continuous improvement process is put into action. All district efforts are focused on the implementation of this plan that represents the achievement of the vision. | A plan for the continuous improvement of the district, with a focus on students, is put into place. There is excellent articulation and integration of all elements in the district due to quality planning. Leadership team ensures all elements are implemented by all appropriate parties. |
| **Implementation** | There is no knowledge of or direction for quality planning. Budget is allocated on an as-needed basis. Many plans exist. | School district community begins continuous improvement planning efforts by laying out major steps to a shared vision, by identifying values and beliefs, the purpose of the district, a mission, vision, and student learning standards. | Implementation goals, responsibilities, due dates, and timelines are spelled out. Support structures for implementing the plan are set in place. | The quality management plan is implemented through effective procedures in all areas of the district. Everyone commits to implementing the plan aligned to the vision, mission, and values and beliefs. All share responsibility for accomplishing district goals. | Districtwide goals, mission, vision, and student learning standards are shared and articulated throughout the district and with feeder schools. The attainment of identified student learning standards is linked to planning and implementation of effective instruction that meets students' needs. Leaders at all levels are developing expertise because planning is the norm. |
| **Outcome** | There is no evidence of comprehensive planning. Staff work is carried out in isolation. A continuum of learning for students is absent. | The school district community understands the benefits of working together to implement a comprehensive continuous improvement plan. | There is evidence that the district plan is being implemented in some areas of the district. Improvements are neither systematic nor integrated districtwide. | A districtwide plan is known to all. Results from working toward the quality improvement goals are evident throughout the district. Planning is ongoing and inclusive of all stakeholders. | Evidence of effective teaching and learning results in significant improvement of student achievement attributed to quality planning at all levels of the district organization. Teachers and administrators understand and share the district mission and vision. Quality planning is seamless and all demonstrate evidence of accountability. |

## District Continuous Improvement Continuums
## PROFESSIONAL LEARNING

| | One | Two | Three | Four | Five |
|---|---|---|---|---|---|
| **Approach** | There is no professional development. Teachers, principals, and staff are seen as interchangeable parts that can be replaced. Professional development is external and usually equated to attending a conference alone. Hierarchy determines "haves" and "have-nots." | The "cafeteria" approach to professional development is used, whereby individual teachers and administrators choose what they want to take, without regard to an overall district plan. | The shared vision, district plan and student needs are used to target focused professional development for all employees. Staff is inserviced on relevant instructional and leadership strategies. | Professional development and data-gathering methods are used by all teachers and administrators, and are directed toward the goals of the shared vision and the continuous improvement of the district and schools. Teachers have ongoing conversations about student achievement data. All staff members receive training in their content areas. Systems thinking is considered in all decisions. | Leadership and staff continuously improve all aspects of the learning organization through an innovative, data-driven, and comprehensive continuous improvement process that prevents student failures. Effective job-embedded professional development is ongoing for implementing the vision for student success. Traditional teacher evaluations are replaced by collegial coaching and action research focused on student learning standards. Policies set professional development as a priority budget line-item. Professional development is planned, aligned, and leads to the achievement of student learning standards. |
| **Implementation** | District staff, principals, teachers, and school staff performance is controlled and inspected. Performance evaluations are used to detect mistakes. | Teacher professional development is sporadic and unfocused, lacking an approach for implementing new procedures and processes. Some leadership training begins to take place. | The district ensures that teachers are involved in year-round quality professional development. The school community is trained in shared decision making, team building concepts, effective communication strategies, and data analysis. | Teachers, in teams, continuously set and implement student achievement goals. Leadership considers these goals and provides necessary support structures for collaboration. Teachers utilize effective support approaches as they implement new instruction and assessment strategies. Coaching and feedback structures are in place. Use of new knowledge and skills is evident. | Teams passionately support each other in the pursuit of quality improvement at all levels. Teachers make bold changes in instruction and assessment strategies focused on student learning standards and student learning styles. *A teacher as action researcher* model is implemented. Staffwide conversations focus on systemic reflection and improvement. Teachers are strong leaders. |
| **Outcome** | No professional growth and no staff or student performance improvement. There exists a high turnover rate of employees, especially administrators. Attitudes and approaches filter down to students. | The effectiveness of professional development is not known or analyzed. Teachers feel helpless and unsupported in making schoolwide changes. | Teachers, working in teams, feel supported by the district and begin to feel they can make changes. Evidence shows that shared decision making works. | A collegial school district is evident. Effective classroom strategies are practiced, articulated schoolwide. These strategies, focused on student learning standards, are reflective of professional development aimed at ensuring student learning and the implementation of the shared vision. | True systemic change and improved student achievement result because teachers are knowledgeable of and implement effective, differentiated teaching strategies for individual student learning gains. Teachers' repertoire of skills is enhanced and students are achieving. Professional development is driving learning at all levels. |

# District Continuous Improvement Continuums
## LEADERSHIP

| | One | Two | Three | Four | Five |
|---|---|---|---|---|---|
| **Approach** | The School Board is decision maker. Decisions are reactive to state, district, and federal mandates. There is no knowledge of continuous improvement. | A shared decision-making structure is put into place and discussions begin on how to achieve a district vision. Most decisions are focused on solving problems and are reactive. | District leadership team is committed to continuous improvement. Leadership seeks inclusion of all school sectors and supports study teams by making time provisions for their work. | District leadership team represents a true shared decision-making structure. Study teams are reconstructed for the implementation of a comprehensive continuous improvement plan. | A strong continuous improvement structure is set into place that allows for input from all sectors of the district, school, and community, ensuring strong communication, flexibility, and refinement of approach and beliefs. The district vision is student focused, based on data and appropriate for district/school/community values, and meeting student needs. |
| **Implementation** | The School Board makes all decisions, with little or no input from administrators, teachers, the community, or students. Leadership inspects for mistakes. | District values and beliefs are identified; the purpose of district is defined; a district mission and student learning standards are developed with representative input. A structure for studying approaches to achieving student learning standards is established. | The district leadership team is active on study teams and integrates recommendations from the teams' research and analyses to form a comprehensive plan for continuous improvement within the context of the district mission. Everyone is kept informed. | Decisions about budget and implementation of the vision are made within teams, by the school board, by the leadership team, by the individual schools, and by the full staff, as appropriate. All decisions are communicated to the leadership team and to the full staff. | The vision is implemented and articulated across all grade levels and into feeder schools. Quality standards are reinforced throughout the district. All members of the district community understand and apply the quality standards. Leadership team has systematic interactions and involvement with district administrators, teachers, parents, community, and students about the district's direction. Necessary resources are available to implement and measure staff learning related to student learning standards. |
| **Outcome** | Although the decision-making process is clearly known, decisions are reactive and lack focus and consistency. There is no evidence of staff commitment to a shared vision. Students and parents do not feel they are being heard. | The mission provides a focus for all district and school improvement and guides the action to the vision. The school community is committed to continuous improvement. Quality leadership techniques are used sporadically. | The district leadership team is seen as committed to planning and quality improvement. Critical areas for improvement are identified. Faculty feel included in shared decision making. | There is evidence that the district leadership team listens to all levels of the organization. Implementation of the continuous improvement plan is linked to student learning standards and the guiding principles of the school. Leadership capacity for implementing the vision throughout the district is evident. | Site-based management and shared decision making truly exists. Teachers understand and display an intimate knowledge of how the school and district operate. Schools support and communicate with each other in the implementation of quality strategies. Teachers implement the vision in their classrooms and can determine how their new approaches meet student needs and lead to the attainment of student learning standards. Leaders are standards-driven at all levels. |

## District Continuous Improvement Continuums
## PARTNERSHIP DEVELOPMENT

| | One | Two | Three | Four | Five |
|---|---|---|---|---|---|
| **Approach** | There is no system for input from parents, business, or community. Status quo is desired for managing the school district. | Partnerships are sought, but mostly for money and things. | School district has knowledge of why partnerships are important and seeks to include businesses and parents in a strategic fashion related to student learning standards for increased student achievement. | School district seeks effective win-win business and community partnerships and parent involvement to implement the vision. Desired outcomes are clearly identified. A solid plan for partnership development exists. | Community, parent, and business partnerships become integrated across all student groupings. The benefits of outside involvement are known by all. Parent and business involvement in student learning is refined. Student learning regularly takes place beyond the school and district walls. |
| **Implementation** | Barriers are erected to close out involvement of outsiders. Outsiders are managed for least impact on status quo. | A team is assigned to get partners and to receive input from parents, the community, and business in the school district. | Involvement of business, community, and parents begins to take place in some schools and after school hours related to the vision. Partners begin to realize how they can support each other in achieving district goals. District staff understand what partners need from the partnership. | There is systematic utilization of parents, community, and businesses districtwide. Areas in which the active use of these partnerships benefit student learning are clear. | Partnership development is articulated across all district groupings. Parents, community, business, and educators work together in an innovative fashion to increase student learning and to prepare students for the Twenty-first Century. Partnerships are evaluated for continuous improvement. |
| **Outcome** | There is little or no involvement of parents, business, or community at-large. The district is a closed, isolated system. | Much effort is given to establishing partnerships. Some spotty trends emerge, such as receiving donated equipment. | Some substantial gains are achieved in implementing partnerships. Some student achievement increases can be attributed to this involvement. | Gains in student satisfaction with learning and school are clearly related to partnerships. All partners benefit. | Previously non-achieving students enjoy learning with excellent achievement. Community, business, and home become common places for student learning, while school becomes a place where parents come for further education. Partnerships enhance what the school district does for students. |

## District Continuous Improvement Continuums

# CONTINUOUS IMPROVEMENT AND EVALUATION

| | One | Two | Three | Four | Five |
|---|---|---|---|---|---|
| **Approach** | Neither goals nor strategies exist for the evaluation and continuous improvement of the district organization or for elements of the organization. | The approach to continuous improvement and evaluation is problem-solving. If there are no problems, or if solutions can be made quickly, there is no need for improvement or analyses. Changes in parts of the system are not coordinated with all other parts. | Some elements of the district organization are evaluated for effectiveness. Some elements are improved on the basis of the evaluation findings. | All elements of the district's operations are evaluated for improvement. Efforts are consistently made to ensure congruence of the elements with respect to the continuum of learning that students experience. | All aspects of the district organization are rigorously evaluated and improved on a continuous basis. Students, and the maintenance of a comprehensive learning continuum for students, become the focus of all aspects of the school district improvement process. |
| **Implementation** | With no overall plan for evaluation and continuous improvement, strategies are changed by individual schools, teachers, and/or administrators only when something sparks the need to improve. Reactive decisions and activities are a daily mode of operation. | Isolated changes are made in some areas of the district organization in response to problem incidents. Changes are not preceded by comprehensive analyses, such as an understanding of the root causes of problems. The effectiveness of the elements of the district organization is not known. | Elements of the district organization are improved on the basis of comprehensive analyses of root causes of problems, client perceptions, and operational effectiveness of processes. | Continuous improvement analyses of student achievement and instructional strategies are rigorously reinforced within each classroom and across learning levels to develop a comprehensive learning continuum for students and to prevent student failure. | Comprehensive continuous improvement becomes the way of doing business throughout the district. Teachers continuously improve the appropriateness and effectiveness of instructional strategies based on student feedback and performance. All aspects of the district organization are improved to support teachers' efforts. |
| **Outcome** | Individuals struggle with system failure. Finger pointing and blaming others for failure occur. The effectiveness of strategies is not known. Mistakes are repeated. | Problems are solved only temporarily and few positive changes result. Additionally, unintended and undesirable consequences often appear in other parts of the system. Many aspects of the school district are incongruent, keeping the district from reaching its vision. | Evidence of effective improvement strategies is observable. Positive changes are made and maintained due to comprehensive analyses and evaluation. | Teachers become astute at assessing and in predicting the impact of their instructional strategies on individual student achievement. Sustainable improvements in student achievement are evident at all grade levels due to continuous improvement supported by the district. | The district becomes a congruent and effective learning organization. Only instruction and assessment strategies that produce quality student achievement are used. A true continuum of learning results for all students and staff. The impact of improvements is increasingly measurable. |

## School Continuous Improvement Continuums
# INFORMATION AND ANALYSIS

| | One | Two | Three | Four | Five |
|---|---|---|---|---|---|
| **Approach** | Data or information about student performance and needs are not gathered in any systematic way; there is no way to determine what needs to change at the school, based on data. | There is no systematic process, but some teacher and student information is collected and used to problem solve and establish student learning standards. | School collects data related to student performance (e.g., attendance, achievement) and conducts surveys on student, teacher, and parent needs. The information is used to drive the strategic quality plan for school change. | There is systematic reliance on hard data (including data for subgroups) as a basis for decision making at the classroom level as well as at the school level. Changes are based on the study of data to meet the needs of students and teachers. | Information is gathered in all areas of student interaction with the school. Teachers engage students in gathering information on their own performance. Accessible to all levels, data are comprehensive in scope and an accurate reflection of school quality. |
| **Implementation** | No information is gathered with which to make changes. Student dissatisfaction with the learning process is seen as an irritation, not a need for improvement. | Some data are tracked, such as drop-out rates and enrollment. Only a few individuals are asked for feedback about areas of schooling. | School collects information on current and former students (e.g., student achievement and perceptions), analyzes and uses it in conjunction with future trends for planning. Identified areas for improvement are tracked over time. | Data are used to improve the effectiveness of teaching strategies on all student learning. Students' historical performances are graphed and utilized for diagnostics. Student evaluations and performances are analyzed by teachers in all classrooms. | Innovative teaching processes that meet the needs of students are implemented to the delight of teachers, parents, and students. Information is analyzed and used to prevent student failure. Root causes are known through analyses. Problems are prevented through the use of data. |
| **Outcome** | Only anecdotal and hypothetical information is available about student performance, behavior, and satisfaction. Problems are solved individually with short-term results. | Little data are available. Change is limited to some areas of the school and dependent upon individual teachers and their efforts. | Information collected about student and parent needs, assessment, and instructional practices is shared with the school staff and used to plan for change. Information helps staff understand pressing issues, analyze information for "root causes," and track results for improvement. | An information system is in place. Positive trends begin to appear in many classrooms and schoolwide. There is evidence that these results are caused by understanding and effectively using data collected. | Students are delighted with the school's instructional processes and proud of their own capabilities to learn and assess their own growth. Good to excellent achievement is the result for all students. No student falls through the cracks. Teachers use data to predict and prevent potential problems. |

# School Continuous Improvement Continuums
## STUDENT ACHIEVEMENT

| | One | Two | Three | Four | Five |
|---|---|---|---|---|---|
| **Approach** | Instructional and organizational processes critical to student success are not identified. Little distinction of student learning differences is made. Some teachers believe that not all students can achieve. | Some data are collected on student background and performance trends. Learning gaps are noted to direct improvement of instruction. It is known that student learning standards must be identified. | Student learning standards are identified, and a continuum of learning is created throughout the school. Student performance data are collected and compared to the standards in order to analyze how to improve learning for all students. | Data on student achievement are used throughout the school to pursue the improvement of student learning. Teachers collaborate to implement appropriate instruction and assessment strategies for meeting student learning standards articulated across grade levels. All teachers believe that all students can learn. | School makes an effort to exceed student achievement expectations. Innovative instructional changes are made to anticipate learning needs and improve student achievement. Teachers are able to predict characteristics impacting student achievement and to know how to perform from a small set of internal quality measures. |
| **Implementation** | All students are taught the same way. There is no communication with students about their academic needs or learning styles. There are no analyses of how to improve instruction. | Some effort is made to track and analyze student achievement trends on a school-wide basis. Teachers begin to understand the needs and learning gaps of students. | Teachers study effective instruction and assessment strategies to implement standards and to increase their students' learning. Student feedback and analysis of achievement data are used in conjunction with implementation support strategies. | There is a systematic focus on implementing student learning standards and on the improvement of student learning schoolwide. Effective instruction and assessment strategies are implemented in each classroom. Teachers support one another with peer coaching and/or action research focused on implementing strategies that lead to increased achievement and the attainment of the shared vision. | All teachers correlate critical instructional and assessment strategies with objective indicators of quality student achievement. A comparative analysis of actual individual student performance to student learning standards is utilized to adjust teaching strategies to ensure a progression of learning for all students. |
| **Outcome** | There is wide variation in student attitudes and achievement with undesirable results. There is high dissatisfaction among students with learning. Student background is used as an excuse for low student achievement. | There is some evidence that student achieve-ment trends are available to teachers and are being used. There is much effort, but minimal observable results in improving student achievement. | There is an increase in communication between students and teachers regarding student learning. Teachers learn about effective instructional strategies that will implement the shared vision, including student learning standards, and meet the needs of their students. They make some gains. | Increased student achievement is evident schoolwide. Student morale, attendance, and behavior are good. Teachers converse often with each other about preventing student failure. Areas for further attention are clear. | Students and teachers conduct self-assessments to continuously improve performance. Improvements in student achievement are evident and clearly caused by teachers' and students' understandings of individual student learning standards, linked to appropriate and effective instructional and assessment strategies. A continuum of learning results. No students fall through the cracks. |

# School Continuous Improvement Continuums
## QUALITY PLANNING

| | One | Two | Three | Four | Five |
|---|---|---|---|---|---|
| **Approach** | No quality plan or process exists. Data are neither used nor considered important in planning. | The staff realize the importance of a mission, vision, and one comprehensive action plan. Teams develop goals and timelines, and dollars are allocated to begin the process. | A comprehensive school plan to achieve the vision is developed. Plan includes evaluation and continuous improvement. | One focused and integrated schoolwide plan for implementing a continuous improvement process is put into action. All school efforts are focused on the implementation of this plan that represents the achievement of the vision. | A plan for the continuous improvement of the school, with a focus on students, is put into place. There is excellent articulation and integration of all elements in the school due to quality planning. Leadership team ensures all elements are implemented by all appropriate parties. |
| **Implementation** | There is no knowledge of or direction for quality planning. Budget is allocated on an as-needed basis. Many plans exist. | School community begins continuous improvement planning efforts by laying out major steps to a shared vision, by identifying values and beliefs, the purpose of the school, a mission, vision, and student learning standards. | Implementation goals, responsibilities, due dates, and timelines are spelled out. Support structures for implementing the plan are set in place. | The quality management plan is implemented through effective procedures in all areas of the school. Everyone commits to implementing the plan aligned to the vision, mission, and values and beliefs. All share responsibility for accomplishing school goals. | Schoolwide goals, mission, vision, and student learning standards are shared and articulated throughout the school and with feeder schools. The attainment of identified student learning standards is linked to planning and implementation of effective instruction that meets students' needs. Leaders at all levels are developing expertise because planning is the norm. |
| **Outcome** | There is no evidence of comprehensive planning. Staff work is carried out in isolation. A continuum of learning for students is absent. | The school community understands the benefits of working together to implement a comprehensive continuous improvement plan. | There is evidence that the school plan is being implemented in some areas of the school. Improvements are neither systematic nor integrated schoolwide. | A schoolwide plan is known to all. Results from working toward the quality improvement goals are evident throughout the school. Planning is ongoing and inclusive of all stakeholders. | Evidence of effective teaching and learning results in significant improvement of student achievement attributed to quality planning at all levels of the school organization. Teachers and administrators understand and share the school mission and vision. Quality planning is seamless and all demonstrate evidence of accountability. |

# School Continuous Improvement Continuums
## PROFESSIONAL LEARNING

| | One | Two | Three | Four | Five |
|---|---|---|---|---|---|
| **Approach** | There is no professional development. Teachers, principals, and staff are seen as interchangeable parts that can be replaced. Professional development is external and usually equated to attending a conference alone. Hierarchy determines "haves" and "have-nots." | The "cafeteria" approach to professional development is used, whereby individual teachers choose what they want to take, without regard to an overall school plan. | The shared vision, school plan, and student needs are used to target focused professional development for all employees. Staff is inserviced on relevant instructional and leadership strategies. | Professional development and data-gathering methods are used by all teachers and are directed toward the goals of the shared vision and the continuous improvement of the school. Teachers have ongoing conversations about student achievement data. Other staff members receive training in their content areas. Systems thinking is considered in all decisions. | Leadership and staff continuously improve all aspects of the learning organization through an innovative, data-driven, and comprehensive continuous improvement process that prevents student failures. Effective job-embedded professional development is ongoing for implementing the vision for student success. Traditional teacher evaluations are replaced by collegial coaching and action research focused on student learning standards. Policies set professional development as a priority budget line-item. Professional development is planned, aligned, and lead to the achievement of student learning standards. |
| **Implementation** | Teacher, principal, and staff performance is controlled and inspected. Performance evaluations are used to detect mistakes. | Teacher professional development is sporadic and unfocused, lacking an approach for implementing new procedures and processes. Some leadership training begins to take place. | Teachers are involved in year-round quality professional development. The school community is trained in shared decision making, team building concepts, effective communication strategies, and data analysis at the classroom level. | Teachers, in teams, continuously set and implement student achievement goals. Leadership considers these goals and provides necessary support structures for collaboration. Teachers utilize effective support approaches as they implement new instruction and assessment strategies. Coaching and feedback structures are in place. Use of new knowledge and skills is evident. | Teams passionately support each other in the pursuit of quality improvement at all levels. Teachers make bold changes in instruction and assessment strategies focused on student learning standards and student learning styles. A teacher as action researcher model is implemented. Staffwide conversations focus on systemic reflection and improvement. Teachers are strong leaders. |
| **Outcome** | No professional growth and no staff or student performance improvement. There exists a high turnover rate of employees, especially administrators. Attitudes and approaches filter down to students. | The effectiveness of professional development is not known or analyzed. Teachers feel helpless about making schoolwide changes. | Teachers, working in teams, feel supported and begin to feel they can make changes. Evidence shows that shared decision making works. | A collegial school is evident. Effective classroom strategies are practiced, articulated schoolwide, are reflective of professional development aimed at ensuring student achievement, and the implementation of the shared vision, that includes student learning standards. | True systemic change and improved student achievement result because teachers are knowledgeable of and implement effective, differentiated teaching strategies for individual student learning gains. Teachers' repertoire of skills are enhanced, and students are achieving. Professional development is driving learning at all levels. |

# School Continuous Improvement Continuums
## LEADERSHIP

| | One | Two | Three | Four | Five |
|---|---|---|---|---|---|
| **Approach** | Principal as decision maker. Decisions are reactive to state, district, and federal mandates. There is no knowledge of continuous improvement. | A shared decision-making structure is put into place and discussions begin on how to achieve a school vision. Most decisions are focused on solving problems and are reactive. | Leadership team is committed to continuous improvement. Leadership seeks inclusion of all school sectors and supports study teams by making time provisions for their work. | Leadership team represents a true shared decision-making structure. Study teams are reconstructed for the implementation of a comprehensive continuous improvement plan. | A strong continuous improvement structure is set into place that allows for input from all sectors of the school, district, and community, ensuring strong communication, flexibility, and refinement of approach and beliefs. The school vision is student focused, based on data, and appropriate for school/community values, and meeting student needs. |
| **Implementation** | Principal makes all decisions, with little or no input from teachers, the community, or students. Leadership inspects for mistakes. | School values and beliefs are identified; the purpose of school is defined; a school mission and student learning standards are developed with representative input. A structure for studying approaches to achieving student learning standards is established. | Leadership team is active on study teams and integrates recommendations from the teams' research and analyses to form a comprehensive plan for continuous improvement within the context of the school mission. Everyone is kept informed. | Decisions about budget and implementation of the vision are made within teams, by the principal, by the leadership team, and by the full staff as appropriate. All decisions are communicated to the leadership team and to the full staff. | The vision is implemented and articulated across all grade levels and into feeder schools. Quality standards are reinforced throughout the school. All members of the school community understand and apply the quality standards. Leadership team has systematic interactions and involvement with district administrators, teachers, parents, community, and students about the school's direction. Necessary resources are available to implement and measure staff learning related to student learning standards. |
| **Outcome** | Decisions lack focus and consistency. There is no evidence of staff commitment to a shared vision. Students and parents do not feel they are being heard. Decision-making process is clear and known. | The mission provides a focus for all school improvement and guides the action to the vision. The school community is committed to continuous improvement. Quality leadership techniques are used sporadically. | Leadership team is seen as committed to planning and quality improvement. Critical areas for improvement are identified. Faculty feel included in shared decision making. | There is evidence that the leadership team listens to all levels of the organization. Implementation of the continuous improvement plan is linked to student learning standards and the guiding principles of the school. Leadership capacities for implementing the vision among teachers are evident. | Site-based management and shared decision making truly exists. Teachers understand and display an intimate knowledge of how the school operates. Teachers support and communicate with each other in the implementation of quality strategies. Teachers implement the vision in their classrooms and can determine how their new approach meets student needs and leads to the attainment of student learning standards. Leaders are standards-driven at all levels. |

## School Continuous Improvement Continuums
# PARTNERSHIP DEVELOPMENT

| | One | Two | Three | Four | Five |
|---|---|---|---|---|---|
| **Approach** | There is no system for input from parents, business, or community. Status quo is desired for managing the school. | Partnerships are sought, but mostly for money and things. | School has knowledge of why partnerships are important and seeks to include businesses and parents in a strategic fashion related to student learning standards for increased student achievement. | School seeks effective win-win business and community partnerships and parent involvement to implement the vision. Desired outcomes are clearly identified. A solid plan for partnership development exists. | Community, parent, and business partnerships become integrated across all student groupings. The benefits of outside involvement are known by all. Parent and business involvement in student learning is refined. Student learning *regularly* takes place beyond the school walls. |
| **Implementation** | Barriers are erected to close out involvement of outsiders. Outsiders are managed for least impact on status quo. | A team is assigned to get partners and to receive input from parents, the community, and business in the school. | Involvement of business, community, and parents begins to take place in some classrooms and after school hours related to the vision. Partners begin to realize how they can support each other in achieving school goals. School staff understand what partners need from the partnership. | There is a systematic utilization of parents, community, and businesses schoolwide. Areas in which the active use of these partnerships benefit student learning are clear. | Partnership development is articulated across all student groupings. Parents, community, business, and educators work together in an innovative fashion to increase student learning and to prepare students for the 21st Century. Partnerships are evaluated for continuous improvement. |
| **Outcome** | There is little or no involvement of parents, business, or community at-large. School is a closed, isolated system. | Much effort is given to establishing partner-ships. Some spotty trends emerge, such as receiving donated equipment. | Some substantial gains are achieved in implementing partnerships. Some student achievement increases can be attributed to this involvement. | Gains in student satisfaction with learning and school are clearly related to partnerships. All partners benefit. | Previously non-achieving students enjoy learning with excellent achievement. Community, business, and home become common places for student learning, while school becomes a place where parents come for further education. Partnerships enhance what the school does for students. |

## School Continuous Improvement Continuums
# CONTINUOUS IMPROVEMENT AND EVALUATION

| | One | Two | Three | Four | Five |
|---|---|---|---|---|---|
| **Approach** | Neither goals nor strategies exist for the evaluation and continuous improvement of the school organization or for elements of the school organization. | The approach to continuous improvement and evaluation is problem solving. If there are no problems, or if solutions can be made quickly, there is no need for improvement or analyses. Changes in parts of the system are not coordinated with all other parts. | Some elements of the school organization are evaluated for effectiveness. Some elements are improved on the basis of the evaluation findings. | All elements of the school's operations are evaluated for improvement and to ensure congruence of the elements with respect to the continuum of learning students experience. | All aspects of the school organization are rigorously evaluated and improved on a continuous basis. Students, and the maintenance of a comprehensive learning continuum for students, become the focus of all aspects of the school improvement process. |
| **Implementation** | With no overall plan for evaluation and continuous improvement, strategies are changed by individual teachers and administrators only when something sparks the need to improve. Reactive decisions and activities are a daily mode of operation. | Isolated changes are made in some areas of the school organization in response to problem incidents. Changes are not preceded by comprehensive analyses, such as an understanding of the root causes of problems. The effectiveness of the elements of the school organization, or changes made to the elements, is not known. | Elements of the school organization are improved on the basis of comprehensive analyses of root causes of problems, client perceptions, and operational effectiveness of processes. | Continuous improvement analyses of student achievement and instructional strategies are rigorously reinforced within each classroom and across learning levels to develop a comprehensive learning continuum for students and to prevent student failure. | Comprehensive continuous improvement becomes the way of doing business at the school. Teachers continuously improve the appropriateness and effectiveness of instructional strategies based on student feedback and performance. All aspects of the school organization are improved to support teachers' efforts. |
| **Outcome** | Individuals struggle with system failure. Finger pointing and blaming others for failure occurs. The effectiveness of strategies is not known. Mistakes are repeated. | Problems are solved only temporarily and few positive changes result. Additionally, unintended and undesirable consequences often appear in other parts of the system. Many aspects of the school are incongruent, keeping the school from reaching its vision. | Evidence of effective improvement strategies is observable. Positive changes are made and maintained due to comprehensive analyses and evaluation. | Teachers become astute at assessing and in predicting the impact of their instructional strategies on individual student achievement. Sustainable improvements in student achievement are evident at all grade levels, due to continuous improvement. | The school becomes a congruent and effective learning organization. Only instruction and assessment strategies that produce quality student achievement are used. A true continuum of learning results for all students and staff. The impact of improvements is increasingly measurable. |

# GLOSSARY OF TERMS

This glossary provides brief definitions of data analysis, data warehouse, and database terms used throughout *Translating Data into Information to Improve Teaching and Learning*.

▼ **Academic Performance Index (API)**

The cornerstone of California's Public Schools Accountability Act of 1999 (PSAA). The purpose of the API is to measure the academic performance and growth of schools. It is a numeric index (or scale) that ranges from a low of 200 to a high of 1000.

▼ **Access**

The act of retrieving data from the data warehouse databases.

▼ **Adequate Yearly Progress (AYP)**

As defined through federal legislation, requires all public schools to annually report student progress toward proficiency on state Reading, Writing, and Math standards.

▼ **Ad Hoc Query**

A request for information that is normally fabricated and run a single time and cannot be anticipated in advance. It consists of a Structured Query Language (SQL) statement that has been constructed by an knowledgeable user or through a data access tool.

▼ **Ad Hoc Query Tool**

A specific kind of end-user data access tool that invites users to form their own queries by directly manipulating relational tables and their joins.

▼ **Aggregate**

Combining the results of all groups that make up the sample or population.

▼ **American Standard Code for Information Interchange (ASCII)**

An industry-standard, text-only file format.

▼ **Analysis**

The act of evaluating data retrieved from the data warehouse.

▼ **Analytical Data Tools**

Software that provides analyses of data through the connection of many data sources.

▼ **Analytical Systems**

Databases that assist with the analysis of curriculum alignment, instructional coherence, and assessment of learning standards.

▼ **Attribute**

Otherwise known as a field. A characteristic of an entity, such as name, ethnicity, or gender.

▼ **Attribute Specifications**

Specifications that control the kind of information that can be entered into the attribute, such as data type (e.g., number, text, or date) or properties (e.g., field size, format, and validation rule).

▼ **Authentic Assessments**

Refers to a variety of ways to evaluate a student's demonstration of knowledge and skills but does not include traditional testing. Authentic assessments may include performances, projects, exhibitions, and portfolios.

▼ **Balanced Scorecard**

A method and a tool that includes a strategy map where strategic objectives are placed over four perspectives in order to clarify the strategy and the cause and effect relationships that exists among them.

▼ **Batch Processing**

Group processing of tasks by a computer, in which processing-intensive activities are grouped and processed as units, rather than being processed immediately on demand.

▼ **Benchmark**

A specific statement of knowledge and skills within a content area's continuum that a student must possess to demonstrate a level of progress toward mastery of a standard.

▼ **Business Intelligence (BI) Tools**

Tools dedicated to the analysis of business data.

▼ **Business Rules**

A set of rules for entering data in a database that are specific to an organization's methods of conducting its operations.

▼ **Cell**

A box into which a piece of data is entered as in a spreadsheet. A spreadsheet is composed of rows and columns of cells.

▼ **Cell Size**

The amount of data reported in a cell.

▼ **Cleaning Data**

A process used to determine inaccurate, incomplete, or unreasonable data and then improving the quality through correction of detected errors and omissions.

▼ **Cohort**

Refers to a group of individuals sharing a particular statistical or demographic characteristic, such as the year they were in a specific school grade level. Matched cohort studies follow the same individuals over time, and unmatched cohort studies follow the same group over time.

▼ **Column**

Represents one attribute (field) of an entity. A column is the vertical line in a table.

▼ **Confidentiality**

Guarantees that personal data that can be tracked to an individual will not be released.

▼ **Cooperative Educational Service Agency (CESA)**

A regional agency, created by the Wisconsin legislature, serving 45 public school districts and governed by an eleven-member Board of Control representing the public school districts in the region.

▼ **Criterion-Referenced Tests (CRTs)**

Evaluations that judge how well a test taker does on explicit objectives relative to a pre-determined performance level. There is no comparison to any other test takers.

▼ **Cross Tabulation**

The simultaneous tabulation of two or more variables.

▼ **Cube**

Describes a database for multidimensional analysis. Each cube contains a set of measures (quantitative data) and dimensions (descriptive data such as grade). Queries are sent to the cube to be answered.

▼ **Cube Browser**

User interface for browsing data that is stored in an On-Line Analytical Processing (OLAP) cube. This software is meant as an exploratory tool.

▼ **Dashboard**

A user interface that organizes and displays critical data in a way that is easy to read. The name refers to the fact that it can sometimes look like the dashboard of a car.

▼ **Data Aggregator**

An information provider or tool that gathers content from several sources and brings it together.

▼ **Data Analysis**

The act of transforming data with the aim of extracting useful information and facilitating decisions.

▼ **Data Archaeologist**

A person whose job it is to locate and "cleanse" historical data before the data are entered into the database. Data archaeologists verify data accuracy and consistency and make the data compatible and relatable.

▼ **Data Architect**

A person or team who defines how the environment for the data warehouse, analytics application, or operational system is built.

▼ **Data Architecture**

The framework for organizing the planning and implementation of data resources.

▼ **Data Cleansing**

The process of ensuring that all values in a dataset are consistently and correctly recorded.

▼ **Data Cubes**

Multidimensional representations of relational data usually created using a star or snowflake schema. Each cube can be its own database. (Also, see cube, above)

▼ **Data Dictionary**

A database of definitions and representations of data elements within a database management system. A list of all the files in a database, along with the number of records in each file and the names and types of each field.

▼ **Data Discovery**

The process of determining what data need to be included in a data warehouse and how the data will be used.

▼ **Data-Driven Decision Making (D$^3$M)**

The act of making decisions based on data.

▼ **Data Element**

The most elementary unit of data that can be identified and described in a dictionary or repository.

▼ **Data-Entry Protocol**

A standardized format that determines how information is placed into the data base (i.e., do not input names in all caps; use Ms/Mrs/Mr with no periods, etc.). It is important that everyone who inputs data knows and uses the standardized protocols.

▼ **Data Integrity**

The quality of correctness, completeness, wholeness, soundness, and compliance with the intention of the creators of the data. It is achieved by preventing accidental or deliberate but unauthorized insertion, modification, or destruction of data in a database.

▼ **Data Mapping**

The process of assigning a source data element to a target data element.

▼ **Data Mart**

A collection of databases designed to help managers make strategic decisions about their business. Whereas a data warehouse combines databases across an entire enterprise, data marts are usually smaller and focus on a particular subject or department.

▼ **Data Mining**

A technique using software tools geared for users who typically do not know exactly what they are searching for but are looking for patterns or trends. Data mining is the process of sifting through large amounts of data to produce data content relationships. This is also known as data surfing.

▼ **Data Model**

The logical map to the data in a database. This includes the source of tables and columns, the meanings of the keys, and the relationships among the tables.

▼ **Data Ownership**

Responsibility for determining the required quality of the data, for establishing security and privacy for the data and for determining the availability and performance requirements of the data. Data originators who have the authority, accountability, and responsibility to create and enforce organizational rules and policies for business data.

▼ **Data Profiles**

Comprehensive data analyses that describe a school or district context.

▼ **Data Quality**

Also Quality Data. Accurate, timely, meaningful, and complete data.

▼ **Data Quality Campaign (DQC)**

The Data Quality Campaign (DQC) is a national, collaborative effort to encourage and support state policymakers to improve the collection, availability, and use of high-quality education data and to implement state longitudinal data systems to improve student achievement. The campaign aims to provide tools and resources that will assist states in their development of quality longitudinal data systems, while also providing a national forum for reducing duplication of effort and promoting greater coordination and consensus among the organizations focusing on improving data quality, access, and use.

▼ **Data Scrubbing**

The process of filtering, merging, decoding, and translating source data to create validated data for the data warehouse.

▼ **Data Staging Area**

A storage area and set of processes that clean, transform, combine, reduplicate, hold, archive, and prepare source data for use in the data warehouse. The data staging area is everything in between the sources system and the presentation server.

▼ **Data Teams**

A group of people who are committed to using data to improve student achievement. At the district level, a data team would include IT personnel who would coordinate hardware and software purchases and be responsible for maintaining the hardware and coordinating data management. At the building level, data teams would include knowledgeable teachers who might serve as "building techs" and who would plan and coordinate professional development activities so all teachers could use the available data.

▼ **Data Visualization**

Techniques for turning data into information by using the high capacity of the human brain to visually recognize patterns and trends.

▼ **Data Warehouse**

A queryable source of data. Typically, a data warehouse is fed from one or more data marts. The data from the data marts need to be cleansed and restructured to support queries, summaries, and analyses.

▼ **Database**

A system of complete, retrievable, and organized information that is accessible electronically and that can be easily manipulated.

▼ **Database Designer**

Person who creates the Entity Relation Diagrams (ERDs) for a relational database system. The database designer should have coursework and experience in computer science, statistics, and education.

▼ **Database Management System (DBMS)**

A series of programs that manage large sets of data. The DBMS may control the organization, storage, and retrieval of data in a database, in addition to controlling the security and integrity. The three most common types of a DBMS are hierarchical, network, and relational.

▼ **Deciles**

The values of a variable that divide the frequency distribution into ten equal frequency groups. The ninth decile is the value below which 90% of the norming group lie.

▼ **Decision Support System**

A computerized system that gathers and presents data from a wide range of sources, typically for business purposes.

▼ **Demographics**

Statistical characteristics of a population, such as average age, number of students in a school, percentages of ethnicities, etc. Disaggregation with demographic data allows us to isolate variations among different subgroups.

▼ **Denormalization**

The inclusion of derived data, the merging of tables, and the creation of arrays of data. One would denormalize by sacrificing some normalization to achieve speed increases.

▼ **Dimension Data**

An entity used to describe, qualify, or otherwise add meaning to "facts" in a star schema fact table. Dimensions are the "by" items in analysis of facts "by" gender, ethnicity, time, etc. Descriptive data that describe the measurements (facts) that users wish to analyze.

▼ **Dimensional Hierarchy**

Refers to the different levels of data within a dimension that data can be rolled up to or down to for analysis. This can be represented in a data model by a series of related tables with parent-child relationships (snow-flaked schemas) or by multiple columns within a dimension table (standard star schemas) called hierarchy columns. Example: the dimensional hierarchy of an education organization could include the following levels: student, teacher, classroom, school, district.

▼ **Dirty Data**

In a data warehouse, is a database record that contains errors.

▼ **Disaggregate**

Separating the results of different groups that make up the sample or population.

▼ **Disparate Data**

Data that are distinctly different in kind, quality, or character. They are unequal and cannot be readily integrated to adequately meet the business information demand.

▼ **Drill-down**

Allows a user to move between levels of data ranging from the most summarized (up) to the most detailed (down).

▼ **Drill-up**

This feature does the opposite of the drill-down; going from the smallest level of detail to higher and higher levels.

▼ **ECTL**

The Extract, Cleanse, Transform, and Load process for getting data into the database. This term is used interchangeably with ETL.

▼ **End-user Access Tool**

A client of the data warehouse; a tool that interacts with the server and returns a screen of data or a report, a graph, or some other higher form of analysis to the user. An end user data access tool can be as simple as an ad hoc query tool or as complex as a sophisticated data mining or modeling application.

▼ **End-user Application**

A collection of tools that query, analyze, and present information targeted to support a need. A minimal set of such tools would consist of an end user data access tool, a spreadsheet, a graphics package, and a user interface facility for eliciting prompts and simplifying the screen presentations to end users.

▼ **Entity**

A person, place, thing, concept, or event about which an organization collects data.

▼ **Entity Relation Diagram (ERD)**

Represents the arrangement and relationship of data entities for the logical data structure, such as boxes and lines to show relationships among tables. ERDs are created to reduce redundant data. Star Schema and Snowflake Schema are ERDs.

▼ **Enumeration**

One of a list of values that are allowed in a given attribute.

▼ **Extensible**

In information technology, something, such as a program, programming language, or protocol that is designed so that users (or later designers) can extend its capabilities. Extensibility can be a primary reason for the system, as in the case of the Extensible Markup Language (XML), or it may be only a minor feature.

▼ **Extensible Markup Language (XML)**

A programming language or protocol that facilitates sharing and movement of data across data systems. Contrast with HTML.

▼ **Extract/Transform/Load (ETL)**

The process of pulling data from operational data sources or external data sources; cleansing, aggregating, summarizing, and integrating data; and loading the data into some form of the data warehouse. ETL can also refer to the vendor software that performs these processes.

▼ **Family Educational Rights and Privacy Act (FERPA)**

The Family Educational Rights and Privacy Act (FERPA is a Federal law that protects the privacy of student education records. The law applies to all schools that receive funds under an applicable program of the U.S. Department of Education. FERPA gives parents certain rights with respect to their children's education records. These rights transfer to the student when he or she reaches the age of 18 or attends a school beyond the high school level.

▼ **Flat File**

A simple data structure with no directories; a file that has no structured interrelationship between its data records.

▼ **Flow Chart**

Illustrates steps in a process; can help identify inefficiencies where a process can be improved.

▼ **Focus Group**

A gathering of people, usually facilitated by a moderator, whose function it is to gather data and information on a particular issue or topic.

▼ **Formative Assessment**

Ongoing assessments designed to monitor student achievement over time; allows staff to determine what part of a task a student knows and does not know.

▼ **Frequency Distribution**

A tabulation of scores from high to low, or low to high, showing the number of individuals who obtain each score or whose scores fall in each score interval. Frequency distributions are used to determine tables of percentile ranks. For example, a frequency distribution of a class of 45 students may indicate that 25 were male and 20 were females.

▼ **Front End**

The part of the software program first seen by the user, usually with icons or text links to the underlying functionality of the application.

▼ **Gain Score**

The change of difference between two administrations of the same test. Gain scores are calculated by subtracting the previous score from the most recent score. Gain scores can be negative, which are actually losses.

▼ **Grade Point Average (GPA)**

The average grade earned by a student, figured by dividing the grade points earned by the number of credits attempted.

▼ **Granularity**

The level of the measures within a fact table represented by the lowest level of the dimensions.

▼ **Graphic Reports**

Presenting data using pictorial representations.

▼ **Graphical User Interface (GUI)**

The use of pictures (e.g., icons, buttons, dialog boxes, etc.) to manipulate the input and output of programs. The user selects objects with a pointer, usually controlled with a mouse.

▼ **Historical Data**

Data from previous time periods, in contrast to current data. Historical data is used for trend analysis and for comparisons to previous periods.

▼ **Host**

A computer with a Web server that serves the pages for one or more Web sites. A host can also be the company that houses a district's data, which is known as hosting.

▼ **Hypertext Markup Language (HTML)**

Standard markup language used to create documents on the World Wide Web.

▼ **Import Manager**

A piece of software that allows the user to import data into a database from other sources.

▼ **Infrastructure**

The architectural elements, organization support, corporate standards, methodology, data, processes, and physical hardware/network, etc., that make up the data warehouse environment.

▼ **Integrate**

Sharing common or multiple data and processes; accessing these data is generally accomplished through querying.

▼ **Interface**

The visible part of a computer system or database allowing the user to select items to view and enter information into the system.

▼ **Interoperability**

With respect to software, describes the capability of different programs to exchange data via a common set of business procedures, and to read and write the same file formats and use the same protocols.

▼ **Item Analysis**

Identifying how many students within a population selected each answer to a specific question on an assessment.

▼ **Legacy System**

An old hardware or software system that may be outdated in some way, either based on obsolete hardware or using an older user interface (e.g., a character-based interface rather than a GUI). A system that may not be able to interact easily with other computer systems.

▼ **Local Education Agency (LEA)**

An LEA might be a district, county, or intermediate educational organization.

▼ **Longitudinal Study**

A study that analyzes data for subjects who continue to participate over an extended period.

▼ **Maximum**

The highest actual score or the highest possible score on the test.

▼ **Mean**

Average score in a set of scores. Calculate by summing all the scores and dividing by the total number of scores.

▼ **Median**

The score that splits a distribution in half: 50 percent of the scores lie above and 50 percent of the scores lie below the median. If the number of scores is odd, the median is the middle score. If the number of scores is even, one must add the two middle scores and divide by two to calculate the median.

▼ **Metadata**

The descriptive information about the data in the database—data about data. Metadata describe the structure and relationships of data pieces. This includes such items as the names of the source fields that the data come from, the calculations to transform the data before loading them into the target database, the names of the columns that the data are going into in the target database, and meaningful end-user oriented descriptions of the target database tables and columns.

▼ **Microsoft**

A supplier of operating systems and other software for IBM PC compatible computers.

▼ **Minimum**

The lowest score or the lowest possible score on the test.

▼ **Mode**

The score that occurs most frequently in a scoring distribution.

▼ **Modularity**

A quality of hardware or software that breaks projects into smaller units (modules) that can stand alone or work with other parts of the program.

▼ **Narrative Report**

A report that tells a story or plot.

▼ **Non-proprietary**

Software application that is not owned or controlled solely by one company or institution.

▼ **Normal Curve Equivalent (NCE)**

Standard scores with a mean of 50 and a standard deviation of 21.06 and a range of 1 to 99.

▼ **Normal Distribution**

Also known as a normal curve. A bell-shaped distribution of scores where most of the scores group in the middle.

▼ **Normalization**

The process of decomposing large tables (files) into smaller tables in order to eliminate redundant data and duplicate data and to avoid problems with inserting, updating, and deleting data. Normalization is a way of organizing the data to prevent data duplication and to preserve strict relationship semantics.

▼ **Normalized Standard Score**

A transformation procedure used to make scores from different tests more directly comparable.

▼ **Norm-Referenced Tests (NRTs)**

Evaluations in which the scores are compared to a norm group, a representative sample of a specified population.

▼ **Norms**

Representative standards or values for a given group against which individual scores can be compared.

▼ **Online**

The status of being connected to a computer or network or having access to info that is available through the use of a computer or network.

▼ **Online Analytical Processing (OLAP)**

Refers to tools developed to store data sets retrieved from data marts and databases that allow users to see the data in multi-dimensional formats. OLAP tools are not databases, and, unlike data mining tools, OLAP tools do not create new knowledge.

▼ **Online Transaction Processing (OLTP)**

The technology that allows access to a small number of tables during a given transaction.

▼ **Open Data Base Connectivity (ODBC)**

A Microsoft standard, now adopted by most database programs, that allows a database, spreadsheet, and other programs to link to other databases. It then allows for the importing/exporting of data.

▼ **Operational Database**

Database that creates, updates, and accesses production systems. Does not access or update decision support systems.

▼ **Percent Correct**

A calculated score implying the percentage of students meeting and exceeding some number, usually a cut score, or a standard. Percent passing=the number passing the test divided by the number taking the test.

▼ **Percent Proficient**

Represents the percentage of students who passed a particular test at a "proficient" level, as defined by the test creators or the test interpreters.

▼ **Percentile Rank (PR)**

Percentage of students in a norm group (e.g., national or local) whose scores fall below a given score. Range is from 1 to 99. A 50th percentile ranking would mean that 50 percent of the scores in the norming group fall below a specific score.

▼ **Perceptions Data**

Information that reflects opinions and views of students, staff, or parents, often gathered through questionnaires.

▼ **Pivot Table**

A statistical software program output table, which summarizes data that can be pivoted interactively. Some pivoting options include rearranging rows and columns, creating multidimensional layers, and showing and hiding cells.

▼ **Portal**

A website that acts as a "doorway" to the Internet or a portion of the Internet, targeted toward one particular subject.

▼ **Pre-defined Report**

A report that has been previously developed. A "canned" report.

▼ **Presentation Server**

The target physical machine on which the data warehouse data are organized and stored for direct querying by end users, report writers, and other applications.

▼ **Primary Key**

An attribute(s) that uniquely identifies one record from another.

▼ **Privacy**

The principle of protecting information about people, especially in shared or collaborative systems.

▼ **Processes**

Measures that describe what is being done to get results, such as programs, strategies, and practices.

▼ **Proprietary Software**

Software that has restrictions on using and copying it.

▼ **Public Education Information Management System (PEIMS)**

Encompasses all data requested and received by the Texas Education Agency (TEA) about public education, including student demographic and academic performance, personnel, financial, and organizational information.

▼ **Quartiles**

There are 3 quartiles—Q1, Q2, Q3—that divide a distribution into 4 equal groups (Q1=25th percentile; Q2=50th percentile; Q3=75th percentile).

▼ **Query**

A request one makes to a database that is returned to the desktop. Understanding and knowing how to set up queries or to ask questions of the database is very important to the information discovery process.

▼ **Range**

A measure of the spread between the lowest and the highest scores in a distribution. Calculate by subtracting the lowest score from the highest score.

▼ **Raw Scores**

A person's observed score on a test or subtest. Number of questions answered correctly on a test or subtest; simply calculated by adding the number of questions answered correctly.

▼ **Refresh**

The mechanism whereby materialized views are updated to reflect new data.

▼ **Relational Database**

A type of database that allows the definition of data structures, storage, retrieval operations, and integrity constraints (requirements that must be satisfied for the database to maintain integrity). The data and relations between them are stored in table form. Relational databases are powerful because they require few assumptions about how data are related and how they will be extracted from the database.

▼ **Relational Database Management System (RDBMS)**

A type of database management system that uses a series of joined tables of rows and columns to store data.

▼ **Reliability**

Indicates the consistency of an assessment instrument to obtain similar scores over time.

▼ **Requirements Gathering**

Defining the scope of the data warehouse project. Includes understanding all data sources, how data are stored and enumerated, and current hardware, software, and networking.

▼ **Return on Investment (ROI)**

For a given use of money in an enterprise, how much profit or cost saving is realized. A ROI calculation is sometimes used along with other approaches to develop a business case for a given proposal. The overall ROI for school/district is sometimes used as a way to grade how well the data warehouse is managed.

▼ **Roll-up**

The process of centralizing.

▼ **Row**

Represents one occurrence of an entity (record). A row is the horizontal line in a table.

▼ **Rubric**

A scoring tool that rates performance according to clearly stated levels of criteria. The scales can be numeric or descriptive. For instance, school process rubrics are used to give schools an idea of where they started, where they want to be with respect to implementation, and where they are right now.

▼ **Scalability**

The ability of a system or data warehouse to accommodate future needs by "growing."

▼ **Scaled Scores**

A mathematical transformation of a raw score.

▼ **School Indicators**

The combination of data such as norm-referenced and standards-based assessments, dropout rates, completion rates, etc., that together provides information about the success of a school in fostering successful student learning.

▼ **Schools Interoperability Framework (SIF)**

A collaboration of school data stakeholders that sets data exchange standards to enable software packages to communicate with one another. SIF-compliant data tools, which should have this term on the label, interact as one system; data that are entered into one of the data tools will be entered into the other tools automatically. (See www.sifinfo.org for more information.)

▼ **Security**

Protecting equipment, performance, and contents when using technology.

▼ **Server**

Hardware that houses server applications.

▼ **Snowflake Schema**

A database architecture for building cubes. The snowflake schema divides the dimension tables into multiple tables by reintroducing a level of normalization.

▼ **Standard**

Something that is considered a basis of comparison or a guideline that is used as a basis for judgment.

▼ **Standard Deviation**

Measure of variability in a set of scores. The standard deviation is the square root of the variance.

▼ **Standard Scores**

A group of scores having a desired mean and standard deviation.

▼ **Standardized Tests**

Tests that are uniform in content, administration, and scoring. They can be used for comparing results across classrooms, schools, school districts, and states.

▼ **Stanines**

A nine-point normalized standard score scale. It divides the normal curve distribution of scores into nine equal points: 1 to 9. The mean of a stanine distribution is 5 and the standard deviation is approximately 2.

▼ **Star Schema**

A popular database architecture. A star schema model consists of fact tables surrounded by and related to dimension tables. Fact tables contain the information that you report and analyze.

▼ **Structured Query Language (SQL)**

The standard database language used by database programs. In most database programs, actions you take to add and retrieve data are converted behind the scenes to SQL commands to communicate your requests between and among database tables.

▼ **Student Achievement Data**

Information that reflects a level of knowledge, skill, or accomplishment, usually in something that has been explicitly taught.

▼ **Summative Assessments**

Assessments that are usually administered at the conclusion of a unit, chapter, course, or year.

▼ **Supervisory Union (SU)**

An administrative, planning, and educational service unit of two or more school districts created by the state Board of Education, primarily in Vermont.

▼ **Survey**

A data collection method that asks direct questions of a person or group.

▼ **System Architecture**

A description of the design and contents of a computer system, including a detailed inventory of current hardware, software, and networking capabilities; a description of long-range plans and priorities for future purchases; and a plan for upgrading and/or replacing outdated equipment and software.

▼ **System Integration**

The combining of two or more computer systems and/or software packages enabling these systems to work together efficiently.

▼ **Systems Programmer**

A non-specific job title that encompasses a variety of specialist roles. Typically, experience in specific operating systems, networking, electronic mail, operating and network security, and hardware devices are required.

▼ **T-score**

A calculated standard score with a mean of 50 and a standard deviation of 10.

▼ **Table**

A data structure for relational databases, comprised of rows and columns, like a spreadsheet.

▼ **Tabular Reports**

Reports formatted to look like a table.

▼ **Total Cost of Ownership (TOC)**

A calculation designed to assess both direct and indirect cost of purchasing, maintaining, and using computer hardware and software.

▼ **Total Information Management Solution**

Solution deployed by Western Heights Public Schools to integrate and manage their disparate database systems.

▼ **Transactional System**

Handles the day-to-day operations of collecting, processing, and storing operational data, such as Student Information Systems, Financial Management Systems, etc.

▼ **Triangulation**

Term used for combining three or more measures to get a more complete picture of student achievement.

▼ **User Interface**

The way a user interacts with data or communicates with the system.

▼ **Validity**

Indicates the effectiveness of an assessment instrument to measure what it is intended to measure.

▼ **Variance**

A measure of the dispersion, or variability, of scores about their mean. The population variance is calculated by taking the average of the squared deviations from the mean—a deviation being defined as an individual score minus the mean.

▼ **z-score**

A standard score with a mean of zero and a standard deviation of one.

▼ **Zone Integration Server**

In a SIF installation, the program that serves as a "central nervous system" by tying together all of the SIF-compliant applications, facilitating their communication and regulating their activities.

# REFERENCES AND RESOURCES

Adriaans, P. & Zantinge, D. (1996). *Data mining.* White Plains, NY: Addison-Wesley Longman.

Armstrong, J., & Anthes, K. (2001). How data can help. *American School Board Journal,* 188(11), 38-41.

Barker, J. (1992). Paradigms: *The business of discovering the future.* New York: HarperCollins.

Barth, R. (2004). *Learning by heart.* San Francisco: Jossey-Bass.

Beaudoin, M-N., & Taylor, M. (2004). *Creating a positive school culture: How principals and teachers can solve problems together.* Thousand Oaks, CA: Corwin Press.

Bergeson, T. & Heuschel, M.A. (2004). *Characteristics of improved school districts: Themes from research.* Olympia, WA: Office of Superintendent of Public Instruction.

Bernhardt, V.L. (2006). *Using data to improve student learning in school districts.* Larchmont, NY: Eye on Education, Inc.

Bernhardt, V.L. (2005). *Using data to improve student learning in high schools.* Larchmont, NY: Eye on Education, Inc.

Bernhardt, V.L. (2004). *Data analysis for continuous school improvement.* (2nd ed.). Larchmont, NY: Eye on Education, Inc.

Bernhardt, V.L. (2004). Data Analysis. In L. Easton (Ed.), *Powerful designs for professional learning.* Oxford, OH: National Staff Development Council (NSDC).

Bernhardt, V.L. (2004). *Using data to improve student learning in middle schools.* Larchmont, NY: Eye on Education, Inc.

Bernhardt, V.L. (2003). *Using data to improve student learning in elementary schools.* Larchmont, NY: Eye on Education, Inc.

Bernhardt, V.L. (2002). *The school portfolio toolkit: A planning, implementation, and evaluation guide for continuous school improvement.* Larchmont, NY: Eye on Education, Inc.

Bernhardt, V.L. (2000). *Designing and using databases for school improvement.* Larchmont, NY: Eye on Education, Inc. (Now out of print.)

Bernhardt, V.L. (1999). *The school portfolio: A comprehensive framework for school improvement.* (2nd ed.). Larchmont, NY: Eye on Education.

Bernhardt, V.L., & Geise, B.J. (2008). *Questionnaires: Powerful tools for improving teaching and learning.* Larchmont, NY: Eye on Education, Inc.

Bernhardt, V.L. & Others. (2000). *The example school portfolio, a companion to the school portfolio: A comprehensive framework for schoolwide improvement.* Larchmont, NY: Eye on Education.

Bischoff, J., & Alexander, T. (1997). *Data warehouse: Practical advice from the experts.* Upper Saddle River, NJ: Prentice Hall.

Blink, R. (2007). *Data-driven instructional leadership.* Larchmont, NY: Eye on Education, Inc.

Bolman, L.G., & Deal, T.E. (2001). *Leading with soul: An uncommon journey of spirit* (re. ed.). Indianapolis, IN: Jossey-Bass.

Bolman, L.G., & Deal, T.E. (1997). *Reframing organizations: Artistry, choice, and leadership.* San Francisco: Jossey-Bass.

Boudett, K.P., Murnane, R.J., City, E. & Moddy, L. (2005). Teaching educators how to use student assessment data to improve instruction: Lessons from a workshop. *Phi Delta Kappan,* v86 n9 p700 May 2005. Bloomington, IN: Phi Delta Kappa International, Inc.

Brackett, M.H. (1996). *The data warehouse challenge: Taming data chaos.* New York: John Wiley & Sons, Inc.

Brassard, M. & Ritter, D. (1994). *The memory jogger II.* Salem, NH: Goal/QPC.

Clark, D.L., Lotto, L.S., & Astuto, T.A. (1984, Summer). Effective schools and school improvement: A comparative analysis of two lines of inquiry. *Educational Administration Quarterly,* 20(3), 41-68.

Cohen, D., & Ball, D.L. (1999). *Instruction, capacity, and improvement.* CPRE Research Report Series RR-43. University of Pennsylvania, PA: Consortium for Policy Research in Education.

Collins, J. (2001). *Good to great: Why some companies make the leap… and others don't.* New York: Harper Business.

Deal, T., & Peterson, K. (2003). *Shaping school culture: The heart of leadership.* San Francisco: Jossey-Bass.

Deming, W.E. (1993). *Out of crisis.* Cambridge, MA: Massachusetts Institute of Technology Center for Advanced Engineering Study.

Deming, W.E. (1993). *The new economics for industry, government, education.* Cambridge, MA: Massachusetts Institute of Technology Center for Advanced Engineering Study.

Drucker, P. (1980). *Managing in turbulent times.* New York: Harper and Row.

Fullan, M. (2001). *Leading in a culture of change.* San Francisco: Jossey-Bass.

Fullan, M., Cuttress, C., & Kilcher, A. (Fall, 2005). Eight forces for leaders of change: Presence of the core concepts does not guarantee success, but their absence ensures failure. *Journal of Staff Development,* 26(4), 54-64.

Hall, G.E. & Hord, S.M. (2006). *Implementing change: Patterns, principles, and potholes* (2nd ed.). Boston: Pearson Education.

Harrington, J.L. (1998). *Relational database design clearly explained.* London: Academic Press.

Hernandez, M. (1997). *Database design for mere mortals: A hands-on guide to relational database design.* Reading, MA: Addison-Wesley Publishing Co.

Heritage, M. & Chen, E. (2005). Why data skills matter in school improvement. *Phi Delta Kappan,* v86 n9 p707 May 2005. Bloomington, IN: Phi Delta Kappa International, Inc.

Hoerr, T.R. (2005). *The art of school leadership.* Alexandria, VA: Association for Supervision and Curriculum Development.

Hogan, R. (1990). *A practical guide to database design.* Englewood Cliffs, NJ: Prentice Hall.

Holcomb, E.L. (2004). *Getting excited about data: Combining people, passion, and proof to maximize student achievement* (2nd ed.). Thousand Oaks, CA: Corwin Press.

Imhoff, C., Galemmo, N., & Geiger, J. (2003). *Mastering Data Warehouse Design: Relational and Dimensional Techniques.* Indianapolis, IN: Wiley Publishing, Inc.

Inmon, W., Welch, J., & Glassey, K. (1996). *Managing the Data Warehouse.* New York: John Wiley & Sons.

Johnson, R.S. (2002). *Using data to close the achievement gap.* Thousand Oaks, CA: Corwin Press.

Juran, J.M. (2006). *Juran on quality by design: The new steps for planning quality into goods and services.* New York, NY: The Free Press, A Division of Simon & Schuster, Inc.

Juran, J.M. & Godfrey, A.B. (1998). *Juran's quality handbook.* New York, NY: McGraw Hill.

Kimball, R., & Merz, R. (2000). *The data webhouse toolkit: Building the web-enabled data warehouse.* New York: Wiley Computer Publishing.

Kimball, R., Reeves, L., Ross, M., & Thornthwaite, W. (1998). *The data warehouse lifecycle toolkit.* New York: Wiley Computer Publishing.

Kimball, R. & Ross, M. (2002) *The data warehouse toolkit: The complete guide to dimensional modeling* (2nd ed.). New York: Wiley Computer Publishing.

Lezotte, L. (1997). *Learning for all.* Okemos, MI: Effective Schools Products, Ltd.

Marzano, R.J. (2003). *What works in schools: Translating research into action.* Alexandria, VA: Association for Supervision and Curriculum Development

McGuff, F., & Kador, J. (1999). *Developing analytical database applications.* Upper Saddle River, NJ: Prentice Hall PTR.

Mercurius, N. (2005). Scrubbing data for D3M. *T.H.E. Journal,* 33(3), 15-18.

Moller, G. & Pankake, A. (2006). *Lead with me: A principal's guide to teacher leadership.* Larchmont, NY: Eye on Education, Inc.

National Center for Education Statistics. (2006). *Forum guide to demystifying decision support systems: A resource for educators and education constituents* (NFES 2006-XXX). U.S. Department of Education. Washington, DC: National Center for Education Statistics.

National Center for Education Statistics (2005). *Forum guide to building a culture of quality data: A school and district resource: 2004* (NCES 2005-801). U.S. Department of Education, National Center for Education Statistics. Washington, DC: U.S. Government Printing Office.

National Center for Education Statistics (2005). *Forum guide to education indicators: 2005* (NCES 2005-802). U.S. Department of Education, National Center for Education Statistics. Washington, DC: U.S. Government Printing Office.

National Center for Education Statistics (2004). *Forum guide to protecting the privacy of student information: state and local education agencies: 2004* (NCES 2004-330). U.S. Department of Education, National Center for Education Statistics. Washington, DC: U.S. Government Printing Office.

National Center for Education Statistics (2003). *NCES nonfiscal data handbook for early childhood, elementary, and secondary education: 2003* (NCES 2003-419). U.S. Department of Education, National Center for Education Statistics. Washington, DC: U.S. Government Printing Office.

Parsaye, K., & Chignell, M. (1993). *Intelligent database tools and applications.* New York: John Wiley & Sons, Inc.

Parsaye, K., Chignell, M., Khoshafian, S., & Wong, H. (1989). *Intelligent databases: Object-oriented, deductive hypermedia technologies.* New York: John Wiley & Sons, Inc.

Petry, F. (1996). *Fuzzy databases: Principles and applications.* Boston: Kluwer Academic Publishers.

Popham, W.J. (2000). *Modern educational measurement: Practical guidelines for educational leaders.* Boston: Allyn & Bacon.

Schmoker, M. (2006). *Results Now: The key to continuous school improvement.* Alexandria, VA: Association for Supervision and Curriculum Development.

Sharratt, G. (2005). Principals establish the culture and set the tone in high-performing schools. *Journal of the International Teaching and Learning Consortium,* 20(1), 12-14.

Shea, M., Murray, R., & Harlin, R. (2005). *Drowning in data? How to collect, organize, and document student performance.* Portsmouth, NH: Heinemann.

Simon, A.R. (1998). *Data warehousing for dummies.* Foster City, CA: IDG Books Worldwide, Inc.

Simon, A.R. (1998). *90 days to the data mart.* New York: John Wiley & Sons, Inc.

Stein, M. (2003). *Making sense of the data, overview of the K-12 data management and analysis market.* Pg.12. Eduventures, Inc.

Streifer, P. (2004). *Tools and techniques for effective data-driven decision making.* Lanham, MD: Scarecrow.

Tenopir, C., & Lundeen, G. (1988). *Managing your information: How to design and create a textual database on your microcomputer.* New York: Neal-Schuman Publishers.

Teorey, T. (1998). *Database modeling and design.* San Francisco: Morgan Kaufmann Publishers, Inc.

Wayman, J. & Stringfield, S. (Ed.). (August 2006). Data use for school improvement. *American Journal of Education* (Special Issue), 112 (4). University of Chicago Press.

Wayman, J.C., Midgley, S. & Stringfield, S. (2005). *Collaborative teams to support data-based decision making and instructional improvement* (Paper presented at the 2005 Annual Meeting of the American Educational Research Association, Montreal, Canada). Baltimore, MD: John Hopkins University, Center for Social Organization of Schools.

Wheatley, M.J. (1999). Bringing schools back to life as living systems in *Creating successful school systems: Voices from the university, the field, and the community.* Norwood, MA: Christopher-Gordon Publishers.

## ONLINE RESOURCES

American Society for Quality (ASQ). Home page available from *http://www.asq.org/*

Chilton School District, Wisconsin (2007). Available from *http://www.cesa7.k12.wi.us/content/chilton/index.asp*

Columbia Public Schools, Missouri (2007). Available from *http://www.columbia.k12.mo.us/*

Connecticut Data Warehouse (2007). Available from *http://www.eastconn.org/TechnologySolutions_DataSolutions.htm*

Edmonds School District #15, Washington (2007). *http://www.edmonds.wednet.edu*

Education for the Future Website. (2007). Available from *http://eff.csuchico.edu*

Inspiration Software, Inc. (2007). Available from: *http://www.inspiration.com*

McIntire, T. (2004). *Eight buying tips: Data warehouses.* San Bruno, CA: Technology and Learning. Available from *http://www.techlearning.com/story/showArticle.jhtml?articleID=26806926*

National Center for Education Statistics. Home page available from *http://nces.ed.gov*

National Center for Education Statistics. Electronic catalog available from *http://nces.ed.gov/pubsearch*

National Center for Education Statistics. Forum home page available from *http://nces.ed.gov/forum*

National Center for Education Statistics (2005). *Forum unified education technology suite: online.* Available from *http://nces.ed.gov/pubs2005/tech_suite*

Northview Public Schools, Michigan (2007). Available from *http://www.nvps.net/*

Power, D.J. (1995-2005). *Decision Support Systems Resources.* Retrieved (August 2005) from *http://dssresources.com*

Rudo, Z. (2005). J. Buttram, K. Hebert, M. Vaden-Kiernan, D. Pan, T.L. Thompson (Ed.). *Enhancing data use and quality to shape education policy.* Insights on Education Policy, Practice, and Research, Number 18. Available online from Southwest Educational Development Laboratory (SEDL), *http://www.sedl.org/*

San Jose Unified School District, California (2007). Available from *http://www.sjusd.k12.ca.us/*

Schools Interoperability Framework, *SIF Specification.* Retrieved (September 2005) from *http://www.sifinfo.org*

Statsoft. (1999). Available from *http://www.statsoft.com*

TechLEARNING Hot Topic: Data Management (2007). Available from *http://www.techlearning.com/hot_topics/data_management.jhtml*

Togneri, W. & Anderson, S. (2003). *Beyond islands of excellence: What districts can do to improve instruction and achievement in all schools.* Washington, DC: Learning First Alliance. Available from *http://www.learningfirst.org*

Tyler Independent School District, Texas (2007). Available from *http://www.tylerisd.org/*

Vermont Data Consortium (2007). Available from *http://vermontdata.org/*

Vermont Department of Education (2006). *Collecting and reporting quality data: A best practices guide for completing the Vermont DOE core data collections.* Springfield, IL: Marucco, Stoddard, Ferenbach & Walsh, Inc. Available from *http://www.state.vt.us/educ/new/pdfdoc/pgm_finance_data/collection/best_practices_guide.pdf*

Wade, H. (December 2001). Data inquiry and analysis for educational reform. *ERIC Digest 153.* University of Oregon. Available from *http://cepm.uoregon.edu/publications/digests/index.html*

Webopedia online dictionary and search engine (2007). Available from *http://www.webopedia.com*

Western Heights Public Schools, Oklahoma (2007). Available from *http://www.westernheights.k12.ok.us/*

Wikipedia online free-content encyclopedia (2007). Available from *http://www.wikipedia.com*

# INDEX

# BOOKS by Victoria L. Bernhardt

## Using Data to Improve Student Learning

A four-book collection of using data to improve student learning—

▼ *Using Data to Improve Student Learning in Elementary Schools* (2003)

▼ *Using Data to Improve Student Learning in Middle Schools* (2004)

▼ *Using Data to Improve Student Learning in High Schools* (2005)

▼ *Using Data to Improve Student Learning in School Districts* (2006)

This series helps you make sense of the data your school collects, including state student achievement results as well as other qualitative and quantitative data. Each book shows real analyses focused on one education organizational level and shows the actual descriptive analyses. You will see that no matter how much or how little data your school or district has, the data can tell the story. The study questions at the end of each chapter serve as guides for the reader. For readers who want feedback, the author describes what she saw in the analyses following the study questions at the end of each chapter.

The goal with these books is for anyone to be able to set up these analyses, regardless of the statistical resources available. Therefore, in addition to showing the analyses in the text, templates are provided on an accompanying CD-Rom for leaders to use for gathering, graphing, and analyzing data in their own learning organizations.

**TO ORDER:** Contact Eye on Education, (888) 299-5350, www.eyeoneducation.com

# BOOKS by Victoria L. Bernhardt

## *The School Portfolio Toolkit: A Planning, Implementation, and Evaluation Guide for Continuous School Improvement*

*The School Portfolio Toolkit* (2002) and CD-Rom is a compilation of over 500 ideas, examples, suggestions, activities, tools, strategies, and templates for producing school portfolios that will lead to continuous school improvement. *The Toolkit* suggests approaches for bringing entire staffs along in the work of the school portfolio.

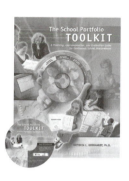

## The School Portfolio

A school portfolio is a non-threatening self-assessment tool which exhibits a school's goals, progress, achievements, and vision for improvement. *The School Portfolio: A Comprehensive Framework for School Improvement* (Second Edition, 1999) describes the theory behind the school portfolio.

## The Example School Portfolio

*The Example School Portfolio* (2000) shows what a completed school portfolio looks like and further supports schools in developing their own school portfolios. After reading this book, teachers and administrators will see how easy it is to develop a school portfolio so they can look at their own school with new eyes and find the elements that, if pulled in alignment, could make all the difference.

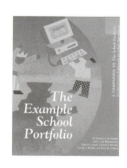

**TO ORDER:** Contact Eye on Education, (888) 299-5350, www.eyeoneducation.com

# EDUCATION FOR THE FUTURE

## Victoria L. Bernhardt, Executive Director

## *About Us*

*Education for the Future* is a not-for-profit initiative located on the California State University, Chico campus that focuses on working with schools, districts, state departments of education and other educational service centers and agencies on systemic change and comprehensive data analyses that lead to increased student learning.

The staff of Education for the Future is a group of highly committed individuals who work in this business because we want to make a difference in the lives of children. We are passionate about our mission, which is to support and build the capacity of schools to provide an education that will prepare students to be anything they want to be in the future.

Contact us to learn more about Education for the Future professional development opportunities, to schedule a workshop, for contract questionnaire services, or to answer your questions

Education for the Future

400 West First Street, Chico, CA  95929-0230

Tel. (530) 898-4482 ~ Fax (530) 898-4484

E-mail: EFFInfo@csuchico.edu

*http://eff.csuchico.edu*

*"Never doubt that a small group of thoughtful, committed citizens*

*can change the world. Indeed, it is the only thing that ever has."*

Margaret Mead